Chinese Studies in History
SPRING–SUMMER 1998/VOL. 31, NOS. 3–4

Chinese Business History
Interpretative Trends and
Priorities for the Future

Guest Editors:
Robert Gardella, U.S. Merchant Marine Academy
Jane K. Leonard, University of Akron
Andrea McElderry, University of Louisville

Routledge
Taylor & Francis Group
LONDON AND NEW YORK

First published 1998 by M.E. Sharpe

Published 2015 by Routledge
2 Park Square, Milton Park, Abingdon, Oxon OX14 4RN
711 Third Avenue, New York, NY 10017, USA

Routledge is an imprint of the Taylor & Francis Group, an informa business

ISBN 13: 9780765603463 (pbk)

Chinese Studies in History, vol. 31, nos. 3–4, Spring–Summer 1998, pp. 3–15.
ISSN 0009–4633/1998 $9.50 + 0.00.

ROBERT GARDELLA
AND ANDREA MCELDERRY

Guest Editors' Introduction

Interpretative Trends and Priorities for the Future

Why business history and why China? What has the study of business structure and activities over time to contribute to an understanding of China's past and present condition? What might analyses utilizing the rich resources of Chinese history do to enrich the understanding of the history of business—surely fundamental to shaping modern civilization—in comparative and global terms rather than singularly Western ones? The first question is directly addressed in the essays to follow, which trace the ways in which Chinese business history has been pursued by scholars in both China and the West. Logically enough, since business history has heretofore been grounded in case studies limited largely to America and Europe, the second question has barely begun to engage the attention of the scholarly community itself.

The phenomenal resurgence of China's economy since the late 1970s, and its increasing integration with international markets over the past two decades, has been a strong proximate inspiration for the present volume. If Chinese business, and foreign business in China, were not subjects important enough and sufficiently newsworthy to engage the interest of today's readership, a monograph tracing the past and present comprehension of Chinese business might well seem arcane or esoteric. That it is neither should be apparent to anyone who regularly scans the *New York Times*, the *Wall Street Journal*, the *Economist, Business Week*, or *Forbes*. The ups and downs of Chinese business are now the staple ingredients of worldwide media mills.

Customarily relegated to the very bottom rungs of a premodern Confucian ladder (in proper ranking behind scholars, farmers, and craftsmen), a vigorous Chinese business class—whether in Taiwan, Hong Kong,

Southeast Asia, or the People's Republic—has come to the forefront as China enters the postmodern twenty-first century. From Beijing to Guangzhou, brazenly procapitalist slogans—"To get rich is glorious" is typical—elbow aside Maoist nostrums, such as "Serve the people," in the world's largest surviving ostensibly socialist party-state. Chinese family firms and far-flung, much elaborated business networks have demonstrated increased capacity and growing determination to wield their economic clout, and, on occasion, political influence around the globe.

But present-day preoccupations with the vicissitudes of China's rapid economic development and its global implications in and of themselves are insufficient justifications for an avowedly historical study. It is not only useful to consider the history of Chinese business in the light of contemporary issues, it is essential to examine Chinese business history to gain a sounder understanding of China's (and the world's) historical record.

How did an increasingly commercialized late imperial Chinese economy (from approximately the sixteenth through the late nineteenth centuries) actually function? What parameters did it establish that would affect China's subsequent development? Multifaceted relationships ranging from collaboration to confrontation grew up between imperial and postimperial Chinese governments and Chinese and foreign businesses—how are we to interpret them? Did Confucianism, strong family and kinship ties, weak formal traditions of civil law, or other characteristics of Chinese civilization affect economic rationality and efficiency? If so, have they on balance been negative or positive influences? Foreign businesses have operated in China over the past three centuries. From the days of the tea trade and opium clippers to today's joint ventures and Special Economic Zones, foreign investment has been linked to some of the best and worst aspects of Sino–Western relations. What do business records reveal about the highly contested record of foreign "economic imperialism" in China, an issue upon which much ink (and no little blood) has been spilled since the early 1800s?

These questions have framed the basic issues in Chinese business history, a new but steadily developing subfield of Chinese economic history. Research in economic history has usually been framed within an analytical system: neoclassical economics in the West, Marxism in East Asia and the West, and Weber's "rise of capitalism" in the West and Taiwan. Chinese and foreign scholars have certainly applied (or at times misapplied) assorted models to interpret the data of Chinese economic and business history. In post-1949 China, the official ideology has, of course, set the general terms of academic communication, at times utterly stifling scholarly discourse, and, at others, actively encouraging fruitful debates. As Man Bun Kwan's essay and Madeleine Zelin's response show, the consistencies and inconsistencies in Chinese Marxist approaches to business history mirror the checkered course of Communist Party dogma and policies. Recurrent themes such as class analysis, protocapitalism, anti-imperialism, and, most recently, hagiography have not always been the surest guides to unraveling China's past. By contrast, Man-houng Lin's article portrays how a less ideologically constrained and much more eclectic academic climate on Taiwan has produced a less coherent yet lively body of scholarship. Modernization theory, economic analysis, anticolonialism, nationalism in both orthodox (pan-Chinese) and local (Taiwanese) guises, and social theorists from Marx to Weber have attracted the attention of Taiwan's business and economic historians.

Western scholarship on China's economy, as Yen-p'ing Hao's essay shows, has mirrored Western interpretations of modern Chinese history in general. The "impact of the West," modernization theory, Marxist, neo-Marxist, and China-centered interpretations have all had their advocates. Hao finds the time is ripe for developing a Chinese model rooted in "China's own unique history." Wellington Chan's essay focuses on Western views of the family firm, and he, too, argues against a deterministic approach that fails to appreciate the changing cultural and institutional contexts of Chinese family firms. Albert Feuerwerker's essay is itself an interpretation of Chinese business history and suggests some continuities (and by implication differences) in three historical periods dating from around 1600 to the present.

China scholars in the West have naturally been influenced by models of Western business development. In the Western world, business history per se emerged as a stronger academic presence in America than in Europe, dating from early twentieth century exposés of the evils of U.S. megacorporations. In this volume, Daniel Nelson's survey of the historiography of American business, along with Keith Bryant's rejoinder, center around the most influential historian of American corporate industrial development—Alfred D. Chandler, Jr. The power of Chandler's several studies lays in their explicit and comparative focus upon organizational changes in modern industrial enterprises, changes summarized under the rubric of "the managerial revolution." Driven by technological innovations and growing markets, corporate managers devised effective institutions to realize economies of scale and scope. Chandler's model has taken root in Europe and Japan, where historical comparisons with America have proved most fruitful. While his approach appears less appropriate to China, Chandler's work has nonetheless become canonical reading for any and all historians of business. It has, in dialectical fashion, inspired revisionist criticism and provoked alternative paradigms, thus immensely vitalizing the field as a whole.

The Articles

The articles herein were initially papers presented at a workshop held at the Buchtel College of Arts and Sciences of the University of Akron, on October 27–29, 1995. The guiding force behind this event was Professor Jane Kate Leonard; she and her staff and colleagues at Akron provided all the participants with a congenial and stimulating atmosphere for the exchange of ideas. Revised contributions from ten of the workshop participants are represented here.[1] Our discussions were also greatly enhanced by papers presented by Rajeswary Brown, School of Oriental and African Studies, University of London, and by Takeshi Hamashita of the Oriental Institute, Tokyo University. While not included in this publication, their comments on Chinese business history from the vantage points of Southeast Asia and Japan were essential and invaluable.

Albert Feuerwerker of the University of Michigan adopts a synchronic comparison of three periods in Chinese history—late imperial China (pre-1842), China under the unequal treaty system (1842–1949), and the People's Republic (post-1949). In each of these eras he discerns five aspects of "doing business": the precedence of politics over economics, the vested interest of conservative social elites in that status quo, a qualified private property regime in the economy, the prevalence of personal ties (*guanxi*) and a corresponding need for brokers or intermediaries, and the weakness of formal civil law institutions to resolve disputes. Feuerwerker contends that business in China still operates (often quite successfully) without a truly unified and effective polity, as China has yet to develop the basic political and values systems appropriate to its ongoing revival as a great civilization.

Man Bun Kwan of the University of Cincinnati examines Chinese business history as pursued in the People's Republic of China [PRC] over the past half-century. After briefly reviewing scholarship during the PRC's first two decades, Kwan closely examines the 1979–89 era, which coincided with rapid economic reforms, and concludes by assessing recent trends from 1990 to 1996. A vast amount of scholarship and archival compilation work of uneven quality has marked these turbulent years, but even more evident are ideologically toned, shifting topics and modes of interpretation. PRC historians have diligently, if not always convincingly, explored the emergence of "protocapitalism" in late imperial China, debated the class nature of domestic businessmen, argued about the pros and cons of late Qing industrialization efforts, and damned or praised the activities of foreign business investors. Recent scholarship has veered away from Marxist pieties to study China's marketing systems, property rights, and the actual operations of firms—evidence that the "modernity of tradition" has formed a substructure for contemporary economic growth.

Taiwan's scholarship is, in the terms of Hu Shi, more focused upon "problems, not isms," as ideology has commonly been subordinated to issues. Man-houng Lin of the Academia Sinica in Taiwan provides a fine overview of the academic context of Taiwan research covering the past three and a half centuries, especially of the central themes engaging scholars of that epoch. Her chapter first addresses the sustaining role of religion in commercial contexts, then examines state–merchant relations in the late imperial era. She moves on to structural concerns—the partnership form as the prevalent one for Chinese business enterprises in the early modern period, and the ubiquity of small firms at all levels of business activity. Whether traditional business can withstand Western competition is an open question, as are the evolving relationships between business interests and the weak governments of the late Qing and early Republic. Lin concludes by tracing the evolution of merchant organizations and activities in Taiwan from the seventeenth century to the present day.

In a trenchant commentary on Kwan's and Lin's essays, Madeleine Zelin of Columbia University points out how the general issue of China's economic development in the PRC has been skewed by political and ideological desiderata—the sprouts of capitalism, the evils of domestic and foreign capitalism as well as imperialism, backward commercial capitalism versus progressive industrial capitalism, and so on. Research agendas were institutionalized, but little attention was paid to the nitty gritty, such as labor practices, the actual day-to-day running of enterprises, and the need to reexamine the state's role in the late imperial and Republican eras. Zelin is encouraged by recent trends in the PRC and even more so in Taiwan, where scholars are taking on the "hard task of figuring out how business worked." Still there is a long way to go. Among the most neglected topics of investigation has been the impact of China's legal system upon business practices, especially the handling of liability and credit.

The themes and issues manifested in Western language scholarship (predominantly in English) on Chinese business history over the past half-century are well delineated in the next contribution by Yen-p'ing Hao of the University of Tennessee. Chief among these themes has been the analysis of business firms and types of "merchants" (*shangren*), the nature of entrepreneurship, the roles of key socioeconomic institutions (such as the family, guilds, business networks, and markets), and the general political and cultural environment in which business firms operated. This last includes the influence of the state and of pervasive cultural values such as Confucianism. Extended treatment is accorded to China's overseas or maritime linkages and, most importantly, to Western enterprises in China, thereby bringing up the crucial issues of economic imperialism and Sino–foreign business competition. Hao concludes that, while scholarship on Chinese business history has often been comparative, its basic task is still to understand the specificities of business in China's rich cultural context.

Wellington Chan of Occidental College zeroes in on a critical component of Chinese business past and present, the family firm. After briefly tracing past Western language efforts to analyze Chinese business competence, Chan turns to the family firm as indicative of the structural and behavioral features of Chinese enterprise. Core features stressed in the literature are identified— congruence between business ownership and control, the relatively small size of firms, lean structures with emphasis on networking strategies—but Chan strongly urges that these be understood in a contextual rather than a conclusive sense. As business conditions changed and adapted from late imperial times to the present, so did family firms. Rather than being artifacts of the past, family firms remain flexible shapers of the business present. In Chan's words, "the ability of the family firm to re-create itself to a new mix of various elements— cultural, institutional, and organizational—in order to maximize opportunities within each new environment," gives these institutions considerable flexibility, hence long-term staying power.

In his comments on the Hao and Chan chapters, Parks Coble of the University of Nebraska–Lincoln notes "the enduring scholarship of many of the works cited" in contrast to the ahistorical, superficial tone of much contemporary writing on the Chinese economy. Far from being marginal, studies in Chinese business history enrich our understanding of current and long-standing issues. Coble, however, cautions that "academic studies are a captive of sources." In the PRC, enterprises lost control of their archives, and scholars' access to these archives has greatly improved in recent years. But we continue to lack archival sources on the various forms of Chinese business outside of China. He concludes by emphasizing the salience of cross-cultural comparisons between Western and Chinese business history and sets forth his own agenda of key research themes for the proximate future.

An explicitly comparative dimension—essential to the study of business history—is introduced by Daniel Nelson of the University of Akron. Writing from the vantage point of the historiography of American business, Nelson states that "business history thus serves as a forceful reminder of the power of economics and technology over culture." Such a view contrasts greatly with the Chinese experience, as does the relative economic freedom and rapid economic change associated with the American historical record. American business history developed around the turn of the twentieth century as a response to the shock of America's industrialization—at first it was polemical (exposés), then empirical (case studies), then moralistic in tone or entrepreneurial in focus, and finally macroanalytical and broadly comparative in the writings of Alfred Chandler. Chandler's work emerged from a revisionist context (the more positive postdepression view of business), and embodied more sophisticated content (a painstaking scrutiny of the managerial and organizational dynamics of industrial corporations). Since the 1950s, Chandler's voice has been dominant in Western business history (including Europe and, lately, Japan), but Nelson notes certain lacunae in his work. There is no human dimension to the managers he empowers or the laborers on their payrolls and no emphasis whatever on the role of government and public policy. But business history is larger than Chandler's focus depicts, and it embraces those areas he ignored and more.

Keith Bryant of the University of Akron critiques his colleague's interpretation by doubting that U.S. business history really exhibits the subordination of culture and society to economics and technology. While acknowledging Chandler's overriding influence in transforming an ill-defined subfield of economic history into a sharply delineated, coherent domain, Bryant points up the limits of rationality in business decisions past and present. Wider social, political, and moral or religious concerns sway behavior, which results in failures as well as successes. Chandler's work is informative for all business historians, not excepting China specialists, but must be used with discretion.

Finally, Chi-kong Lai of the University of Queensland, Australia, addresses a new and very promising area of research in Chinese business history—the analysis of individual business enterprises from the late nineteenth century until the present. A recent upsurge of interest in such case studies has reflected the increasing availability of primary sources, such as company archives, legal materials, survey reports, and government documents. While listing numerous published studies, Lai introduces readers to the valuable archival collections in Shanghai, Nanjing, Hong Kong, Taiwan, and Australia. He indicates that these archives will prove essential in understanding the structure, operations, and cultural as well as technological context of Chinese business enterprises in the modern era. These archives also contain material that will elucidate basic issues in Chinese business history.

Taken together these essays indicate that earlier views of Chinese business have undergone significant revision in both Chinese and Western studies. One can also detect a growing convergence in the views of scholars in the PRC, Taiwan, and the West. Why this has occurred is hardly obscure: the "success" of Chinese business in the Pacific Rim, economic developments in the PRC, easier access to archives in China, and more interaction among scholars from various places. How it is manifested in the literature is best understood by examining some of the issues covered in this volume.

The Issues

"What is Chinese business history?" is the logically first issue to address. As both Hao and Kwan point out, there is no Chinese equivalent for the term "business history." Kwan, writing on PRC scholarship, identifies it as a genre of economic history, "loosely defined as the history of an enterprise, whether it be handicraft or industrial, commercial or financial, public or private" (p. 35), which in Chinese would be *qiye lishi* (enterprise history). On the other hand, writing on Taiwan scholarship, Lin focuses on commercial history, which in Chinese would be *shangye lishi*. Hao points out that "there is no generally accepted definition of business history, even in the United States, where this discipline started and has thrived" (p. 106), and his point is borne out by a disagreement between the two Western business historians on its exact nature. Nelson writes, "Business history . . . serves as a forceful reminder of the power of economics and technology over culture," but Bryant thinks, "Corporate cultures often reflect the values of the society in which they operate to the detriment of the firm" (p. 167). With respect to Chinese business history, Hao basically agrees with Bryant, writing that it "provides an eloquent testimony to the importance of history over economics and technology" (p. 122). As the essays indicate, the role of culture in shaping Chinese business practice remains an issue and is influenced by the model chosen by a particular scholar.

The question of which models might best inform the Chinese business historian brings up a second issue. Nelson and Bryant do agree on the importance and significance of Alfred Chandler's paradigms for the study of business history. However, it remains problematic to what extent Chandler's model, which sees technology as the engine driving the transition from family firm to corporate management hierarchies (from the market to the "visible hand"), can be applied to China. One could certainly argue that technology in the guise of external military threats led to a transformation of the economy into state-controlled management hierarchies but has not yet led to capitalism. Most basically, Chandler is concerned with the rise of capitalism and accepts it as a given, while Chinese scholars have been concerned with the nondevelopment of capitalism and ambivalent toward it.

Nelson and Bryant also concur on the "flaws in the Chandlerian world": Chandler does not recognize that "personality often had (and has) a decisive impact"; he does not take into account the influence that the "chorus and orchestra, the employees who made up the base of the corporate hierarchy" had on the organization; and he neglects the role of government and public policy. According to Bryant, "these omissions are not only critical, but they also suggest the limitations in applying the Chandlerian hypotheses to Chinese business history." As the essays in this volume bring out, these omissions are all areas that, in one way or another, have received attention from historians of Chinese business. The interest in entrepreneurs, although not particularly concerned with individual personalities, is, on one level, concerned with the impact of personality. Many of the enterprise histories in the PRC have been "written from the perspective of class struggle" and "preserved a from-the-bottom voice of the past" as Kwan points out. And the role of governments and government policy is a central issue in Chinese business history.

Chandler or not, there is no question that Chinese business history has been shaped by Western paradigms. As Zelin points out, scholarship on both sides of the Taiwan straits has been concerned not so much with business as with economic development, particularly with the question of "Why didn't China modernize?" The same might be said of Western scholarship. Kwan's essay shows how in the early years of the PRC a Marxist paradigm led to a search for China's capitalist past and saw the publication of the first collections of archival materials on various business enterprises and the first salvos in the "sprouts of capitalism" debate. Hao's essay shows how during the same period, Western works on Chinese business history sought "answers to China's 'tardy' modernization" under the general paradigm of "China's response to the West" with "a corresponding emphasis on the weaknesses of Chinese economic and business institutions." In framing answers, Weber, not Marx, was more influential.

Recent scholarship has been less tied to such negative paradigms, as a review of three specific issues—state–business relations, the role of culture, and the problem of foreign influence—illustrates. The view of government–business relations that has seeped into the general academic consciousness sees Chinese governments as hostile to business activity and attributes this hostility to culture. For example, in the chapter on Ming–Qing history in a recent edition of one of the most widely used world civilization textbooks, the authors quote Han Fei—erroneously identifying him as a sixth–century B.C. Confucian rather than a second–century B.C. Legalist—to the effect that an enlightened ruler will suppress the merchant class in the interest of social order. They disingenuously comment, "Revering such classical Confucian texts, officials in the seventeenth and eighteenth centuries looked on merchants with distrust and distaste."[2] A number of recent studies have paid attention to historical context and made it impossible to make such sweeping generalizations about officials and official policy. The late Qing period (ca. 1800–1911) has perhaps received the most attention from scholars.

"Symbiotic" is the word that both Lin and Hao use to describe the revisionist view of official–merchant relations in the late Qing. Simply put, officials invested in businesses to further their family fortunes, and the merchants received the patronage essential to doing business. In earlier scholarship, although this "symbiosis" was recognized, it tended to be cast more in the form of a morality play where officials represented a rapacious state. More recent scholarship, as Chan writes, "is inclined to believe that the professional roles of officials and merchants were not immovable categories, but interchangeable functional parts."

This shift is evident in evaluations of self-strengthening enterprises, particularly the *guandu shangban* (officially supervised, merchant-managed) enterprises in the late nineteenth century. While recognizing that these enterprises had problems of bureaucratism, corruption, and mismanagement stemming from their close association with the Qing state, some Western and PRC scholars have stressed positive aspects: unprecedented attempts to vertically integrate, spin off industries, and develop skills. One study from Taiwan argues that the self-strengthening period represents a shift from noninterventionist to interventionist state policies as the state came to depend more on commercial and less on agricultural taxes. Another scholar finds the failure of intervention in the late Qing reforms was due to inadequate abilities and not to conflict between the state and business. Feuerwerker sees the self-strengthening movement in terms of certain continuities in Chinese economic history: Although the state was not hostile to commercial activity, politics took precedence over economics in the interest of a political and social elite. During the self-strengthening period the location of an officially sponsored enterprise was likely to be determined by the "regional political interest of their bureaucratic patrons. . . . And political convenience might overcome cost-benefit analysis." Feuerwerker's interpretation sees culture, or at least political culture, as one determinant in Chinese business history.

Culture as a primary factor in determining the nature of economic enterprise is most readily associated with Max Weber, who attributed China's failure to develop capitalism to Chinese values or the lack of a Protestant ethic. A much less sophisticated version of this view is still embalmed in textbooks:

> According to Confucian philosophy, any promotion of trade would encourage people to aspire to a different lifestyle and to a higher social status, and such aspirations would bring change and social disorder. Moreover, Chinese thinkers held that merchants produced nothing: They bought something from its grower or maker and sold it at a higher price than they had paid; thus they were parasites living off the labor of others.[3]

The success of many Chinese business enterprises in the late twentieth century and the recognition that this acumen is not a recent phenomenon has led to a post-Weberian view of Chinese values. In the West, this has centered on the reevaluation of Confucian values in relation to business. In Taiwan, scholars have found elements in Zen Buddhism, Daoism, and guild religious rituals that supported business activity. However, as Lin notes, these studies do not negate "Weber's assertion that Chinese religious values hindered the rise of capitalism since capitalism is not equivalent to mercantile activities." On the other hand, insofar as the Chinese firms have become transformed into transnational capitalist enterprise groups but retain certain particularistic values, culture continues to be an issue.

The big question in the "culture" debate has concerned the efficacy of particularistic business relationships, notably family firms, lineage trusts, partnerships, and business networks based on family and regional ties, and powerful exclusionary guilds. In the both the past and present, these ties have been viewed as "dysfunctional." As recently as 1996, Francis Fukuyama argued that these particularistic values inhibited the development of a universal "social trust," and thus the ability to create a business organization large or flexible enough to compete in the global economy.[4] Chan disputes this view with an analysis of two contemporary transnational Chinese family firms, one in Hong Kong, the other in Thailand. He shows how the values and organizational structure of these and other Chinese firms have changed in response to changes in their economic, cultural, and institutional context. The core values, essentially particularistic ones, remain but do not preclude the possibility of a more impersonal trust in government, financial, and legal institutions.

Chan's analysis follows other recent work that seeks to understand Chinese business organization and management on its own terms. This trend has led generally to a reassessment of particularistic values in more positive terms. Increasingly, Western scholars have debated whether there is a "Chinese-style of management and organization" distinct from the Chandlerian model. In the PRC, the Marxist model has been modified in certain "capitalist sprouts" studies. Kwan finds that these studies, taken together, "paint a picture of a vibrant economy. Far from stagnant, or locked in a trap, businesses evolved to meet changing needs, and while some failed because of mismanagement and disasters, natural or otherwise, such sprouts of capitalism did not wither. Indeed, they laid the foundation of China's modern economy." Similarly in Taiwan, a plethora of recent case studies on topics including partnerships and merchants' associations, significantly modify textbook generalizations about Chinese business development.

The role of foreign investment and foreign trade in modern Chinese economic and business development has been one of the field's most controversial issues and is particularly subject to political judgments given that foreign economic penetration was part and parcel of gunboat diplomacy. Nor have the political polemics been laid to rest, as demonstrated by reactions to the recently released Chinese film *The Opium War*. The film presents the classic Chinese nationalist view of British exploitation, and more than one article in the Western press has hastened to point out that Chinese smoked opium before the British sold it, Chinese complied in the opium trade, and the war was over China's closed markets, not over opium. Fortunately, scholarly interpretations have become less polemical. Until recently, studies in the PRC began with the premise that foreign investment and foreign companies were exploitative, but, as Kwan points out, with the need to cultivate foreign investment, "this overwhelmingly nationalist approach has been ameliorated in more recent studies." Hence Butterfield and Swire can be condemned for its part in the coolie trade, but praised for its business acumen. Many studies recognize the significance of foreign investment in developing China's modern industries, and even gunboat diplomacy can be seen as positive insofar as it tore down China's "feudal economy." In Taiwan, recent studies focusing on the impact of foreign trade on the traditional economy have demonstrated the resilience of Chinese merchants in the face of foreign competition, both at home and abroad. Chinese merchants continued to dominate the interregional trade in China and linked the treaty ports to the hinterland. Their profit or loss can be tied to world economic trends, not simply to foreign privileges in China. In Western scholarship, the issue continues to be debated from neoclassical and neo-Marxist theoretical perspectives. But overall, as Hao's concise and lucid summary indicates, much of the research is pragmatic, making it more difficult to generalize about foreign influence. Hao is not hedging when he writes, "It is probably safe to say that its beneficial and deleterious effects on the Chinese economy occurred concurrently and that, on balance, its effects were neither uniformly destructive nor wholly beneficial" (p. 119).

As the reader will discover, the above discussion only touches upon the current issues in Chinese business history. The reader will also find that much of the research related to these issues is not readily apparent in book catalogues. With some notable exceptions, most of the specifically business history studies are found in journals and edited volumes (often conference volumes) and in theses and papers. Thus, the reviews of the literature here are all the more valuable to the study of Chinese business history. They are also valuable for setting research priorities for both "old business history hands" and newcomers to the field.

The consensus among the workshop participants was that Chinese business historians had best develop a specific model for the investigation of

Chinese business. How to achieve this was the subject of much discussion, which has been more fully summarized in the spring 1996 issue of *Chinese Business History*.[5] There was general agreement that more problem-oriented studies of business activities are essential. As Hao succinctly puts it, "The main business of Chinese business history is business in history" (p. 122). But there was also recognition that attention must be paid to the context. Zelin makes a strong case for understanding the legal context. A similar case could be made for understanding the religious context. Chan insists that this context must be understood historically, not theoretically. At this point, exactly how the field develops cannot be projected by any theory or model but will certainly take its cues from what has gone before, as indicated by the research reviewed in the following essays. It will also be informed by the developments in Chinese business in the Pacific Rim and in the global economy. These developments are rooted in a complex history that demands further clarification.

Notes

1. Professor Leonard and her staff and colleagues at Akron provided all the participants with a congenial and stimulating atmosphere for the exchange of ideas. The editors would like to thank, in particular, Ms. Jacci Baker, who took care of everything from coffee to transcription. We also received crucial support from the History Department staff at the University of Louisville and special thanks goes to business manager Rita Hettinger and to Shirley Taylor who scanned and edited a number of the chapters.
2. John McKay, Bennett Hill, and John Buckler, *A History of World Societies*, 4th ed., vol. 2 (Boston: Houghton Mifflin, 1996), p. 714.
3. Ibid.
4. See Francis Fukuyama, *Trust* (New York: Free Press, 1995).
5. Andrea McElderry, "Time and Space: Periodizing Chinese Business," *Chinese Business History* 6, no. 1 (spring 1996), pp. 5–6.

Chinese Studies in History, vol. 31, nos. 3–4, Spring–Summer 1998, pp. 16–34.
ISSN 0009–4633/1998 $9.50 + 0.00.

ALBERT FEUERWERKER

Doing Business in China over Three Centuries

Many Chinese, long used to being shut out of the political process, seemed unaware or uninterested in the most recent (September 1995) Chinese Communist Party (CCP) Central Committee meeting. "Who cares, really?" asked a Chinese manager of a joint-venture enterprise to an Associated Press reporter. For him, the shift to a partial market economy had brought a degree of prosperity and freedom that has made the leaders' decisions seem less important. But, the leaders are not impotent yet: The manager also earnestly requested that the reporter not use his name.

Above all I am going to be talking about the state and the economy. My aim is to suggest some continuities—and therefore, by implication, differences as well—in the matter of "doing business" in China over three centuries: (1) toward the end of the era of the Ming–Qing "tribute system," which came to a close with the "Opium Wars" of the mid-nineteenth century; (2) under the "unequal treaties" imposed by the foreign victors from 1842 through World War II; and (3) since 1949 in the People's Republic of China (PRC). My comments, which can barely skim this immense subject, will consider both Chinese domestic business practice and the matter of foreigners doing business in China.

Of course the Chinese economy in, say, 1800 differed from the economy in 1933, and even more so from that in 1995.

1. In the first of these eras, imperial China stood basically unchallenged at the center of an East Asian system of international relations and com-

From a paper presented as the keynote address at the workshop on Scholarly Research on Chinese Business History: Interpretative Trends and Priorities for the Future, University of Akron, October 27–29, 1995.
Albert Feuerwerker is A.M. and H.P. Bentley Professor Emeritus of History at the University of Michigan.

merce. At the end of the eighteenth century, China's population was perhaps 325 million, of whom more than 80 percent were farmers ("peasants" is the term usually employed). Although there had been improvements in the sense of a wider dissemination of the best available practices, the technology used in agriculture, handicraft manufacture, and transport—as well as the organizational forms and managerial techniques employed—was essentially that which had been elaborated in the Song dynasty (960–1279). But by contemporary world standards, that is, the world before the European scientific and industrial revolutions, China would be counted as a developed, relatively high-income country.

2. In the century inaugurated by the 1842 Treaty of Nanking, China was enclosed in a system of unequal treaties that made it a passive object rather than an autonomous actor in international relations. Its sovereignty and self-image had both been fractured. China's population in 1850 was perhaps 400 million and grew to 500 million by 1933. Of 1933's 500 million, 73 percent lived in families whose main occupation was agriculture, and farm output accounted for 60 percent of GDP. But changes had occurred over the century—still limited, to be sure, and excluding agriculture, which barely kept up with population growth—so that 7 percent of GDP now originated in "modern" industry, mining, and transport. In the most optimistic view, per capita GDP may have increased slightly in the two or three decades before 1937. What is certain is that, by both nineteenth- and twentieth-century measures, China, which in the pre-Industrial Revolution era would have been counted as a high-income country, in this new world was a poor and underdeveloped nation beset with very large political and economic problems.

3. China's economy in 1995, of course, differs greatly from that of 1933. The vital political context has also vastly changed. Today, for China's neighbors in Asia and for Europe and America, the critical question is whether or not a proud nation comprising one-fifth of the earth's people and experiencing remarkable economic growth will easily become a normal and responsible participant in a world system that, in Maoist days, it once scorned and even hoped to overturn. China's population will be 1.212 billion by the end of 1995; two-thirds of this population lives in rural areas, where average incomes are only 40 percent of average urban incomes. There are at least 120 million "surplus" workers in rural China. The coastal cities are swollen by floods of rural dwellers flocking to more prosperous urban areas in search of work. And even among the relatively favored workers in state-owned enterprises, with their proverbial "iron rice bowls," 15–20 percent are in fact redundant.

But the World Bank's strikingly low official estimate of China's GNP—U.S. $370 per capita in urban areas in 1994—is totally at variance with reality, which may be three or four times as large as this politically convenient number that has justified loans to China at concessional rates. Even with the enormous negative burden of Maoist political disasters (e.g., the Great Leap Forward, the Cultural Revolution) that produced deep economic crises, China's economic growth averaged 3–4 percent per capita in the four decades after 1949. From 1979 to 1989 gross national product escalated at an annual rate of 8 percent. The growth rate jumped to 13 percent in each of 1992 and 1993, and was 11.8 percent in 1994.

This resurgent expansion must be severely qualified by the continued poor performance of China's inefficient state-owned industries, and by the lag in agricultural growth where very large problems—the supply of food grains and cotton, for example—loom ahead. And Beijing's expansionary monetary policy, which was a major catalyst of the rapid growth, can once again boost inflation dangerously and bring on that cycle of boom and bust that has marked the reform years since 1979. Consumer price inflation was at least 24.1 percent in 1994, and while it has slowed in the first half of 1995, this was largely due to administrative measures rather than the curbing of the underlying causes of the inflation.

Actual, as opposed to "contracted," foreign investment in China reached $34 billion in 1994, up from $27 billion in 1993. From 1978 through 1994, foreign investment totaled $100 billion. The share of industrial output from state-owned industries fell to 40 percent in 1994, from 54 percent in 1993 and 77 percent in 1978. And the state share of GDP is shrinking along with the falling income from state-owned enterprises (SOEs) and very mixed results so far from efforts to revise the tax system. Foreign trade continues to grow, but some perspective is needed here—indeed, it is called for by all of this data that has fanned an inane China fever, even among supposedly sophisticated investors who ought to know better—like the College Retirement Equities Fund (CREF), which has put $50 million of my money and yours into Shanghai and Shenzhen B shares, and invested in companies whose financial records are risible and for whose shares there is no true market. Thus, even if China's total foreign trade turnover reaches $280 billion in 1995, up from $237 billion in 1994, China will then overtake only Spain (population 40 million!) to become the world's tenth-largest trading nation!

Over the three time periods, the economies of which I have just hastily sketched, I want to consider five large aspects of doing business in China, both by Chinese among themselves and by foreigners trading with or investing in China, whose characteristics tend to prevail through all or most of this lengthy time span. There were always countervailing tendencies, and reality is, for the most part, more complex than my abstractions, but for this occasion let me focus on the not unimportant continuities.

   1. *Precedence of politics over economics.* I put this item first because it

underlies so much else of what I intend to say. What I want to convey, with regard to Chinese decision-makers, is the saliency of the ends of political control and political stability over those of economic growth and economic control. "Merchants," regardless of nationality, of course, are in business for gain, and "farmers" everywhere seek to sell their crops for a profit (although, if they are "peasants" we are told it is household consumption that they strive to maximize). But even when, in the twentieth century, economic growth became a recognized goal, its priority could frequently be subordinate to getting or keeping power.

Here are some examples: In the late imperial era, before the advent of the *lijin* transit levy, the taxation of domestic trade was only a minor source of state income, but indirect regulation of markets in the interest of social stability through the licensing of traders/brokers (*yahang*) was carefully elaborated as a Qing state policy. The Qing granary system was a sophisticated adjunct to the private market in food grains, and the two together worked remarkably well at the height of the dynasty to respond to local food crises brought on by natural disasters and annual harvest fluctuations. But in extreme times, the magistrate at every level faced enormous pressures to keep all the grain he could within his jurisdiction, in the interest of local order and control, thus beggaring both the private market and the restocking of state granaries. The salt gabelle brought revenue to the dynasty and critical dietary salt to the populace, but, perhaps even more important, its operation brought the possibly largest concentrations of private wealth in China within the purview and control of the state—and similarly with other types of "official merchants." Above all, I suppose, the concept of growth of per capita output and its potential utility was largely absent. The Grand Canal was maintained, as it was in good times, largely to facilitate the flow of tax grains from the Yangzi valley provinces to the political center in North China, not in the first instance for the benefit of the numerous private shippers who clogged its waterways.

This distinctive emphasis on the political control side of matters is even more clearly evident in the case of foreigners doing business with the Qing. For the Chinese state the political functions of the tribute system were paramount. By containing foreign contact within a set of practices that were characterized by regularity (no surprise démarches), caution (only official relations were sanctioned), the mutual exchange of favors (tribute and imperial gifts), and the symbolic acknowledgment of China's superiority (the kowtow), the Qing state could achieve a sense of security, maintain a rudimentary international intelligence network, and enhance its prestige. Trade under the guise of tributary relations was, naturally, profitable to the Chinese merchants and officials of the frontier and coastal cities through which the embassies entered China. And customs revenues were of possible importance to the Imperial Household Agency. But for Beijing the possible economic gains, while they were not neglected, were very clearly secondary to the pursuit of stability and order. Not so, of course, for many of the foreign tributaries whose motive was frequently the opportunity to trade with China, while for others commercial gain was mixed with the cultural attraction of Chinese civilization.

International trade as tribute, as is well known, was only a portion of the total maritime commerce of Ming or Qing China. While China was still strong and self-confident, it was not necessary that the assumptions of the tribute system be taken too literally—just that their function as part of the justification for the Mandate of Heaven of the Qing emperor not be directly challenged within China. Indeed, there was no possibility that the tribute ideology could be literally applied. It was in the path of the expanding private trade among Fujian and Guangdong and the Philippines, Malacca, and the like, that the Europeans first began to appear on the Chinese coast in the sixteenth century, assuring that the future would not be humdrum.

The second of our three periods, the century of the unequal treaties, is divided between the last seventy years of the Qing dynasty and the briefer reign of the Republic of China. Domestic business underwent changes, but the saliency of political considerations remained a characteristic. Many of the early industrialization efforts of the late Qing were embedded in an "official supervision and merchant management" (guandu shangban) format that supported the regional political interests of their bureaucratic patrons as much as the economic interests of the investors. And political convenience might overcome cost–benefit analysis as, for example, in governor-general Zhang Zhidong's decision to locate China's first iron and steel plant across the river from his yamen rather than at a site better suited to the assembly of the necessary coke, iron ore, and coal. Even when they were not formally guandu shangban enterprises, late nineteenth- and early twentieth-century firms were rarely successful without official backing, which could entail choices by quasi-official entrepreneurs like Zhang Jian and Zhou Xuexi, who favored their political networks more than the firms' balance sheets. This weight of political considerations is evident in another guise even in the "rights recovery" movement in the first decade of the twentieth century among Jiangnan and other gentry, who sought, and in a few cases actually succeeded, but at an uneconomic cost, to reclaim railway and mining concessions that the foreign concessionaires had not exploited as they had engaged to do.

Under the Republic, we may point to the constant diversion of the government railroads to the carriage of warlord troops and munitions, to the severe detriment of normal commerce, as part of the big game of who would win Beijing and nominally be in control of China. If warlordism of this type ended with the establishment of the Guomindang's Nanjing government in 1927–28, the dominion of power and control over economic expansion and profit continued in the ambiguous relationship of Chiang Kai-shek and the Guomindang (GMD) to the wealthy capitalists of Shanghai and elsewhere. A sort of Sun Yat-sen–inspired, "socialist" (*san minzhuyi*) ideology underlay the persistent suspicion of these "bourgeois" elements, the limited government support for market-based economic development, and the direct and indirect drain of their resources to support GMD power and eventually the "bureaucratic capitalism" of the notorious "Four Great Families." Only in the late 1950s on Taiwan was this deep anticapitalist strain in the GMD overwhelmed by the realities of survival in a hostile world.

As to the treatment of foreign business in China during this century, the salience of concern with political control and social order over a cost–benefit outlook is not hard to discern. In the formation of the treaty system, the Manchu court was, for a long time, more concerned with prestige (such matters as not ceding audiences with the emperor for foreign envoys) than with the implications of the economic aspects of the treaties. And later, economic concessions to the imperialist powers were arranged—as in the case of the Trans-Siberian Railroad route across Chinese territory—in a political context where corruption was rampant. Among the foreigners themselves, with their rival "spheres of influence," there was surely tension between the more strictly economic efforts of the manufacturers and merchants in China and the maneuverings of their ministers and consuls, who were engaged in choosing up sides for the opposing alliances that were to face each other in World War I. Moreover, in the Republican decades the foreign impact on China was far greater in the political and psychological realms than the conventional accounts of economic "imperialism" by Sun Yat-sen, Chiang Kai-shek, or Mao Zedong would allow.

In the third of our time periods, in the PRC since 1949, surely the shape of the domestic economy in the Maoist years was distinctly the consequence of this man's misplaced "voluntarist" outlook, of extremism unchecked, of his bizarre turning of the party against itself in murderous factional struggles. When what was required was slowly and tentatively to build political and economic institutions and a new culture, the Maoists, in their zealous belief in the power of the human will, opted for a goal of rapid and total transformation. Hurried collectivization (and the anti-Rightist campaign), the Great Leap Forward, and then the Great Proletarian Cultural Revolution brought near economic disaster. Ignorance of opportunity costs and cost–benefit analysis, the manipulation of data and statistics, the control of information to restrict access for political ends, and a horrible *bagu* language [lit., eight-legged essay] that embraced official and much of public discourse—all this lessened in the reign of Deng Xiaoping, in the era of reform and opening to the outside world (*kaifang*) that began in 1979. But there are mounds of evidence to confirm that, although moderated, politics is still very much in command.

Take, as an example, the case of China's biggest new bank, the State Development Bank (SDB) that was set up in 1994 to finance priority projects with long pay-back periods, particularly large-scale infrastructure schemes. The World Bank noted, in a report of October 1994, that "the biggest issue facing the SDB is the degree of autonomy that it is to enjoy." Critics fear that "it may become the lender of last resort for the pet projects of Beijing's most powerful cadres."[1] Some see it as only outwardly something new, and expect that it will function in quite "traditional ways."

We must be cognizant of the importance of an enormous change that has taken place in China over the past ten years: The central regime in Beijing (i.e., the CCP and the gerontocracy that dominates it) has proceeded very far in giving up economic power to the provinces and localities so that freewheeling economic expansion can occur, while keeping its firm hold on political power. The synoptic slogan for the "socialist macroeconomics" of today is decentralization and relinquishment (*fangquan rangli*)—the direct antithesis of "planner's sovereignty." This has come about because, after Mao and the Cultural Revolution, and then after Tiananmen, economic growth became the only goal of the CCP, the only source of legitimacy for its continued political monopoly. The paradox is, I suppose, that the more economic power is decentralized, the more in fact it is embedded in a political nexus that determines outcomes as much as the supposedly objective workings of the market and the economists' production functions. The controversial Three Gorges dam project fits under this rubric as an example of gigantism (reminiscent of Stalin) pushed forward by intraleadership factionalism, in spite of serious questions about costs and how much electric power it will in fact produce—not to mention grave environmental issues and the small likelihood that the 1.3 million people to be displaced will ever be decently resettled.

For foreigners doing business in China the precedence of politics over economics may be expressed as part of such ambiguous actions as the selection of Mercedes-Benz rather than Ford or Chrysler as a partner in a minivan joint venture in July 1995 at the time of the to-do about Taiwan's president entering the United States. (In this particular case, a Chrysler official recently told me that Chrysler was not, in fact, very actively pursuing the minivan deal because of problems about protecting its technology.) The restrictive regulations imposed upon providers of foreign business news in China in January 1996—criticized by foreign investors and journalists as a retreat from "economic reform"—seemed to stem from both the avarice of the Xinhua News Agency and the desire of the wary central leadership to exclude news reports that, in their eyes, "slander China and jeopardize China's national interests." More broadly, this issue may be expressed in the questions: Will the PRC's interest in keeping and expanding the very large investments that have come from Taiwan help to moderate its recent bellicosity? Or will the factional maneuvering in the shadow of Deng Xiaoping's anticipated ascension to join Marx and Engels, if not Mao Zedong, undermine sound economic and political judgment with respect to both Taiwan and the future of Hong Kong? And even *more* broadly, in the longer run will not rational economic interest prevail both domestically and for foreign business in China as the CCP decays even further?

2. *Politics in command in the interest of a political and social elite.* By this rubric, I intend to suggest that in doing business in China, in the late imperial past and at present, one is confronted with a remarkably conservative society. The precedence of politics over economics was always in the interest of a particular political and social elite, for the purpose of maintaining social order and discipline so as to protect and enhance the dominance of this elite. Disorder (*luan*)—whether in the form of individual dissidence, or heterodox syncretic sects, or secret society rebels, or opposition political parties—was perceived as a danger in all three of the eras we are examining. More broadly, as Donald Munro has noted, there was a strong tendency to deny uncertainty in all aspects of life, and perhaps ever more so as society and the economy became more complex.[2] The omnipresent "that has not been solved yet" (*hai meiyou jiejue*) in contemporary Chinese discourse is in tune with Munro's observation that in traditional Chinese thought there was an appropriate model for everything, and no uncertainly is possible if minds are truly in tune. Thus we find a declaration by the State Statistical Bureau of July 13, 1995, on the matter of curbing inflation: "The situation is still serious. . . . So we must pay attention to unified thinking and strictly control price adjustments."[3] Let me speculate that it was not always quite so closed a society. Tang and especially Song China were surely more imaginative and innovative times, when the philosophical supports, the political institutions, and the technological resources of late imperial China were shaped. Until, let us say, 1500, Chinese agricultural and industrial technology continued to be superior or equal to European technology on the eve of the Renaissance. It remains a challenging historical question to explain the apparent inability of Ming and Qing China to continue the uncommon technological advances and economic growth of the Song era.

Society in the first of our three epochs, as in the other two, was sharply hierarchical, in the Qing characterized by the Manchu court and nobility at the top, a Manchu–Han bureaucracy spanning state and society, and local society dominated by a Confucian-educated, Han gentry-elite. Perhaps it was the "conquest" origins of the dynasty that moved it to the sponsorship of the more conservative strains of imperial Confucianism as the basis for its Mandate of Heaven. But it was a genuine conservatism that pervaded society, a dedication to continuity not as a reaction to modernist challenges, but from commitment to a philosophic–religious orthodoxy that claimed to comprehend the total meaning of life and humanity. At least among the literate elite there were few dissenters, no "Sunday" Confucians. The socially dominant gentry-elite, whose interests overlapped only in part with the *raison d'état* of the dynasty and its top bureaucrats, was prepared to lead a mobilization against rebels—the momentous mid–nineteenth-century Taiping rebellion—who were enemies not only of the Manchu court but also of that conservative and hierarchical Confucian social and political order of which they, the gentry, were both the transmitters–interpreters and the beneficiaries.

Conservative thought and politics in support of a stratified, hierarchical society persisted throughout the century of the unequal treaties, although at the end of that epoch it was sorely challenged and then overthrown by a competing all-inclusive, hierarchical mode of envisioning and organizing society. The end of the nearly thousand-year-old examination system in 1905 only formally marked what was an ongoing process of differentiation within a social elite that had had strong roots in rural landholding. Their sons (and now for the first time, some of their daughters, too) were starting to include modern intellectuals, school teachers, journalists and editors, professionals, party politicians, warlords, industrialists, and bankers. When the Qing dynasty failed both to roll back the foreign imperialist presence in China and to afford sufficient political participation to this elite that was increasingly mobilized by nationalist, anti-imperialist doctrine, the elite made China's first urban revolution and replaced China's last imperial dynasty with a republic. But they remained *the* elite; however bitter their internal conflicts, however feckless their factionalism, these descendants of the gentry of imperial times, increasingly urban in location and outlook, remained at the top on all of the scales of wealth, power, and social status, separate from the stiff, inert, and relatively illiterate rural population, and even from the growing number of urban residents (who were also increasingly politically aware). Thus, the impiety of "total Westernization" was an indictment hurled at some intellectuals who sought to discard the omnipresent models and restricted modes of inquiry of traditional thought—and traditional ways of doing business. And the Guomindang, standing with one leg in past convictions and the other in modern uncertainties, might, as I have suggested, look at the unfettered economy of Shanghai with much the same hostility as the traditional Confucian's scorn of profit (*li*), as opposed to old-fashioned virtue (*de*).

The most striking social change that the PRC brought was the end of gentry society, the replacement—for millions the violent physical extinction—of the rural and urban elite of whom I have been speaking with a new CCP hierarchy. The process of establishing Communist rule was accompanied by the emergence, after 1949, of a new "red aristocracy," party and state cadres (*ganbu, apparatchiks*) of successive generations (those of the Long March, the anti-Japanese united front, the civil war, land reform, etc.), whose vested interests, as each wave found its niche, increasingly limited the capacity of the party-state to undertake further change. The newly privileged *ganbu* elite was a genuine problem in Mao's China—as it proved to be a central shortcoming of the rule of Marxist–Leninist parties everywhere. Its origins in the semiliterate peasantry of North China combined with the Chairman's anti-intellectualism to stifle creativity, including economic and enterprise innovation, in the first three decades of the PRC.

In the era of Deng Xiaoping, self-reliance (*zili gengsheng*) gave way to *kaifang* (opening to the outside world and export-led economic development), and mere nativist conservatism was somewhat out of fashion. But the reformers of the Deng era inherited a state that was weaker at the center than one would have imagined possible in the 1950s. The orthodox cultural and ideological hegemony that the Maoists had sought to impose could no longer be persuasive. To establish their legitimacy and power, the post-Mao coalition under Deng, composed, on the one hand, of CCP reformers (many were younger cadres) and, on the other, of anti-Maoist orthodox Leninists (Stalinists?) had only the option of accomplishing the economic growth promised in 1949 and so often derailed by Maoist utopian extremism. The reformers were willing to modify the "socialist system" in the interest of economic expansion, and perhaps some were led (or would have been led at some point in the future) by the inner logic of the process of reform to question socialism itself. The other half of the coalition—those with real power as shown in the spring of 1989, many of them elderly leaders retired from actual party or state office—blamed Mao's excesses for the failure to achieve a Stalinist-type socialism. As the Deng era comes to a close, the apprehension of *luan* as the succession of power is brokered still makes Beijing extremely wary about uncontrolled business, both domestic and foreign, and about critical economic reforms without which continued rapid growth is uncertain, but that might unleash *luan* to threaten the already weakened party-state, which, for the CCP elders, is all that they possess after seven decades of revolution.

3. *An economy of private property—with qualifications.* With the qualifications that I shall note for the PRC, since at least the Tang dynasty (618–907), by far, most land in China has been privately owned and farmed, commerce basically in private hands, and manufacturing (handicraft until modern times) similarly conducted by private (often household-based) enterprises.

In the first of our three periods, the state had some participation in the salt monopoly and in copper and silver mining for coinage. The "official" pottery kilns (as at Jingdezhen) and silk manufactories (as at Nanjing) were, over time, transformed into supervising offices for private contractors. The system of semifree labor by enrolled artisans of the Ming dynasty disappeared in the Qing, as did unfree personal status for most peasants. While markets were regulated and taxed, except for official salt merchants (and a few others), entry to the market was basically free. In foreign trade there were government licensed "monopolies," the "cohong" to deal with European traders and others for Southeast Asia. But these were monopolies of privileged (and highly "squeezed") participation; they were not usually price monopolies. Smugglers and pirates appear frequently in the annals of both domestic and foreign trade; and they were, of course, very "private" (when they were not the gendarmerie on their day off).

In agriculture the treaty-system century saw a further erosion of quasi-public banner land. While the *guandu shangban* industrial enterprises of the 1870s and later might include some government funds as well as "supervision," their assets came mainly from private investors (including some officials, of course). Some government shipyards and arsenals were opened, but the first iron and steel plant was quickly "privatized." The telegraph lines, started as private ventures, were nationalized, as were failing private railroad lines (this was one cause of the 1911 revolution). Although official patronage was often useful, the largest part of Chinese-owned modern industry was privately owned—and all of the foreign-owned sector was private. Private banks existed alongside the more powerful government banks, while domestic commerce was almost entirely in private hands. In the course of war and civil war from 1937 to 1949, groups of enterprises controlled by cliques of high GMD bureaucrats and their followers ("bureaucratic capitalism") grew in significance. These were frequently based on former Japanese-controlled (or "collaborator") assets in the wartime occupied areas.

There was little foreign role in Chinese agriculture. Foreign trade was private on both sides. The piratical commerce of the Opium War era gradually gave way to a more "normal" trade that was no longer a zero-sum game, but one in which both Chinese and their foreign partners profited, although not necessarily equally. Foreign traders increasingly saw their role circumscribed to serving as importers supplying a thriving private Chinese commercial distribution network. Most businesses and property over this century were thus usually in private hands.

But when we come to Mao's China, agriculture has been collectivized and industry and commerce, for the most part nationalized. After the mid-1950s there was no private sector remaining apart from petty crafts. In smaller-scale manufacturing some enterprises continued to operate as "collectives." Beginning in 1979, in the era of Deng Xiaoping, the agricultural collectives were dismantled and agriculture, for good or ill, became essentially private again. Farmers' land contracts, introduced in 1979 for terms of one or two years duration, have since then been extended for varying periods, differing by locality, of up to thirty years. "Ownership" is still technically "collective"; in fact, farmers pay annual fees (a land tax, in essence) and may transfer land to others or subcontract. Beijing's hope is for larger, more efficient farms, as many leave the land seeking employment in township and urban enterprises.

In industry and commerce the state-owned sector is shrinking, with many of the state-owned industrial enterprises—a third or more—operating at a loss and producing products that no one wants to buy. Much cotton yarn, for example, is made with antiquated machinery and is of a low quality unsuitable for export goods, thus wasting scarce raw cotton supplies. Many in the CCP leadership understand that the critical next stage of the reforms is to withdraw state subsidies and cheap capital from failing SOEs, but so far have been unwilling to face the daunting obstacles to such fateful changes. Standing in the way of reforms are: remnants of "socialist" ideology, especially at the center, while the provinces and localities are keen on privatization; huge interenterprise debts and their unrepayable bank loans; lack of a social security system for redundant workers, and hence fear of worker unrest; immature legal and banking systems unable to discipline enterprises; and weak labor and housing markets. There are some experiments underway to separate state ownership from management, but it is still very unclear how this will operate. Debate over privatization, as the wary participants well know, is also debate over the future of the CCP. Once assets and money pass out of the hands of the state, what will the role of the party be?

In Guangdong, and to a lesser extent in Fujian, the dynamic industrial sector of the past decade includes a substantial, genuinely private component—much of it linked to investments from Hong Kong and Taiwan. Much more common in the rest of China is the phenomenon of local, mainly township-level, officials as entrepreneurs, a sort of semiprivate industry almost completely out of the control of the center. This has produced enhanced regional inequality and local protectionism, and what one legal expert has termed a "local corporatism," wherein the local officials and local enterprise leaders are one and the same, and are effectively removed from discipline by the center in the absence of serious legal and banking systems. And that localism, too, prevents cooperation on the increasingly grave environmental issues facing China.

There was little foreign presence doing business under Mao. For the Deng reforms *kaifang* were central—even if, as Deng Xiaoping has colorfully put it, when you open the door the flies will come in. Most of the flies, so far, have been compatriots (*tongbao*) from Hong Kong, Taiwan, and Southeast Asia, whose investments have been mainly in low-wage manufacturing for export or in hotels and other urban real estate. This is all private investment; in addition, China has received some government-backed advances (e.g., from Japan) as well as concessional loans from international agencies. To date, there remain unresolved problems about foreign investment in infrastructure projects (the Chinese would like it, but balk at providing the returns that investors in such risky undertakings demand). Foreign direct investment in high-tech projects (the third wave, à la Toffler) remains limited, constrained in part by problems relating to the protection of technology; and even the second wave (automobiles, railroads, power) has yet to be achieved. In Beijing's eyes at least, private foreign investors will come anyway, drawn now not by the emperor's "virtue" (*de*), which supposedly lured the tributaries of Ming and Qing times, but by the perennial attraction not of merely "400 million customers" but of 1.2 billion and growing.

4. *Particularistic criteria* (guanxi) *and the importance of intermediaries.* If the conventional "objective" situation—say technology, demand and supply, and prices—may take second place to political motives, then the personal character of the participants in any transaction assumes a particular importance. Thus "particularistic" criteria loom large in doing business in China in all three of our time periods. I refer especially to the importance of kinship as a basis for business organization and the selection of management; or of other personal relations such as a common place of origin, common schooling, or contemporary military or bureaucratic service. Not uncommonly, in large gentry families in the past or in high *ganbu* families of today, some relatives will occupy bureaucratic offices while others pursue mercantile interests—and the two will, of course, at least be conscious of each other's interests even if not commonly contriving to further them by illicit means. The business ventures of the "princelings" of the PRC today—from Chen Yun's son to Deng Xiaoping's own children—evoke memories of the Soongs and the Kungs of the last days of the GMD.

Institutions such as the merchant guilds (*huiguan*) of the late imperial era were important loci for face-to-face transactions, colored by common place of origin or common line of business, in a society that lacked other facilities for nonlocal decision-making (such as a satisfactory banking system, or rapid communications). Qing merchant handbooks emphasized the importance of proper human relations to business success—not as something inherently separate from economic interests, but as a means to protect and enhance them. But *guanxi*, personal relations, as a basis for business organization has its drawbacks, too: it tends to limit enterprise size; it is a hostage to chance with respect to the qualities of second and later generation descendants of the original entrepreneurs; and it can obstruct technological changes, especially organizational innovation, away from family-based face-to-face management.

I believe that the frequent reference in Chinese writing to such-and-such economic cliques reflects a pervasive behavioral style in which factionalism is integral much more than it does a penchant for *waishi*, the tabloid-type inside history that few of us "scholars" deign to read. The salt merchants of Yangzhou and the Shaanxi bankers of the Qing era, for example, formed particularistic groupings and interacted with official patrons. In the late Qing, Li Hongzhang and Zhang Zhidong, among others, presided over regional economic and political satrapies, including the client entrepreneurs who undertook China's early industrialization efforts. Zhou Xuexi's business empire, including the pioneer Chee Hsin Cement Company, got its start with the backing of President Yuan Shikai.

This emphasis on personal character (or personal relations, extending to "right" thinking) applied to the foreign character, too. Qiying, a Chinese negotiator at the time of the Opium War, may have believed that "their characters are unfathomable," but throughout the late empire and the republic, a succession of foreigners played key roles or served in advisory positions because of their reputed good "character," from Robert Hart who headed the maritime customs for decades, through the advisors to Yuan Shikai and his Beiyang army successors, including also Sun Yat-sen's Japanese friends, and the Germans and Americans who counseled Chiang Kai-shek and the Guomindang. I have not pursued carefully the possible relationship between personal ties and foreign economic opportunities in the republican years, but I would be surprised if it were any less salient than it appears to be in the PRC today.

Andersen Consulting and the Economist Intelligence Unit recently surveyed foreign corporations operating in China for clues on how to make money in that fast growing economy. "Choosing and building relationships with the wrong Chinese partners will jeopardize the success of even the most promising venture," the Andersen report of September 21, 1995, concluded. "It is the rule of relationships, not the rule of law," commented an

Andersen partner. So, last July, American International Group (AIG) again pulled off a coup by getting the go ahead to set up the first foreign insurance branch office in Guangzhou. AIG became the first foreign insurer permitted back into China, when, in 1992, it established a branch in Shanghai, the city where it had begun in 1920. That breakthrough was the result of years of personal diplomacy by AIG chairman Maurice Greenberg, who cultivated friendships with top Chinese leaders. Last July, Greenberg was named a "senior economic advisor" to the Beijing city government.

Related to this salience of *guanxi* in business and other matters is the characteristic importance of intermediaries for many transactions. This was a major function of the *huiguan* (guilds) to which I referred, of the omnipresence of guarantors (*baozhengren*) for most deals, of the Cohong to treat with the East India Company, and of compradors as critical intermediaries (and often also wealthy participants on their own account) throughout the treaty system century. Westernized Chinese and the "old China hands" of the treaty ports also fall under this rubric. On the contemporary scene, for American business in China these intermediaries are frequently Chinese-Americans, or Hong Kong and Taiwan Chinese—more broadly *huaqiao*, members of the Chinese Diaspora. And because business negotiations are more often than not conducted in English, there is a large role for English-speaking Chinese nationals who are not themselves principals in the deals being discussed.

5. *The weakness of formal legal institutions as loci for dispute settlement.* Maybe it is not such a bad thing to be free of attorneys: The United States with 5 percent of the world's population maintains 75 percent of the world's lawyers! Still, our understanding of how *modern* economic growth (increase of output *per capita*, or *intensive* growth) has come about in the West, reinforced by a Nobel prize to the scholar who elaborated the critical importance of "transaction costs," Douglass North, includes an important place for the institutions of law and property that empower both the predictability and the security of complex economic transactions. Can we speculate that the *premodern* economic growth (increase of *total* output but not *per capita*, or extensive growth) that China experienced before the nineteenth century simply was not so dependent upon formal legal norms and processes as the Kuznetsian-type economic development, set in motion by the Industrial Revolution?

In the Qing dynasty there was a relative paucity of formal legal rules about economic transactions. The Qing law code contained no commercial law section *per se* that might provide substantive or procedural protection for merchants, but some parts of the criminal code did treat property and commerce under the sections devoted, for example, to household law. Here,

I am not repeating the conventional and misleading judgment that there was no "civil" law in late imperial China. There was no *civil code*, but, in fact, county magistrates handled thousands of cases each year originating in suits by both peasants and urban people over property issues. If complex commercial transactions were not formally covered, they frequently were the subject of mediation and regulation in the informal (nongovernmental or quasi-governmental) realm, where, for example, merchant guilds (and later chambers of commerce from the early twentieth century) were the key actors. Functionally there was a similarity between this sophisticated and complex, multistage, informal *guanxi*-based procedure—Madeleine Zelin has described its operation among the salt firms in Zigong, Sichuan—and what a strict legal positivism would expect. The guilds and chambers of commerce had considerable problems, however, in the matter of enforcing their judgments because of the weight of particularistic ties in both the Qing and Republic. And enforcement is a critical shortcoming, too, of the expanded court system of the Deng era in the PRC.

Foreigners doing business in China were removed from the jurisdiction of Chinese criminal law by the extraterritoriality provisions of the Opium War treaties; they had disdained it and avoided it, in any case. By practice, rather than by formal covenant, foreign business in China during the Republic could at times also evade the strict enforcement of civil, including economic, legislation.

A "modern" civil code, based on the European continental model, was adopted in 1929–31. While it included features compatible with the Qing code of the past, it also dealt with much broader commercial areas, and in greater detail. By 1932 there were perhaps 10,000 lawyers in China, located in Shanghai and also Beijing, Tianjin, Suzhou, Hangzhou, and Nanjing. They had few incentives to work outside of urban areas, included few women, and were a disparate group, indeed, in terms of their training. To the successive governments (the Beijing warlords and then the GMD in Nanjing) lawyers were a necessary evil, needed as part of the requirements for the end of extraterritoriality, but trouble. The Shanghai Bar and the GMD did not fit smoothly together, a problem parallel to Chiang Kai-shek's troubles with the Shanghai bourgeoisie.

In Mao's China, formal civil law and most lawyers disappeared along with private property. Criminal law, in the Deng era, remains one area that has been notably resistant to the forces of change affecting the rest of Chinese society. As under Mao, while some excesses are gone, basically the government is not restrained by its own rules. The Communist Party and its members enjoy a sort of "extraterritoriality," subject only to internal CCP discipline. Much of the criminal process is outside of the formal legal system and is handled as administrative control by the police. Foreigners with white or brown or black skins are probably not affected, but a number of overseas Chinese businessmen (possibly not too ethical themselves in these cases) have run afoul of the system.

A substantial amount of civil legislation, especially concerning foreign investment, has come into force during the past decade. The goal of the Ministry of Justice is to have 150,000 lawyers by the year 2000; there are 75,000 now; there were 3,000 in 1980. Concern with "professional responsibility" and "legal ethics" has not developed very far; and the whole matter of separating lawyers from their former role as "state legal workers" is troublesome. Local and provincial courts have proliferated, but there are great problems in executing civil judgments, which makes the legal system a poor vehicle for enforcing business contracts and settling disputes. For one thing, there is an ideological reluctance to use coercive measures; civil disputes are, after all, "contradictions among the people." Judgments against SOEs are difficult to enforce because the courts at each level are under the same jurisdiction that controls the guilty enterprise. The courts are only one bureaucracy among many, and have no overriding jurisdiction. Private households (*getihu*) have no work unit (*danwei*), so that it is difficult to garnishee wages, for example, in divorce or child-support cases. Above all, the localities ignore central regulations and directives when it suits them to do so.

The central government, for ideological and fiscal reasons, has sought to keep control over foreign business activities in China, while, at the same time, encouraging them. We may note such measures as strict review of the contracting process, regulations about the formation and operation of foreign-invested enterprises (including regulations for internal use only [*neibu*] that are not available to the foreigner), control of foreign exchange, and taxation. In practice, policy went back and forth with respect to the degree of "openness" before Deng's 1992 Shenzhen visit set off the latest burst of reform, and it may vacillate again in the course of the pending succession. Decentralization has permitted Beijing's regulations to be contradicted or ignored by the localities. If Beijing cannot control the localities, how can it control foreign investment? "Local corporatism" further undermines the process of establishing a serious legal system as the basis for doing business in China. Corruption has grown to grievous proportions with the use of existing institutions for private gain, illegal and unauthorized fees, the establishment of illegal businesses by government agencies, bribery, the transfer of government assets, the appearance of "local despots" in the countryside, environmental degradation, and the flight of capital. Further, as the center's economic power has decayed, there is the opportunity for foreign investors—mainly Hong Kong and Taiwan Chinese who have no stake in law themselves—to join with township officials (who are also entrepreneurs) both to undercut the wages and working conditions of local workers and to continue to violate Beijing's international agreements in such areas as the protection of intellectual property rights.

That "the rule of law" has yet to take firm hold in China and that this lack affects doing business in China by foreigners is evident. Note, finally, the explanation, given by the Toyota board member responsible for Asia, for Toyota's not making a large equity investment in China: "because the period for a return on our investment is long, we need a more solid foundation, including well-defined policies from Beijing, a legal framework and internationally trusted practice."[4]

Conclusion: Does it all matter? But China was always a complex place, and, of course, the Chinese are "inscrutable." If the five aspects that I have discussed formed a critical part of the context in which business was conducted in China over the centuries, in the longer view and in world comparative terms, they do not seem to have offered substantial obstacles to creditable economic performance. Until the eighteenth century, China's premodern or extensive economic growth was as good as that of any other part of the world. The era of the unequal treaties, to be sure, saw many problems, and was marked by the failure to make a smooth and rapid jump to modern economic growth. But the bases were established (discovered, imported, adopted, adapted); the power of compound interest is not to be gainsaid, but one has to start somewhere. Three decades were lost to Maoist maniacal utopianism, yet since 1980 China has experienced the fastest growing economy in the world and perhaps in world history.

My caution lies not in the matter of economic growth—doing business; in many ways this is the easiest part of the challenges that China confronts on the eve of the twenty-first century. And it will not follow automatically that, because some will become rich by "jumping into the sea" (xiahai) of "doing business," those other importunate issues will be met. The first of these challenges is to construct a unified and effective polity, a political system to replace that of the Qing empire, destroyed in 1911 and never successfully rebuilt. An adequately strong state—it does not have to be either a one-party dictatorship or a Western-style democracy—is necessary if an autonomous legal system is to come into being, or an effective banking system, or the control of foreign investment, or a social safety net for the population, or adequate investment in human capital, or compliance with international norms with respect to human rights, or investment in agriculture, or protection of the environment, or prevention of extreme regional and interpersonal differentials. Doing business alone—the market—will not achieve these common ends.

The other equally large challenge is to forge a set of shared values and beliefs (like the dominant Confucianism of the imperial past) that could glue Chinese society together in the twenty-first-century world, that would provide a genuine identity for the men and women of a truly modern China. I do not anticipate that some imported religion is going to work any better than did Marxism–Leninism, Mao Zedong Thought, now totally in shambles. From where in China's rich tradition such a "civic religion" will emerge I cannot guess. But I am certain that the cramped contemporary message to "make a little money" (*zhuan yidian qian*) by doing some business will not long suffice to nourish hearts and minds in a nation with so long a history and so rich a culture.

Notes

1. *Far Eastern Economic Review*, April 27, 1995, p. 60.
2. See Donald J. Munro, *The Imperial Style of Inquiry in Twentieth Century China: The Emergence of New Approaches* (Ann Arbor, MI: Center for Chinese Studies, University of Michigan, 1996).
3. Reuters, Beijing, July 13, 1995.
4. *Far Eastern Economic Review*, January 26, 1995, p. 45.

Chinese Studies in History, vol. 31, nos. 3–4, Spring–Summer 1998, pp. 35–64.
© 1998 M.E. Sharpe, Inc. All rights reserved.
ISSN 0009–4633/1998 $9.50 + 0.00.

MAN BUN KWAN

Chinese Business History in the People's Republic of China

A Review

Reviewing historiographical development in China, Harold Kahn and Albert Feuerwerker observed in 1964 how Chinese historians moved from the classroom to the platform in "a genuine attempt to find legitimization in China's past for the domestic and external developments of her most recent present."[1] Little seems to have changed thirty-two years later and developments have been attributed to a state-sponsored pluralism.[2] With a decade of economic reform since 1979, and another half-decade since 1991, it is perhaps an opportune time to take stock of changes in historiography, specifically business history, in China.

There is no lack of material from which a conclusion might be drawn. Although there is no Chinese equivalent of the term business history, this genre of economic history, loosely defined as the history of an enterprise, whether it be handicraft or industrial, commercial or financial, public or private, may be traced to Wei Yungong's *Record of the Jiangnan Arsenal* [Jiangnan zhizaoju ji] in 1905. Since 1949, and especially after 1979, selected sources, monographs, and papers in academic journals related to the subject easily exceed 1,000.[3] In addition, the Chinese People's Political Consultative Conferences have published at least 14,000 articles on various

---

From a paper presented at the workshop on Scholarly Research on Chinese Business History: Interpretative Trends and Priorities for the Future, University of Akron, October 27–29, 1995.

Man Bun Kwan is on the faculty of the University of Cincinnati Department of History.

Critical comments by conference participants, especially S. Cochran, A. Feuerwerker, W. Kirby, and M. Zelin have helped me in revising this essay. All errors, of course, are mine.

industries, trades, and businesses in over 2,300 national and local *Historical Materials* [Wenshi ziliao].[4] Memoirs on capitalists and enterprises have appeared in many publications.[5] Less accessible to foreign researchers might be publications of political organizations such as the Chinese Democratic League [Zhongguo minzhu tongmeng], and mass organizations such as the Federation of Industry and Commerce [Gongshangye luanhehui], successor to the various local chambers of commerce before 1949.[6]

This essay obviously cannot do justice to this large body of literature, especially what has accumulated since 1979. Beginning with an overview of the data-collection phase from 1950 to 1966, the essay will focus on the period between 1979 and 1989, and will follow with a section on recent developments (1990 to 1996). In the context of China's shifting politics, the changing interpretive trends on the following issues will be highlighted: the socialist transformation of capitalist enterprise, the sprouts of the capitalism controversy, the sprouts' modern fate, the role of foreign investment, the self-strengthening movement and the "main thread" debate, the lineage of the Chinese national bourgeoisie, marketing, and the recent hagiography surrounding Chinese capitalists (both past and present). While their counterparts in the West labored against a "disdain" for the bourgeois on a subject ignored by both historians and economists, Chinese business historians have provided alternative perspectives to modern Chinese history by focusing on businesses as economic units integral to Chinese society.[7] Voluntarily or otherwise, for better or for worse, they do not have the luxury of the ivory tower.

Chinese Business History, 1949–1966

Uncharacteristic as it may seem in hindsight, Mao Zedong once advocated the development of capitalism in China, declaring that the country had too little of it.[8] After 1949, this policy was endorsed repeatedly by the Chinese Communist Party (hereafter CCP), specifically by Mao himself in the first working conference on the United Front in March 1950. In that spirit, the newly created Chinese Historical Association and the Chinese Economics Association sponsored a group of leading historians and economists, including Chen Hansheng, Fan Wenlan, and Qian Jiaju to form the Editorial Committee for the Publication of Materials on Modern Chinese Economic History [Zhongguo jindai jingjishi ziliao congkan bianji weiyuanhui]. Works in this series pertaining to business history include Wei Zichu's collection of documents on the Kailan Mining Administration, and a four-volume set on Modern China's salt gabelle administration and the salt trade.[9]

A parallel effort was led by Yan Zhongping, then associate director of the Institute of Economics, Chinese Academy of Sciences, who launched in 1953 under the series title *Anthology of Reference Materials on Modern Chinese Economic History* [Zhongguo jindai jingjishi cankao ziliao congkan] an ambitious project covering major topics (statistical overview, industry, agriculture, handicraft, foreign trade, and foreign debt), as well as key industries like railroads and shipping.[10]

Following the completion of the socialist transformation of capitalist enterprises campaign, in 1960, Zhou Enlai initiated a five-year program to summarize China's experience with capitalism. Historians affiliated with research sections of state organizations, such as the Central Bureau for Commerce and Industry, were mobilized.[11] With access to the voluminous archives and interviews of surviving employees, they compiled a series of selected materials on various industries and enterprises under the series title of *Anthology of Historical Materials on Capitalistic Industrial and Commercial Enterprises in China* [Zhongguo zibenzhuyi gongshangye shiliao congkan].

A number of local academies of social sciences and universities also contributed to the enterprise. The Shanghai Academy of Social Sciences led the country in collecting materials on "model" capitalist enterprises, including the Nanyang Brothers Tobacco Company, Dalong Machine Works, Hangfeng Spinning Mill, and the conglomerates of Liu Hongsheng and the Rong family. At the Institute of Economics of Nankai University, research focused on Zhou Xuexi's Chee Hsin Cement Company, and the archives of the Kailan Mining Administration.

Such scholarship has contributed significantly to our understanding of these enterprises and the economic history of the period. However, since such materials came from voluminous archives and other sources, selections were often made, consciously or otherwise, on the basis of how well they fit the theme of modern Chinese history as a struggle against foreign imperialism and feudalism. The publication process provided further opportunity for omissions, if not censorship. Without belittling their value, such compilations must be used with caution. It is imperative that researchers request access to the original archival materials, or failing that, bianyu material left on the cutting room floor.

The Socialist Transformation and the Four-History Movement

Given more time, Chinese historians might be able to move beyond the data-collection phase to analyzing and writing on this rich body of material. Unfortunately, shifting politics cast their capitalistic subjects in an increasingly unfavorable light, culminating in the socialist transformation of capitalist enterprises campaign. A study of this process is Beijing Ruifuxiang, a retailer of silk, foreign imports, tea, and furs, as well as operating a weaving and dyeing mill in Jinan, from which a fascinating model of "traditional" commercial organization and family business emerges.[12] Here we found a powerful owner keeping a tight control on his professional managers, who, in addition to receiving a salary, were also granted a share of the profits as an incentive. These employees, who were often relatives of the owner or his fellow natives from Zhangqiu, would serve faithfully for life as the firm prospered. After the death of the strong-willed owner and family head, however, the firm weakened as dissent and problems of succession forced a division of the owner's household. Warfare further weakened the firm until an infusion of state capital and the socialist transformation gave the firm a new lease on life.

The story of Ruifuxiang became a model for both the "traditional" business and the future of the country's former capitalists. However, as the political pendulum swung against the national bourgeoisie and private enterprise, academic studies gave way to the "Four-History" Movement, including factory history written from the perspective of class struggle. Workers and students, often history majors in various universities, were mobilized to collect data and conduct interviews. To the extent that their work reflected the politics of the time, such publications (and many others that remain unpublished) preserved a from-the-bottom voice of the past.

Sprouts of Capitalism

Impertinent as it may seem in hindsight, just when the CCP was about to transform, if not eradicate, private enterprise, historians embarked upon the "sprouts of capitalism" debate. The theoretical basis of the controversy may safely be attributed to Mao Zedong in 1939—that "[As] China's feudal society developed its commodity economy and so carried within itself the embryo of capitalism, China would of herself have developed slowly into a capitalist society even if there had been no influence of foreign capitalism."[13] That China could change is grounded less in economic history than in political theory, as Lü Zhenyu first articulated the argument in 1937 to combat the "stagnationists" (and hence "capitulationists") in the Nationalist party.[14] Resurrected in 1955, the debate evolved around an exhaustive catalog of the various commodities in circulation, leading to an analysis of the ways in which the commodities were produced, the nature of the labor involved, the development of merchant putting-out systems (*shangren guzhu*), culminating in the appearance of workshops. A business history approach with enough case studies might shed light on the timing and extent of this transformation. Unfortunately, a paucity of such business records left the debate in a circle and, with the onset of the Cultural Revolution, history as a scholarly pursuit ground to a halt.

Recovery from the Cultural Revolution

The era of Deng Xiaoping ushered in not merely economic reforms, but also made it possible for surviving historians to resume their work, resulting in perhaps the most sophisticated work on the development of capitalism in China under the series title of *A History of the Development of Capitalism in China* [Zhongguo zibenzhuyi fazhanshi].[15] Departing from earlier discussions on the subject, which placed the transition as beginning in late Ming, Wu Chengming and his colleagues argue that although prototypes of handicraft workshops had made their appearance by late Ming, they basically disappeared by mid-Qing. There is thus no lineal path of development as previously assumed. Instead, the crucial change occurred in early Qing when merchants began to invest increasingly in putting-out systems and other enterprises such as mining.[16] Other historians have discerned a similar trend for landlords.[17]

Implicit, too, in Wu's theoretical perspective is his modification of the orthodox Marxist position on the inverse relationship between the development of commercial capital and industrial capital while acknowledging the dissolving influence commerce might have on the "feudal" mode of production.[18] Dismissing managerial landlordism as negligible, and workshops such as the salt wells of Zigong as too few to be of significance, Wu focuses on the development of the merchant putting-out system as the major path of transition for commercial capital into productive capital. In accordance with Marx's dual-path model, he allows that this development might be less "revolutionary" than producers becoming owners of workshops.[19]

Recent research, however, has moved beyond this classic Marxist position. In a detailed study of the putting-out systems operated by silk merchants (*changfang*) in Suzhou's silk-weaving industry, Wang Xiang characterizes the dual-path model as "simplistic," a theoretical desideratum rather than one grounded in history.[20] Emphasizing the silk merchants' control of the production process and workers, commercial capital, however "feudalistic," fostered a development that did not wither, but rather continued to grow and evolve. From its small beginnings in 1702, the number of *changfang* grew to twelve by 1840, and their products were shipped to Canton in the south and to Xinjiang in the north and beyond. For the even more commercially developed China proper, studies of the silk, cloth, porcelain, sugar, soybean, grain, lumber, and brokerage businesses, or the sand-boat (*shachuan*) shipping and insurance industries are too numerous to list here.[21] Merchant manuals enjoyed a large circulation, offering advice on practical matters ranging from the training of apprentices to prudent behavior while on the road.[22]

Such a national, if not international, commercial operation is neither unique nor unprecedented. Through detailed comparison of merchant handbooks and tracing of trade routes, Chinese historians have discerned a vast expansion of commerce during the Ming and further developments under the Qing.[23] The long distance trade between China proper and the Northwest, for instance, prospered beginning in 1724, if not earlier, with the establishment of Dashengkui. Until 1929, the firm's camel caravan (*pa*) carried tea, silk, cotton cloth, garlic, tobacco, and other sundries deep into central Asia. On the return trip, furs, hide, wool, and herbal medicine would make up its cargo, in addition to herds of sheep and horses. At its peak, the firm regularly supplied Beijing with at least 100,000 sheep and at least 5,000 horses.[24]

An extensive operation of this scale requires coordination, and these entrepreneurs could draw on the organizational and managerial skills developed by their fellow Shanxi merchants. In the formation of a business, capital could come from an individual or from a partnership among nonrelatives. However, depending on the scale of the business, these investors may or may not have taken an active interest in its operation.[25] Once a trustworthy manager was identified, investors could draw a dividend from their investment and in that sense own the business, but otherwise not be active in its operation. While there were dictatorial and active proprietors who could dismiss their employees at will, both owners and managers increasingly had their duties, liabilities, and rights defined by elaborate contracts enforceable through the courts and customary law.[26] By late Ming, if not earlier, Shanxi merchants had developed "modern" profit-sharing schemes as an incentive for professional managers to work faithfully and hard for their far-flung business.[27] The success of Dashengkui may be explained in part by this system, which eventually gave the professional managers overwhelming authority over the firm, in which the descendants of the firm's three founding partners owned only 3.5 of the firm's 34.5 shares. Under the direction of a head manager at Huhehot, the firm adopted a policy of limiting its annual dividend for each share to 10,000 taels, regardless of the profit from an estimated turnover of over 10 million taels each year.[28] The hefty surplus held in reserve gave it the strength to expand into a conglomerate of native banks (including the *piaohao* Dashengchuan) and subsidiaries specializing in the trading of grain, silk, tea, livestock, wool, and camel hair. These products in turn became raw materials in the production of blankets and rugs and were distributed widely to both nomads on the steppes and the peasant households of North China.

Facilitating the expansion of this commodity economy was an array of financial institutions, the most prominent of which was the *piaohao*. Traditionally dated from the early reign of the Daoguang emperor (r. 1821–1850), documentary evidence suggests that its prototype, matching drafts (*huipiao*), as a private business arrangement among relatives and friends, might be traced to early Qing, if not earlier.[29] Specializing in long-distance remittances, these *piaohao* had been condemned because of their close relationship with the "feudal" Qing state through the purchase of degrees and remittance of state funds, although recent studies suggest that a significant portion of the *piaohao*'s capital financed interprovincial long-distance trade, especially after 1900.[30] For the financing of local trade and production, Chinese merchants could draw upon the support of proto-banks such as the credit house (*changju*) dating from 1736 in North China, or their counterpart the native bank (*qianzhuang*) in other parts of the country.[31]

Taken together, these studies paint a picture of a vibrant economy. Far from stagnant, or locked in a trap, businesses evolved to meet changing needs, and while some failed because of mismanagement and disasters, natural or otherwise, such sprouts of capitalism did not wither. Indeed, they laid the foundation of China's modern economy.

The Modern Fate of Rural Handicrafts

While the continuation of handicraft workshops present a departure from the accepted conventional wisdom, the issue of whether handicraft workshops furnished a link in the evolution toward industrial production remain controversial. Peng Zeyi argues that the handicraft-based workshops remain an important sector, accounting for 79 percent of capitalistic industrial enterprises until 1954. On the other hand, Wang Jingyu argues that there was little or no development toward industrial production of the three handicraft workshop industries that he studied. In other words, they coexisted as a dualistic economy.[32]

Recent regional studies paint a more nuanced picture of the continued survival of rural handicrafts. In the case of Suzhou's silk industry discussed earlier, forty-six new *changfang* appeared between 1845 and 1912, a growth attributed to rising demand from domestic and foreign markets. During this period, several changfang also made the transition from decentralized putting-out systems to their own established workshops.[33] After the 1911 Revolution, a number of *changfang*, led by Yongxingtai, formed the first weaving mill using iron looms and, by the early 1920s, motorized looms.[34]

However, the superiority of factory production is not apparent as *changfang* remained a viable business. Merchants continued the putting-out system, providing a supplemental source of income for rural households by specializing in certain kinds of fabric and maintaining a flexible production schedule. On the other hand, some mill owners leased their mills to silk merchants, preferring to collect a stable rent rather than operating the mills themselves.[35] In other words, the "traditional" and "modern" forms are not mutually exclusive. Indeed, they reinforced and complemented each other.

A similar experience, albeit on different regional cycles, is also seen in cotton weaving in both the Lower Yangzi and North China. Even foreign imperialism did not lead to the demise of this handicraft and business activity. Xu Xinwu's work details the industry's modern fate in Central and South China where imported yarn gradually displaced homespun yarn beginning in the 1870s, but peasants continued to find employment in the production of native cloth by using imported yarn as warp and experienced periods of prosperity.[36] In parts of the Lower Yangzi such as Nantong, an expanding "native" cloth trade to the Northeast sustained a healthy, if not growing, demand for homespun yarn as weft.[37]

In both the Lower Yangzi and North China, cotton yarn and cloth merchants played a critical role in organizing the industry as suppliers of yarn and more efficient iron looms. Firms such as Fufeng of Gaoyang in Hebei Province began in 1902 as a department store cum money lender until its owner Yang Musen identified the opportunity in cotton cloth and pioneered the reproduction in Tianjin of the imported Japanese iron loom.[38] At its peak during the trade's second period of prosperity (1926–29), the putting-out operation controlled over 1,000 looms scattered over several districts, over 2 million yuan in capital, and branch offices that stretched from Outer Mongolia to Chengdu.[39] Competing for the same market were the versatile merchants of Baodi District who, like their Gaoyang counterparts, joined the cloth trade as a sideline business. Originally known as money and grain firms (*qianliang hang*), they branched out into the yarn trade, and then developed putting-out systems, a weaving mill, and established a spinning mill in 1910 using venerated second-hand machinery purchased from Zhang Zhidong's cotton mill in Wuchang.[40] On the other hand, there are case studies detailing how owners of handicraft workshops turned from production to commerce in search of profits.[41] There is, indeed, no one single lineal path.

Foreign Investment

This coexistence of the "traditional" and the "modern" further complicates the debate on the effects of foreign imperialism and investment on China, given the assumed overwhelming superiority of foreign technology and capital. While hundreds of foreign company archives remain untouched, archivists and teams of historians have skillfully and carefully selected a handful and have published materials not available elsewhere. In 1983, under the direction of the History Planning Commission of the State Council, the Editorial Committee on Modern Chinese Economic History [Zhongguo jindai jingjishi congshu bianji weiyuanhui] was established to oversee the national effort. Based at the Shanghai Academy of Social Sciences, the series thus far includes works pertaining to business history, such as the chamber of commerce archives from Suzhou and Tianjin, translations of works on Chinese business history from English, and *Ying–Mei yan gongshi zaihua qiye ziliao huibian* [B.A.T in China] in four volumes. Another American activity covered is the International Banking Corporation (after 1927, the National City Bank of New York), and British companies include the International Export Company, Tianjin (a subsidiary of Union International Company of London).[42] Representing Japanese capital are the Southern Manchurian Railroad, the Han Yeh Ping Iron and Coal Company, and the Yokohama Specie Bank.[43]

These sources provide solid grounds for business history and make a strong case for imperialist exploitation. Few foreign companies, if any, escape condemnation. Zhang Zhongli and Chen Zhenlian's *The Sassoon Conglomerate in Old China* [Saxun jituan zai jiu Zhongguo] studies a conglomerate that, at its peak, controlled assets of at least 2 billion yuan. Beginning as an importer of Indian opium, the company reinvested its estimated profits of 40 million taels from this trade in Shanghai's real estate. Through careful analysis of its archives, the authors documented the company's keen business strategy of insider-trading, manipulation, and exploitation of its extra-territoriality privilege. By 1941, the conglomerate controlled an empire of banks, dockyards, trading companies, real-estate developers, and investment companies, as well as over $20 million thoughtfully remitted abroad—all coming from the "plundering" and "exploitation" of the Chinese people.[44] Other studies on the Oriental Bank, the 1910 Shanghai rubber stock bubble, Japanese investment in China, and the Beijing Syndicate reinforced this line of argument.[45] Foreign companies conduct themselves not with fair and open competition, but rather oligopolistic, if not monopolistic, control and abuse of their extra-territoriality privilege.[46] Even worse are charges of spying and deceit.[47]

With the need to cultivate foreign investors as a result of the economic reforms, however, this overwhelmingly nationalistic approach to foreign investment has been ameliorated in more recent studies. Butterfield & Swire Company, while still being condemned for its role in the coolie trade, is credited for its sound business acumen and entrepreneurship. Readers are exhorted to learn valuable lessons from a concrete analysis of the conglomerate's history in economic terms.[48]

Other historians have gone even further in this shift, if not revision, of emphasis. Surveying foreign enterprises in Sichuan, ranging from bristle processing plants, silk reeling works, and shipping companies on the Yangtze to mines, Zhang Lihong found that they constituted a significant portion of the province's industrial economy. While acknowledging that foreign investments were supported by the gun-boat diplomacy of the powers at the expense of China's sovereignty, she argues that the overwhelming "feudal" economy could only be torn down by force. In this context, foreign enterprises contributed to the development of the province, "in effect an important aspect of modern China's capitalistic industry and commerce."[49] Other historians support this incorporation by pointing out that what had once been classified as foreign capital, such as many of the shipping companies, actually came from Chinese investors.[50] A few even argued that China's economy would have been developing at a "bound-feet" pace had it not been for foreign investment.[51]

The Self-Strengthening Movement and the "Main Thread" Debate

If the role of foreign investment is being reevaluated, state-sponsored enterprises since the self-strengthening movement also generate much controversy. Caught between the anti-feudal/anti-imperialist struggle and the desirability of industrialization, historians found politics a convenient yardstick in their interpretation. The influential historians Fan Wenlan and Hu Sheng both dismissed enterprises such as the China Merchants' Steamship Navigation Company and the Shanghai Weaving Mill sponsored by Li Hongzhang and other "self-strengthening" reformers because of their close association with the Qing state. Mired in corruption and waste, the monopoly that these enterprises enjoyed only served to obstruct the development of these industries by the national bourgeoisie.[52]

A critical reexamination of these "self-strengthening" enterprises has provided a cleavage point for a major debate among modern Chinese historians since the Cultural Revolution. In a series of articles, Li Shiyue emphasizes the progressive nature of these enterprises, their limitations notwithstanding, as the take-off point for China's social productivity, which laid the foundation for the subsequent Hundred Days reforms and the 1911 revolution.[53] Inspired by Li's challenge, other historians began to approach these "self-strengthening" enterprises as economic units of analysis rather than appendages of leading statesmen or the Qing state. When the reorganized

Shanghai Weaving Mill was experiencing difficulty in raising the necessary capital from the state, Chinese investors such as Zheng Guanying and Jing Yuanshan came to the rescue. Concerned with the influx of foreign imports and to protect their investment, they lobbied in 1881 against the establishment of any new mills, foreign or domestic, and constantly struggled against attempts by officials to dominate the enterprise.[54]

While acknowledging the weakness and impurity of the nascent national bourgeoisie, historians have also traced various multiplier effects from these "self-strengthening" enterprises. The experience gained in the management of these enterprises provided valuable lessons when the first generation of Chinese industrial capitalists went on to build other enterprises with the substantial cash flow from these "self-strengthening" enterprises.[55] The Chinese Merchants' Steamship Navigation Company, for instance, provided seed capital for at least twenty mines, steel mills, banks, and weaving mills.[56] Taken together, these enterprises not only provided state sponsorship and inspiration, however limited and limiting, to civilian investors, but also trained a generation of engineers and industrial workers.[57]

This attempt at redefining the "main thread" of modern Chinese history, substituting anti-feudal/anti-imperialist class struggle with development toward capitalism, has provoked a stormy debate, with studies on the "self-strengthening" enterprises providing plenty of ammunition for both sides. Despite the privileges of state loans and monopoly, officials in charge of these enterprises were not interested in protecting the country's interests. Under the direction of Li Hongzhang, for instance, the China Merchants' Steamship Navigation Company repeatedly "surrendered" to foreign shippers by entering into a series of market-sharing agreements to guarantee its profits.[58] The dependence of these enterprises upon foreign advisers and technology merely provided more opportunities for foreign interests to encroach upon China and for bureaucratic graft.[59] The China Merchants' Steamship Company, for instance, was run aground by bureaucrats, like Sheng Xuanhuai, who drained the company of its profits.[60] To the extent that these enterprises were economically successful, they only contributed to the rise of bureaucratic capitalism, thus obstructing the growth of the nascent national bourgeoisie.[61]

The Lineage of the Chinese National Bourgeoisie

Class analysis and struggle thus continue to influence business history in post–Cultural Revolution historiography, and the compradors invite special condemnation because of their close association with the "feudal" state as well as with foreign imperialists. "Hong" merchants, such as the three generations of the Wu family (Howqua I–V), amassed a fortune of at least $26 million from the opium and tea trade of Canton (Guangzhou), squandered it through extravagance, and served the Qing state faithfully with over 1.6 million taels of silver in contributions while earning official titles as rewards.[62] By definition, too, wealth accumulated by anyone serving the foreign firms, with or without a contract, in the exploitation of their countrymen through trade or services falls under this category of comprador capital.[63] They did not merely help in the infiltration of China, but shared an economic interest with their "masters" by investing in the foreign firms, and thus were accomplices in the oppression of the nascent national bourgeoisie.[64]

Equally undesirable are the effects of bureaucratic capitalism that include hundreds of enterprises owned and operated by warlords and government officials. Beginning in the late Qing, bureaucrats such as Sheng Xunhuai and Zhou Xuexi looted the state coffers to finance their investments.[65] Abusing the authority invested in them, these bureaucrats, joined by their warlord brethren, amassed a huge fortune for themselves through plundering and obstructed the healthy development of the national bourgeoisie by limiting competition and favoring the enterprises they owned, directly or indirectly.[66] On the other hand, their corruption, ineptitude, and inconstant political fortune also contributed to the demise of many of these enterprises.[67]

The highest stage of capitalistic development in modern China, however, is reserved for comprador–bureaucratic capitalism whereby compradors and bureaucrats converged after 1927.[68] Under Chiang Kai-shek, compradors north and south colluded with various political cliques, despite their often colliding interests. Together, they began to seize control of the country's economy, first through the major banks, culminating in the formation of the Joint Board of the Four Banks under T.V. Soong, the Central Trust under H.H. Kung, and the Postal Remittances and Savings Bank under the so-called C.C. clique.[69] Through the National Resources Commission, they encroached upon the national bourgeoisie by forced injection of state capital into such companies as the Nanyang Brothers Tobacco Company, or nationalized mines to help fulfill their agreements with Germany and the United States. After World War II, they occupied themselves with confiscating enterprises taken from the national bourgeoisie by the invading Japanese. Recovery of these enterprises by their rightful owners was deliberately obstructed, just as efforts by leading national bourgeois industrialists, seeking state guarantees for foreign loans to develop the country's economy, were repeatedly frustrated.[70]

Many historians have found this politically correct argument debatable. If the bureaucrats of late Qing represented the interests of the feudal state based upon landlordism, then by definition they could not be capitalistic, bureaucratic or otherwise. In this view, a more appropriate classification for these enterprises might be state capitalism.[71] In a careful study of comprador capitalism, Wang Shui estimates that compradors invested at least 5 million taels of silver in various modern enterprises and probably supplied 20 percent of the capital for privately owned factories and mines established between 1872 and 1894, and 12 percent for such enterprises between 1895 and 1913. While the absolute amount involved might be a fraction of the compradors' total estimated wealth, it represents an important boost to the growth of the national bourgeoisie.[72] Not to be overlooked is the contribution of the National Resources Commission in developing critical enterprises, such as the Yumen Oil Field, under adverse conditions, or the fact that an organization of a "reactionary" regime could have both positive and negative effects.[73]

From the perspective of business history, then, perhaps the most significant flaw in this line of argument is the combining of politics and economics. Just as dynasties come and go, warlords, bureaucrats, and compradors often left their positions, voluntarily or otherwise, to become what theoretically should be classified as national bourgeoisie and as a result their businesses acquired a chameleon-like elusiveness. Yuan Shizhuan's Jiawang Colliery at Xuzhou would have been classified as a bureaucratic-warlord enterprise and received a "different" treatment, until a careful historian established that Yuan is not the seventh brother of Yuan Shikai as alleged.[74] Equally daunting is the long career of Tang Tingshu who, after making his tainted fortune as a comprador for Jardine, Matheson and Company, resigned to become a merchant director of the China Merchants' Steamship Navigation Company, and subsequently the Kailan Mining Administration. In this long career, he founded dozens of mines and other enterprises, rendering his classification an estimable task.[75] Nor are such political categories exhaustive for the study of capitalistic development in China, as in the case of the many overseas Chinese who, as holders of foreign passports, fell through the cracks between foreign and national.[76] It was this group of overseas Chinese, together with an increasingly disillusioned and activist merchant community, who supported the 1911 revolution.[77]

On the other hand, the logic of capitalism also reminds us of the role of profit in all these enterprises, regardless of their owners' status or political views. Caught between states that were too weak or too intrusive and foreign competition, the businesses of these nascent national bourgeoisie had to return a profit to survive. To some historians, that some of them did was achieved at the expense of the workers, with exploitation rates estimated to be as high as 1,000 percent in some industries (average: 230 percent in 1933). To make workers work harder, downsizing was routine and essential.[78] Competition among some of them became so keen that dumping below cost to force competitors into bankruptcy and takeovers was commonplace.[79] In their unscrupulous quest for profit, kickbacks, market-sharing, and price-fixing schemes were arranged and broken just as frequently.[80] Nor are these otherwise desirable national bourgeois companies above reproach when it comes to their efforts to cultivate various "reactionary" regimes or to conspire with foreign companies in cartel agreements.[81] If they had had their way, monopolizing the market would not be beneath them, as in the case of Chee Hsin Cement Company.[82] As heuristic categories, comprador–bureaucrat–national bourgeoisie might be an exceedingly sharp instrument for political analysis and policy, but too blunt a tool to deal with the nature and complexities of the Chinese bourgeoisie and their businesses.

Such difficulties might have led to the search for alternative approaches to understanding the nature and origins of capitalism in modern China. Wei Ming, for example, side-stepped the issue of warlord–bureaucratic capitalism by defining their many investments in modern factories and mines as private economic activity.[83] Following his lead, other historians have focused on private–personal, as opposed to public–state, economic activities regardless of one's occupational status, and assessed the social and economic effects accordingly.[84] Making a careful distinction between bureaucratic capital and capital of bureaucrats, Li Lin argues that as bureaucrats like Zhou Xuexi increasingly involved themselves in industrial enterprises, their connections with the state, however undesirable, made it possible for the businesses to survive against foreign competition and thus contribute to the industrialization of the country.[85] Going further, some placed less emphasis on the "tainted" nature of capital—whether it be landlord, bureaucrat, or comprador.[86] Regardless of one's social and political status, there are valuable lessons in management to be learned from them.[87] A study of the Kailan Mining Administration attributed the profitability of the company to the sound business practices of its new British owner. The lesson to be learned is that:

> The slow process of China's early industrialization and the frequent failure of the "Self-Strengthening" enterprises may thus be traced to one fundamental cause—the mere introduction of advanced means of production while attempting to preserve intact (or without complete eradication of) the traditional feudal superstructure and management methods would make the task doubly hard.[88]

Recent Developments

State sponsorship and financial support continue to loom large in the compilation of sources for business history. Initiated by Hu Yaobang in 1979 and endorsed by Hu Qiaomu, the new gazetteer movement launched in 1983 has resulted in a genre of business history too extensive to list here.[89] Such works might cover a trade at the national level, or a regional "trust," or a province.[90] Municipal archives have combed their voluminous collections, resulting in publication of several business archives.[91] Individual state enterprises, such as the Capital Iron and Steel Company, also publish studies for public consumption that soon pass as history.[92]

Since the early 1980s, several state ministries have also been active in the compilation of sources and histories in areas under their jurisdiction. The Ministry of Finance has orchestrated a national effort to comb various local archives of base areas during World War II and the civil war. Together, these recently published documents and memoirs provide a fascinating glimpse into the evolution of the CCP's policy toward private enterprise during these formative years.[93] Similarly, the People's Bank of China has commissioned researchers to work on various local banks from late Qing to 1949.[94] The All-China Federation of Supply and Marketing Cooperatives supports a series of selected historical materials of rural cooperatives.[95] Books emphasizing the patriotism and entrepreneurship of the national bourgeoisie or the tradition of social service and business have also been published by the Chinese People's Political Consultative Conference.[96]

The largest state-sponsored project on business history to date is the series on *The Socialist Transformation of Capitalistic Commercial and Industrial Enterprises in China* [Zhongguo zibenzhuyi gongshangye de shehuizhuyi gaizao]. Since 1987, the CCP's Central Party Historical Material Collection Committee and the United Front Bureau have organized the compilation of case studies as well as directives from the central and local governments. To date, over thirty volumes have been published. Another series, supported by the CCP's Party History Section, has been published on handicraft cooperatives and the development of urban and township industrial collectives. From the perspective of business history, however, missing in this chorus are the effects on businesses, as well as the problems and lingering effects of "undue haste," "inattention to detail," "oversimplification," and "inappropriate employment and treatment of industrialists and merchants" referred to in the "CCP Central Committee's resolution on certain historical problems since 1949."

Markets

Interest in preserving the historical record is not confined to the various state organs. Increasingly, historians are responding to the market reform to the extent that some of them might have shifted their theoretical perspective. "Sprouts of capitalism" has been declared dead, to be replaced by either

"sprouts of modernization," or "sprouts of market economy."[97] In addition
to identifying trade routes, historians have begun reconstructing and understanding the structure of marketing in Chinese history, influenced in part by
G.W. Skinner's seminal work. At the local level were primary markets serving
the needs of the surrounding countryside. Wholesaling and bulking of farm
products took place at the intermediary market towns.[98] By late Qing, a
three-tiered national market comprised of urban, rural, and regional markets
had been identified.[99] In addition to a marketing system predicated on retailing,
Liu Xiusheng traces the formation during the Qing period of two other overlap-
ping, but not contiguous, marketing systems in bulking and wholesaling.[100]

In this expanding and increasingly differentiated market economy, price
formation was affected by a multitude of factors. By the late Ming, if not
earlier, commercial capital increasingly penetrated and controlled the hith-
erto self-sufficient "natural economy" of peasant households, resulting in
higher rates of commercialization than previously estimated.[101] Extensive revisions have also been made on Dwight Perkins's pioneering work
on the size of the country's market (domestic and foreign trade), suggesting
that it has been underestimated by as much as one-third.[102] Whether it is
"involution" or "self-exploitation," the debate surrounding the welfare of
the peasants neglected the role of merchants and the issue of how their
businesses interfaced with the rural sector. Studies of price movements
based on routine official reports and statistics, while telling us a good deal
about state concerns and commodity flows, only made a beginning in addressing the "business" side of the equation.[103] The appearance of an orderly
and efficient rice market in eighteenth-century Guangdong belies considerable anomalies and noneconomic factors, including the interference by the
Manchu garrison, provincial and local officials, in price formation at the
local and provincial levels.[104] Policies of the central government, too, continue to obstruct and interfere with the operation of the market.[105]

On the other hand, the large number of local and regional studies published since the early 1990s helps us to understand the business environment of late Imperial China. On the issue of "feudal" state control and
interference with the civilian economy, Liang Miaotai's study on Jingdezhen
argues that the existence of imperial kilns stimulated rather than obstructed
the development of private kilns. A constant flow of state orders and technological transfer benefited this civilian sector. Drawing upon surviving
ledgers of private kilns, he concludes that the business was at least as
profitable as landholding, although it required much less start-up capital.[106]

Economic reforms also raise the issue of property rights. As the responsibility system in the countryside spread to the cities and applied to factories
and other production units, specifying rights and responsibilities became a

critical issue, renewing interests in studies on civil law, contracts, and forms of business organization, including shareholding.[107] The legal framework affecting business conduct, including liability, debt, inheritance, and property rights, had long been the domain of civil law (as opposed to criminal law) in the West. As a separate code governing such matters was lacking, it has been suggested that China did not have a civil tradition, although a number of Chinese legal scholars argue that such matters were handled by customary law and codes scattered in formally promulgated dynastic compilations.[108]

Even in the absence of a separate civil code, a highly developed legal culture of local customary practices evolved to serve businesses in China. In Sichuan's salt industry, elaborate contracts were designed with terms reflecting the risks assumed by the contracting parties.[109] With drilling often being a time-consuming and capital-intensive undertaking, the landlord and shareholders could enter into a contract in perpetuity [zisunjing, literally son and grandson well], as opposed to a fixed term contract that reverts the property to the landlord after a specified number of years.[110] In packaging together a salt well drilling and production operation, the landlord would receive land rent as well as slots in the production schedule. The syndicator of the package might, in lieu of a fee, be promised slots, as would investors who financed the drilling operation. Should the well turn out to be dry and additional capital be needed, a new group of investors could buy out its predecessor, or receive its allotment of production time when the well began production. These slots (representing shares in the well operation) could be inherited or alienated and bought and sold in the open market (without, of course, the benefit of a Wall Street). With tens of thousands of taels and as many as forty shareholders involved in the drilling and ownership of a well, the industry also evolved the practice of limited liability (jingzhai jinghuan), limiting the shareholders' loss to the amount they invested in the well. Instead of an immediate settlement of all debts incurred for the well, creditors could put a lien on the shares/slots, allowing them to receive income from the well until their debts were cleared and the shares reverted to the holder. Although not every contingency could be provided for, such legally enforceable documents provided a firm foundation to attract capital and business operations.

On the other hand, the rule of law might not be ubiquitous, and a local lineage-based society like Foshan exercised considerable autonomy and operated thriving businesses, such as real estate development and casting of iron implements. To the extent that these enterprises were profit-seeking units, their behavior was affected by considerations of the lineage and the community's welfare. Maximization of the goodwill of household and lineage members was as important as maximization of returns on investment.[111]

On the other hand, the sharing, deployment, and access to a larger pool of capital and human resources beyond individual entrepreneurs and their nuclear families made these businesses stronger. Beyond kinship, native-place ties also cemented solidarity and aided merchant groups such as the Ningbo *bang* in their expansion across the country.[112]

Explaining this success in terms of kinship and other "particularistic" ties has led historians to reconsider the embeddedness of economic action and to shift their focus toward the cultural and psychological matrix of merchants and capitalists.[113] The building of lineage halls and gardens and sponsorship of the arts and scholarship, once dismissed as pretentious and wasteful, are recognized as making important contributions to the development of a vibrant urban culture.[114] Instead of casting Confucianism and profit as mutually exclusive pursuits, Tang Lixing's study on the Huizhou merchants argues that a career in commerce is no less satisfying than the scholar-official path and just as vigorous in the practice of Confucian virtues.[115] Amidst a rising interest in Max Weber, Du Xuncheng found such categories as "Occidental" and "Oriental" at once facile and superficial. In the realms of ethics and values, Weber's ideal-type comparative method exaggerated the differences while ignoring considerable similarities.[116] Indeed, the ability of "traditional" merchants and their values to mobilize resources, human or otherwise, for the good of the group echoes some of the arguments surrounding Confucianism and the economic miracle of modern East Asia.[117]

Regional studies of capital formation confirm the critical role played by "traditional" merchants and commercial capital in the establishment of industrial enterprises. In the case of Wushi, neither the state, nor local government, the landlords, or the peasants played a significant role, and approximately 60 percent of the capital for the many silk reeling works, flour mills, and other businesses came from networks of "traditional" merchants.[118] Based on surveys conducted in the early 1950s, Chen Qingde argues that it was the merchants, rather than the producers, who garnered the bulk of the profits.[119] At the national level, commercial capital (including financial capital) predominated, accounting for as much as 97 percent of the capital belonging to the national bourgeoisie in 1894, 85 percent in 1920, and 78 percent in 1936 (excluding the Northeast).[120] Buoyed by this strength and the rising tide of nationalism as exemplified by the idea of commercial warfare (*shangchan*), merchants and industrialists considered themselves as troops in the service of the country and their capital as fodder. From a historical perspective, the modern Chinese bourgeoisie has rediscovered its strength and place in history.[121]

This rediscovery also affirms and legitimizes the role of entrepreneurship and private enterprise under the current economic reforms. With an eye toward the market and profits, publishing houses have been flourishing with studies that provide models of past success.[122] One ambitious effort is the *Biographies of Major Chinese Capitalists* [Zhongguo dazibenjiazhuan], a ten-volume set on thirty-seven leading captains of industry and commerce from the Republican period, including Zhang Jian and the Guos of Wing On fame.[123] Under preparation is a sequel covering forty overseas Chinese entrepreneurs, to be followed by their successful mainland brethren. Another series of biographies on major capitalists and their businesses, with Xu Dixin as chief editor, has been published with the explicit goal of providing examples for budding entrepreneurs to emulate.[124] Even the CCP's own press, the Red Flag, joined this avalanche.[125] As dozens of "how-to" guides on playing the emerging stock market and inspirational literature of the Horatio Alger variety fill the sidewalk bookstalls in individual runs of over 10,000 copies, publishers are awash in the windfall. Perhaps a new height of hagiography in Chinese business history is achieved by the story of the Haomen Corporation.[126] Business history is a fast-growing business in China.

Chinese historians have benefited from this development. State sponsorship remains important with its support of such major research projects as that on the Huizhou merchants.[127] However, to the extent that the socialist *nouveaux riches* are organizing and involving themselves in shaping the business environment and history, their activities, including family histories, essay competitions, conferences, associations, publications, and appointment as advisers to national and local governments reflect a significant change in contemporary China, intended or not by the CCP.[128] Corporate sponsorship of scholarly meetings is frequent, just as their subsidy might be crucial in deciding the fate of scholarship.[129] Whether such public activities and genres of business history constitute the emergence of a liberal democratic civil society, or the cashing in of a Habermasian bourgeois self-conception are questions for future historians to consider.

Notes

1. Harold Kahn and Albert Feuerwerker, "The Ideology of Scholarship: China's New Historiography," in Albert Feuerwerker, ed., *History in Communist China* (Cambridge: MIT Press, 1968), p. 13.
2. Timothy Wright, ed., *The Chinese Economy in the Early Twentieth Century* (New York: St. Martin's Press, 1992), pp. 1–4.
3. Such as *Zhongguo jingjishi yanjiu* [Studies in Chinese Economic History, hereafter *JJS*]; *Zhongguo shehui jingjishi yanjiu* [Studies in Chinese Social and Economic History, hereafter *SHJJ*]; *Pingzhun xuekan* [Bulletin of the Chinese Association for Commercial Economics]; and on occasion *Lishi yanjiu* [Studies in History, hereafter *LS*]; *Jindaishi yanjiu* [Studies in Modern Chinese History, hereafter *JDS*]; and *Zhongguoshi yanjiu* [Studies in Chinese History, hereafter *ZGS*].

4. A convenient reference is Li Yongpu, ed., *Quanguo geji zhengxie wenshi ziliao bianmu suoyin* [An Index to Historical Materials published by National and Local Political Consultative Conferences], 5 vols. (Beijing: Zhongguo wenshi, 1992), especially vol. 2.

5. *Gongshang shiliao* [Historical Materials on Industries and Commerce], vols. 1–2 (1980–81); *Gongshang jingji shiliao congkan* [Anthology of Materials on Industrial, Commercial, and Economic History], vols. 1–4 (1983–84).

6. Tianjin, for instance, is served by the two organizations publishing jointly the *Tianjin gongshang shiliao congkan* [Anthology of Historical Materials on Tianjin's Industry and Commerce], vols. 1–8 (1983–88). Similar publications can be found for Beijing, Chongqing, and Wuhan. A convenient reference for such literature is Li Yongpu, ed., *Zhongguo shizhilei neibu shukan minglu* [Bibliography of Internal Publications Related to Chinese History and Gazetteers] (Jinan: Renmin, 1988).

7. On the less-than-hospitable climate for business historians, see Charles Jones, *International Business in the Nineteenth Century* (New York: New York University Press, 1987), p. 17.

8. Mao Zedong, "On Coalition Government," in *Mao Zedong ji* [Collected Works of Mao Zedong], 10 vols. (Hong Kong: Yishan, 1976), vol. 9, p. 224. Words uttered by Liu Shaoqi to the same effect became one of his principal crimes during the Cultural Revolution. See Bo Yibo, *Ruogan zhongda juece yu shijian de huigu* [Recalling Major Decisions and Events], 2 vols. (Beijing: Zhonggong zhongyang dangxiao, 1991), vol. 1, pp. 49–58.

9. Wei Zichu, *Diguozhuyi yu Kailuan meikuang* [Foreign Imperialism and the Kailuan Collieries] (Shanghai: Shenzhou guoguangshe, 1954); and Liu Foding et al., *Zhongguo jindai yanwushi ziliao xuanji* [Selected Sources on Modern China's Salt Gabelle and Trade], 4 vols. (Tianjin: Nankai daxue chubanshe, 1985–86).

10. The latest addition to this series is Peng Zeyi, ed., *Zhongguo gongshang hanghui shiliaoji* [Historical Materials on Handicraft and Commercial Guilds of China], 2 vols. (Beijing: Zhonghua shuju, 1995).

11. On this bureau and its predecessor, the *Zhongyang shiying qiyeju* [Central Bureau for Private Enterprises], see Qian Jiaju, *Qishinian de jingli* [Seven Decades of My Life] (Hong Kong: Jingbao, 1986), pp. 191–202; and his *Quguo yousilü* [Concerned Thoughts in Exile] (Hong Kong: Tiandi, 1991), pp. 96–98, 149. Qian served as a nonparty vice-director of the bureau and offers an insider's account of the process.

12. Zhongguo kexueyuan jingji yanjiusuo, Zhongyang gongshang xingzheng guanliju ziben zhuyi jingji gaizao yanjiushi, comp., *Beijing Ruifuxiang* [Ruifuxiang of Beijing] (Beijing: Sanlian, 1959). See also Liu Yueqian, "Shandong Mengjia yu Ruifuxiang" [Ruifuxiang and the Meng family of Shandong], in *Tianjin wenshi ziliao xuanji* [Selected Historical Materials of Tianjin] 2 (1979), pp. 100–117. Another work on the same theme is Zhongguo renmin yinhang Shanghaishi fenhang, comp., *Shanghai qianzhuang shiliao* [Historical Materials on Native Banks in Shanghai] (Shanghai: Renmin, 1960).

13. The 1944 edition of this essay, reportedly ghost-written by Fan Wenlan, did not contain this oft-quoted passage. See Mao Zedong, "Zhongguo geming yu Zhongguo gongchandang" [The Chinese Revolution and the Chinese Communist Party], in *Mao Zedongji* [Collected Writings of Mao Zedong] (Hong Kong: Yishan, 1976), vol. 7, p. 103.

14. Lü Zhenyu, *Zhongguo zhengzhui sixiangshi* [A History of Chinese Political Philosophy] (Shanghai: Liming shuju, 1937; reprinted Beijing: Renmin, 1981), p. 21.

15. The first book from the rejuvenated project is *Jiu Zhongguo de zibenzhuyi shengchan guanxi* [Capitalistic Relations of Production in Old China] (Beijing: Renmin,

1977). It is followed by Xu Dixin and Wu Chengming, eds., *Zhongguo zibenzhuyi de mengya* [The Sprouts of Capitalism in China] (Beijing: Renmin, 1985); idem, *Jiuminzhu zhuyi geming shiqi de Zhongguo zibenzhuyi* [Chinese Capitalism, 1840–1920] (Beijing: Renmin, 1990); and idem, *Xinminzhuzhuyi geming shiqi de Zhongguo zibenzhuyi* [Chinese Capitalism, 1921–1949] (Beijing: Renmin, 1993).

16. Xu Dixin and Wu Chengming, *Zhongguo zibenzhuyi de mengya*, p. 26; Zhongguo Renmin daxue Qingshi yanjiushi et al., *Qingdai de kuangye* [The Mining Industry in the Qing period], 2 vols. (Beijing: Zhonghua shuju, 1983); and Wei Qingyuan and Lu Su, "Qingdai qianqi de shangban kuangye jiqi zibenzhuyi mengya" [Merchant-Operated Mining Industries and the Sprouts of Capitalism in Early Qing], *Qingshi luncong* [Essays on Qing History] 4 (1983), pp. 65–91.

17. Liu Yongcheng and Hao Zhiqing, "Qingdai qianqi de shangren yu shangye ziben" [Merchants and Commercial Capital in Early Qing] (paper presented at the conference on Chinese social and economic history, Chengdu, 1983). This view is contradicted by Xiao Guoliang in his paper at the same conference, subsequently published as "Shilun Qingdai qianqi shangye lirun buneng bupiandi zhuanhuawei chanye ziben de yuanyin" [On the Reasons Why Commercial Profits Did Not Generally Transform into Productive Capital During the Early Qing Period], *ZGS* 4 (1984), pp. 71–80.

18. Karl Marx, *Capital* (New York: International Publishers, 1967), vol. 3, pp. 266–377, especially p. 328. Other historians question this dissolving effect. See Fu Zhufu, "Shangye ziben de erchongxing ji qi zai Zhongguo lishishang de biaoxian" [The Dualistic Effects of Commercial Capital and Its Articulation in Chinese History], *Jingjixue jikan* [Anthology on Economic Studies] 3 (1984), pp. 142–68; and Chen Qingde, "Shangpin jingji xinlun" [New Thoughts on Commodity Economy], *Zhengming* [Contention] 6 (1987), p. 15.

19. Xu Dixin and Wu Chengming, *Zhongguo zibenzhuyi de mengya*, pp. 27–28.

20. Wang Xiang, *Zhongguo zibenzhuyi de lishi mingyun* [The Historical Fate of Chinese Capitalism] (Suzhou: Jiangsu jiaoyu, 1992), p. 81. See also Xu Xinwu, "Zhongguo fangji shougongye zhong weiyi zibenzhuyi mengya" [The Only Sprout of Capitalism in China's Spinning and Weaving Handicraft Industry], *Pingzhun xuekan* 3 (1986), vol. 2, pp. 111–27.

21. A convenient reference for such works is Zhongguo shekeyuan lishisuo jingjishizu, comp., *Zhongguo shehui jingjishi lunzhu mulu* [A Bibliography of Chinese Social and Economic History] (Jinan: Qilu, 1984).

22. On such manuals, see, for example, the works of Yang Zhengtai; and Luo Lun, "Qianlong shengshi Jiangnan zuoshang jingying neimu chutan" [The Inner Workings of Sedentary Merchants in the Lower Yangtze During the Heyday of the Qianlong], *Nanjing daxue xuebao* [Bulletin of Nanjing University] 4 (1989), pp. 1–8.

23. On the expansion of trade routes, see Liu Min, "Zailun Qingdai shangye ziben de zengzhi" [Further Discussions on the Growth of Commercial Capital in the Qing Period], *SHJJ* 3 (1985), pp. 69–73; Wu Chengming, "Lun Qingdai qianqi woguo guonei shichang" [The National Market in Early Qing], *LS* 3 (1983), pp. 96–106; Wu Liangkai, "Qingchao qianqi guoneishichang de fazhan" [Development of the National Market in Early Qing], *Shehuikexue jikan* [Journal of Social Sciences] 2 (1986), pp. 36–43; and Liu Xiusheng, *Qingdai shangpin jingji yu shangye ziben* [Commodity Economy and Commercial Capital During the Qing Period] (Beijing: Zhongguo shangye, 1993).

24. Neimenggu zhengxie wenshi ziliao yanjiu weiyuanhui, comp., *Lumengshang Dashengkui* [Dashengkui in Inner Mongolia] (N.p.: Zhongguo renmin zhengzhi xieshang huiyi Neimenggu zizhiqu weiyuanhui, 1984).

25. Wang Shixin, "Ming–Qing shiqi shangye jingying fangshi de bianhua" [Changes in the Organization of Commercial Enterprises from Ming to Qing], *JJS* 2 (1988), pp. 14–28; Xu Jianqing, "Qingdai shougongye zhong de hehuozhi" [The Partnership System in Qing Handicraft Industries], *JJS* 4 (1995), pp. 124–39.

26. For a collection of such contracts with important implications on transaction costs, see Zigongshi dang'anguan et al., *Zigong yanye qiyue dang'an xuanji* [Selected Contracts from the Salt Archives of Zigong] (Beijing: Zhongguo shehui kexue, 1985). For studies of partnership contracts, see Yang Guozhen, "Ming–Qing erlai shangren heben jingying de qiyue xingshi" [Business Partnership Contracts During the Ming–Qing Period], *SHJJ* 3 (1987), pp. 1–9; Peng Jiucong and Chen Ran, "Zhongguo qiyue gufenzhi gailun" [An Overview of Contractual Partnerships in China], *JJS* 1 (1994), pp. 56–65.

27. Zhang Zhenming, "Qingdai jinshang de gufengzhi" [Employee-share Partnership of Shanxi Merchants During the Qing Period], *SHJJ* 1 (1989), pp. 39–43.

28. Neimenggu zhengxie wenshi ziliao yanjiu weiyuanhui, comp., *Lumengshang Dashengkui*, p. 31.

29. Novels from the late Ming described such practices, although the earliest material evidence came from early Qing. See Wang Zongyi and Liu Xun, eds., "Qingchu jingshi shanghao huipiao" [Sight-draft and Business Establishments in Early Qing Beijing], *Wenxian* [Historical documents] 2 (1985), pp. 93–112. For analysis of these documents, see Huang Jianhui, "Qingchu shangyong huipiao yu shangpin jingji de fazhan" [Commercial Sight Drafts and the Development of the Commodity Economy in Early Qing], *Wenxian* 1 (1987), pp. 3–16; Shi Ruomin, *Piaoshang xingshuaishi* [The Rise and Fall of Sight-draft Banks] (Beijing: Zhongguo jingji, 1992), pp. 56–67.

30. Kong Xiangyi, "Shanxi piaohao ye Qing zhengfu de guojie" [Shanxi *piaohao's* Collusion with the Qing State], *SHJJ* 3 (1984), pp. 1–12; Shanxi piaohao shiliao bianxiezu, comp., *Shanxi piaohao shiliao* [Historical Materials on the Shanxi Sight-draft Banks] (Taiyuan: Shanxi jingji, 1990). In the course of the conversion of the building that housed Rishengchang, the first *piaohao*, into a museum, a cache of fifteen ledgers and forty letter books of the firm was recovered.

31. Wang Jianhui, "Qingdai zhangju chutan" [An Initial Analysis of the *Zhangju* During the Qing], *LS* 4 (1987), pp. 111–24; and his *Shanxi piaohaoshi* [A History of the Shanxi Sight-draft Banks] (Taiyuan: Shanxi jingji, 1992), pp. 10–14.

32. See Peng Zeyi, "Jindai Zhongguo gongye zibenzhuyi jingjizhong de gongchang shougongye" [Handicraft Workshops in Modern China's Capitalistic Industrial Economy], in Fudan daxue lishixi et al., *Jindai Zhongguo zichan jieji yanjiu shuji* [Studies on the Chinese Bourgeoisie, sequel] (Shanghai: Fudan daxue, 1983), pp. 35–50. An expanded version of Wang's essay was published subsequently as "Zhongguo jindai shougongye jiqi zai Zhongguo zibenzhuyi shengchan zhong de diwei" [Handicraft Industries in Modern China and Its Place in Chinese Capitalistic Production], *JJS* 1 (1988), pp. 88–100.

33. Wang Xiang, *Zhongguo zibenzhuyi de lishi mingyun*, p. 113. Other scholars dispute his timing and argue that *changfang* had achieved dominance over the trade and probably peaked before the Opium War. See Duan Benluo et al., *Suzhou shougongyeshi* [A History of Suzhou's Handicraft Industries] (Suzhou: Jiangsu guzhi, 1986), pp. 212–19; and Fan Jinmin and Jin Wen, *Jiangnan sichoushi yanjiu* [A Study of Jiangnan's Silk Industry] (Beijing: Nongye, 1993), pp. 221–30.

34. Wang Xiang, *Zhongguo zibenzhuyi de lishi mingyun*, pp. 183–95.

35. Ibid., p. 305. See also Zhang Deken, "Shichang zurenzhi yuanyin chutan" [An Inquiry into the Leasing of Silk Mills], *Jingji yanjiusuo jikan* 10 (1988), pp. 224–52.

36. Xu Xinwu, ed., *Jiangnan tubushi* [A History of the Native Cotton Cloth Industry in Jiangnan] (Shanghai: Shanghai shehuikexue, 1992).

37. Lin Jubo, *Jindai Nantong tubushi* [A Modern History of the Nantong Native Cotton Cloth industry] (Nanjing: Nanjing daxue xuebao bianjibu, 1984), p. 30.

38. Hebei daxue difangshi yanjiushi et al., *Gaoyang jibuye jianshi* [A Concise History of Gaoyang's Cotton Cloth Industry] (Shijiazhuang: Zhongguo renmin zhengzhi xieshang huiyi Hebeisheng weiyuanhui, 1987), p. 65.

39. In addition to the works of Wu Zhi, H.D. Fong, and Linda Grove, see also Liu Foding and Chen Zhengping, "Gaoyang jibuye de lishi he xianzhuang" [The Past and Present of Gaoyang's Weaving Industry], *Hebei xuekan* 6 (1984), pp. 56–60.

40. The Baohua Weaving Mill as cited in Tianjinshi dang'anguan et al., eds., *Tianjin shanghui dang'an huibian, 1903–1911* [Selected Archival Material from the Tianjin Chamber of Commerce], 2 vols. (Tianjin: Renmin, 1987), vol. 1, pp. 1186–89. On the Lishengxiang Spinning Mill, see Archives of the Tianjin Chamber of Commerce, 128.2.2044 and 128.3.2259; and H.D. Fong and Bi Xianghui, *Rural Industrial Enterprise in North China* (Tianjin: Nankai University, 1936), p. 56.

41. Chen Yuhuan and Liu Zhiwei, "Qingdai houqi Guangdong sizhi gongchang de ge'an yanjiu" [A Case Study of Late Qing Silk Weaving Workshops in Guangdong], *SHJJ* 3 (1987), pp. 50–56, 63.

42. Zhongguo renmin yinhang jinrong yanjiusuo, ed., *Meiguo huaqi yinhang zaihua shiliao* [Historical Material of the International Banking Corporation in China] (Beijing: Zhongguo jinrong, 1990); Liu Yizhong et al., "Tianjin heji yanghang shiliao" [Historical Materials of the International Export Company, Tianjin] *Tianjin lishi ziliao* [Historical Material of Tianjin], p. 6.

43. Manteshi ziliao bianjizu, ed. *Manteshi ziliao* [Historical Materials of the South Manchurian Railroad], part 2, 4 vols. (Beijing: Jilinsheng shehui kexueyuan, manteshi ziliao jizu, Zhonghua Shuju, 1979); Su Chongmin, "Manteshi gaishu" [An Overview of the South Manchurian Railroad], *LS* 5 (1982), pp. 3–20; Wuhan daxue jingjixi, ed., *Jiu Zhongguo Hanyeping gongsi yu Riben guanxi shiliao xuanbian* [Selected Historical Materials of Old China's Han Yeh Ping Iron and Coal Company, and Its Relationship with Japan] (Shanghai: Renmin, 1985); Wang Xi et al., *Hanyeping gongsi* [The Han Yeh Ping Iron and Coal Company], 4 vols. (Shanghai: Renmin, 1986); Fu Wenning, ed., *Riben Hengbin zhengjin yinhang zaihua huodong shiliao* [Historical Materials of the Activities of the Japanese Yokohama Specie Bank, in China] (Beijing: Zhongguo jinrong, 1992).

44. Zhang Zhongli and Chen Zhenlian, *Saxun jituan zai jiu Zhongguo* [The Sassoon Conglomerate in Old China] (Beijing: Renmin, 1985).

45. Wang Jingyu, *Shijiushiji xifang zibenzhuyi dui Zhongguo de jingji qinlüe* [Economic Invasion of China by Foreign Capitalism During the Nineteenth Century] (Beijing: Renmin, 1983); Du Xuncheng, *Riben zai jiu Zhongguo de touzi* [Japanese Investments in Old China] (Shanghai: Shanghai shehui kexueyuan, 1986); Min Jie, "Shanghai xiangjiao fengchao jiqi dui Jiangjie diqu minzujingji de chongji" [The Assault on the Economy of Jiangsu and Jiejiang by the Shanghai Rubber Stock Bubble], *JJS* 1 (1989), pp. 126–42; Xie Yi, *Yingguo Fu gongsi zai Zhongguo* [The Fu Company of Britain in China] (Wuhan: Wuhan daxue, 1992).

46. Nie Baozhang, "1870–1895 nian zai Hua yanghang shili de kuangzhang" [The Expansion of Foreign Firms' Power in China, 1870–1895], *LS* 1 (1987), pp. 145–61; Xiong Xingmei, "Lun Yingguo ziben dui Kailuan meikuang jingying de kongzhi" [British Capital and the Control of the Kailan Mining Administration], *Nankai xuebao* [Bulletin of Nankai University] 2 (1986), pp. 49–63; Ding Changqing, "Cong Kailuan kan jiu Zhongguo meikuangye zhong de jingzheng he longduan" [Competition and Monopoly in Old China's Coal Mining Industry as Seen from the Kailan Mining Administration], *JDS* 2 (1987), pp. 1–26.

47. Yang Peixin, *Hua–E daosheng yinhang* [The Russo–Asiatic Bank] (Hong Kong: Jingji yu falü, 1987), pp. 28–30.

48. Zhang Zhongli et al., *Taigu jituan zai jiu Zhongguo* [The Butterfield and Swire Group in Old China] (Shanghai: Renmin, 1991), pp. 2–3.

49. Zhang Lihong, "Jindai waishang zai Sichuan de touzhi huodong" [Foreign Investments in Modern Sichuan], *JJS* 2 (1993), pp. 31–39.

50. Zhou Guowei, *Zhongguo jindai jingjishi xinlun* [New Studies on Modern Chinese Economic History] (Nanjing: Nanjing daxue xuebao, 1991), pp. 44–60.

51. Such a position provoked a stinging rebuke from Yan Zhongping, which was published posthumously as "Diguozhuyi duihua qinlüe de lishi pingjia wenti huan xuyao taolun" [On Evaluating the History of Foreign Imperialism in China There Should Be Further Discussion], *JJS* 2 (1992), pp. 9–14.

52. Fan Wenlan, *Zhongguo jindaishi* [A modern history of China], 2 vols. (Beijing: Renmin, 1955), vol. 1, pp. 205–19; Hu Sheng, *Cong yapian zhanzheng dao wusi yundong* [From the Opium War to the May Fourth Movement], 2 vols. (Beijing: Renmin, 1981), vol. 1, pp. 318–36.

53. Li Shiyue and Hu Bin, "Yangwupai yu jindai gongye" [The Self-Strengtheners and Modern Industries], *Shandong shifan daxue xuebao* [Bulletin of Shandong Normal University] 3 (1979); Li Shiyue, "Cong Yangu, weixin, dao zichan jieji geming" [From the Self-Strengthening, Reform, to the Capitalist Revolution], *LS* 1 (1980), pp. 31–40; Hu Bin and Li Shiyue, "Li Hongzhang yu lunchuan zhaoshangju" [Li Hongzhang and the China Merchants' Steamship Navigation Company], *LS* 2 (1982); and Li Shiyue, "Zhongguo jindaishi zhuyao xiansu ji qi biaozhi zhi wojian" [My View of the Main Thread in Modern Chinese History and Its Markers], *LS* 2 (1984), pp. 122–32. For a summary of the debate, see Zeng Jingzhong, "Zhongguo jindaishi jiben xiansu taolun pingshu" [A Review of the Discussion on the Main Thread in Modern Chinese History], *JDS* 5 (1985), pp. 164–89.

54. Chen Meilong, "Lun wanqing Shanghai jiqi jibuju de xingzhi" [On the Nature of the Shanghai Weaving Mill in Late Qing], *JDS* 3 (1986), pp. 74–95.

55. Jiang Duo, "Shilun yangwu yundong dui zaoqi minzu ziben de cujin zuoyong" [The Stimulating Effects on Early National Bourgeois Capitalism by the Self-Strengthening Movement], in Huang Yifeng and Jiang Duo, *Zhongguo jindai jingjishi lunwenji* [Anthology on Modern Chinese Economic History] (Nanjing: Renmin, 1981), p. 331.

56. Zhu Yingui, "Lun Qingji lunchuan zhaoshangju de zijin wailiu" [The Outflow of Capital from the China Merchants' Steamship Navigation Company During the Qing], *JJS* 2 (1993), pp. 10–21.

57. See Lin Qingyuan, *Fujian chuanzhengju shigao* [A History of the Fuzhou Arsenal] (Fuzhou: Renmin, 1986), pp. 50–77.

58. Zhang Guohui, *Yangwu yundong yu Zhongguo jindai qiye* [Modern Chinese Industrial Enterprises and the Self-Strengthening Movement] (Beijing: Zhongguo shehui kexue, 1979), pp. 304–8.

59. Wang Xi, "Shilun yangwupai guandu shangban qiye de xingzhi yu zuoyong" [An Inquiry into the Nature and Effects of the Self-Strengtheners' Officially Supervised and Merchant-Operated Enterprises], *LS* 6 (1983), pp. 175–87.

60. Zhang Houquan et al., *Zhaoshangju shi* [A History of the China Merchants' Steamship Navigation Company] (Beijing: Renmin jiaotong, 1988), pp. 237–43.

61. Xia Dongyuan and Yang Xiaomin, "Lun Qingji lunchuan zhaoshangju de xingzhi" [On the Nature of the China Merchants' Steamship Navigation Company], *LS* 4 (1980), pp. 55–66; Luo Yiujiu and Lin Pinghan, "Yangwu yundong de lishi jiaoxun" [The Historical Lessons of the Self-Strengthening Movement], *SHJJ* 1 (1992), pp. 78–85.

62. Zhang Wenqin, "Cong fengjian guanshang dao maiban shangren" [From Feudal Official Merchant to Comprador Merchant], *JDS* 3 (1984), pp. 167–97; 4 (1984), pp. 231–53.

63. Yan Zhongping, "Shilun Zhongguo maiban zichan jieji de fasheng" [On the Rise of the Comprador Capitalist Class in China], *JJS* 1 (1986), pp. 81–98.

64. Nie Baozhang, *Zhongguo maiban zichan jieji de fasheng* [The Rise of Comprador Capitalism in China] (Beijing: Zhongguo shehui kexue, 1979), pp. 146–49.

65. See Zhuo Yen, "Zhou Xuexi er gongkuan banshiye fajia de neimu" [The Inside Story of Zhou Xuexi's Use of Public Funds to Invest in Enterprises for the Enrichment of His Family], *Wenshi ziliao xuanji* [Selected Historical Materials] 53 (1964), pp. 32–34.

66. See, for example, Kong Jingwei et al., *Fengxi junfa guanliao ziben* [Warlord and Bureaucratic Capital of the Fengtian Clique] (Changchun: Jilin daxue, 1989); Jiang Duo, "Lüelun Beiyang guanliao ziben" [A Brief Treatise on the Bureaucratic Capitalism of the Northern Warlords], *JJS* 3 (1990), pp. 42–51; Jing Zhankui, *Yan Xishan yu Xibei shiye gongsi* [Yan Xishan and the Northwestern Industrial Company] (Taiyuan: Shanxi jingji, 1991).

67. Chuan Han-sheng (Quan Hansheng), *Hanyeping gongsi shilüe* [A Concise History of the Hanyehping Iron and Coal Mining and Smelting Company] (Hong Kong: Chinese University of Hong Kong, 1972), pp. 238–40; Zheng Linming, "Longyan meikuang gongsi chuangban shimo" [The Founding and Demise of the Longyan Iron Mining Company], *JDS* 1 (1986), pp. 255–71. This is the precursor to the Capital Iron and Steel Company.

68. Huang Yifeng et al., *Jiu Zhongguo de maiban jieji* [The Comprador Class in Old China] (Shanghai: Renmin, 1982), p. 155. There is a debate over whether the three— that is, comprador, bureaucrat, and comprador–bureaucrat—formed one continuous pedigree or were disjointed. See Wang Jingyu, "Zailun Zhongguo zibenzhuyi he zichang jieji de chansheng" [Further Discussions on the Birth of Capitalism and Capitalist in China], in Fudan daxue lishixi et al., *Jindai Zhongguo zichan jieji yanjiu shuji*, pp. 14–34.

69. Chongqingshi dang'anguan et al. comp., *Silian congchu shiliao* [Historical Materials of the Joint Board of the Four Banks], 3 vols. (Beijing: Dang'an, 1993).

70. Jian Rui, "Guomindang guanliu ziben fazhan de gaishu" [An Overview of the Development of the Nationalist Party's Bureaucratic Capitalism], *JJS* 3 (1986), pp. 97–118; and Wu Taichang, "Guomindang zhengfu ziyuan weiyuanhui longduan huodong shuping" [A Review of the National Resources Commission's Monopolistic Activities], ibid., pp. 119–34.

71. Ding Richu and Shen Zuwei, "Lun wanqing de guojia zibenzhuyi" [On State Capitalism in Late Qing], *LS* 3 (1986), pp. 157–74.

72. Wang Shui, "Qingdai maiban shouru de guji jiqi shiyong fangxiang" [An Estimate of Compradors' Income and Uses During the Qing Dynasty], *Jingji yanjiusuo jikan* [Bulletin of the Institute of Economics, Chinese Academy of Social Sciences] 5 (1983), pp. 298–324, especially pp. 320–23.

73. Cheng Linsun, "Lun kang-Ri zhanzheng shiqi ziyuan weiyuanhui de qiye huodong jiqi lishi zuoyong" [The Entrepreneurial Activities of the National Resources Commission During the Anti-Japanese War and Its Historical Effects], *Zhongguo jindai jingjishi yanjiu ziliao* [Research Bulletin on Modern Chinese Economic History] 5 (1986), pp. 1–26; Zheng Youkui et al., *Jiu Zhongguo de ziyuan weiyuanhui* [The National Resources Commission in Old China] (Shanghai: Shanghai shehui kexueyuan, 1991); Zhang Shuyan, *Yumen youkuang shi* [A History of the Yumen Oil Field] (Xian: Xibei daxue, 1988); and Liu Fushou, "Ziyuan weiyuanhui de xingzhi ji lishi zuoyong

liangmenguan" [The Janus-faced Historical Impact and Nature of the National Resource Commission], *JJS* 3 (1993), pp. 110–16.

74. Yu Mingxia, *Xuzhou meikuang shi* [A History of the Xuzhou Colliery] (Xuzhou: Jiangsu guzhi, 1991), pp. 158–60.

75. As attempted by Wang Jingyu, *Tang Tingshu yanjiu* [A study on Tang Tingshu] (Beijing: Zhongguo shehui kexueyuan, 1983).

76. This necessitated the creation of the more or less neutral term *huaqiao ziben*. See the works of Lin Jinzhi since 1983.

77. Zhu Ying, *Xinhai geming shiqi xinshi shangren shetuan yanjiu* [A Study on the New Merchant Organizations During the 1911 Revolution Period] (Beijing: Renmin daxue, 1990).

78. Quan Weitian, *Zhongguo minzu zibenzhuyi de fazhan* [The Development of Chinese National Bourgeois Capitalism] (Zhengzhou: Renmin, 1982), p. 227; Liu Foding, "Woguo minzu ziben qiye zhaqu shengyu jiazhi de shouduan yu tedian" [On the Methods and Characteristics of Surplus Value Extraction by National Bourgeois Enterprises in China], Nankai jingji yanjiu niankan, 1982–1983 [Annual Anthology of the Nankai Institute of Economics, 1982–1983], pp. 202–18. The exploitation rate is defined as sales-production costs divided by the wage bill of a company.

79. See, for example, Xu Weiyong and Huang Hanmin, *Rongjia qiye fazhanshi* [The Rong Family and Their Enterprises: A History] (Beijing: Renmin, 1985), pp. 71–75; Ling Yaolun et al., *Minsheng gongsishi* [A History of the Ming Sung Company] (Beijing: Renmin jiaotong, 1990), pp. 26–28.

80. Jin Yanshi et al., comp., "Tianjin dongya maofang gongsi shiliao" [Historical Materials on the Oriental Wool Manufacturers, Tianjin], *Tianjin lishi ziliao* 20.

81. On the former "charge," see, for example, the Yudahua Group managed by the father-in-law of Jiang Weiguo. On the group, see Yudahua fangji jituan shiliao bianshezu, comp., *Yudahua fangji ziben jituan siliao* [Historical Materials on the Yudahua Textile Group] (Hubei: Renmin, 1984); and Jiang Duo, "Luelun jiu Zhongguo Yudahua ziben jituan" [A Study of the Yudahua Group of Old China], *Jianghan luntan* 3 (1987), pp. 59–64. On the latter "charge," see, for example, Yu Xiaoqiu, "Yongli jianchang he yingshang Buneimen yangjian gongsi douzheng qianhou jilüe" [Summary of Yungli Chemical Industries' Struggles Against Brunner, Mond and Company of Great Britain], in *Huagong xiandao Fan Xudong* [Fan Xudong: A Pioneer in the Chemical Industry] (Beijing: Zhongguo wenshi, 1987), pp. 79–84.

82. Guo Shihao, "Qixin yanghui gongsi jianbing Hubei shuilichang shimo" [The Takeover of the Hubei Cement Company by the Chee Hsin Cement Company], in Sun Jian, ed., *Zhongguo jingjishi lunwenji* [Essays on Chinese Economic History] (Beijing: Renmin daxue, 1987), pp. 295–323.

83. Wei Ming (Wei Xiaoming), "Lun beiyang junfa guanliao de siren zibenzhuyi jingji huodong" [On the Private Capitalistic Economic Activities of the Northern Warlords], *JDS* 2 (1985), pp. 66–110.

84. See, for example, Chen Zifang, "Lun Qingmo minchu guanliao siren ziben de kuozhang jiqi lishi pingjia" [An Appraisal of the Expansion of Bureaucrats' Private Capital During the Late Qing and the Early Republican Period], *Shixue yuekan* [Historical Monthly] 5 (1990), pp. 48–54.

85. Li Lin, "Cong Zhou Xuexi jituan kan guanliu ziben de zhuanhua" [The Privatization of State Capital in the Late Qing: A Case Study], *Twenty-First Century* 3 (1991), pp. 45–55.

86. Huang Yiping, "Wanqing jindai junshi gongye de qiyin xingzhi ji zuoyong" [The Rise of Modern Defense Industries in Late Qing, Its Nature and Effects], *Huadong shifan daxue xuebao* [Bulletin of East China Normal University] 1 (1990), p. 34.

87. Zhao Jing, ed., *Zhongguo jindai minzu shiye zibenjia de jingying guanli sixiang* [The Entrepreneurial Philosophies of Modern China's National Bourgeois Industrialists] (Kunming: Renmin, 1988), pp. 2–4; Li Gang, *Zhongguo minzu ziben qiye jingying yu guanli* [The Entrepreneurship of National Bourgeois Enterprises] (Xian: Xibei daxue, 1992).

88. Liu Foding, "Kaiping kuangwuju jingying deshi bianxi" [The Management of the Kailan Mining Administration: Successes and Failures], *Nankai xuebao* 2 (1986), p. 36. See also Wang Yuru, "Kailuan meikuang de ziben jicheng he jingying xiaoyi fenxi" [Capital Composition and Management Effectiveness of the Kailuan Collieries] (master's thesis, Institute of Economics, Nankai University, 1988), and a summary of her findings in *JDS* 4 (1989), pp. 148–66.

89. See, for example, Tianjin shihua tongzhi bianwei bangongshi, comp., *Tianjin shihua tongzhi, 1962–1988* [A Comprehensive Gazetteer of the Tianjin Petrochemical Company] (Tianjin: Tianjin kexue jishu, 1990).

90. See, respectively, Xu Zhihe and Xu Jianzhong, *Zhongguo gongyouzhi qiye guanli fazhanshi* [Managing China's Public Enterprises, 1927–1965] (Shanghai: Shanghai shehui kexue, 1992); its sequel (1966); and Zhou Weiqi and Zhu Jiayu, *Wuhan Changjiang lunchuan gongsishi* [A History of Wuhan Changjiang Shipping Trust] (Beijing: Renmin jiaotong, 1991).

91. Beijingshi dang'anguan et al., comp., *Beijingshi zilaishui gongshi dang'an shiliao* [Archival Materials on the Peiping Waterworks Company] (Beijing: Yanshan chubanshe, 1986); Beijingshi dang'anguan et al., comp., *Beijing dianche gongshi dang'an shiliao* [Archival Materials on the Peiping Electric Tramway Company] (Beijing: Yanshan chubanshe, 1988).

92. Shoudu gangtie gongshi et al., *Shougang gaige* [Economic Reform at the Capital Iron and Steel Company], 3 vols. (Beijing: Beijing, 1992).

93. See, for example, *Dongjiang geming genjudi shuishou shiliao* [Historical Materials on Taxation in the Dongjiang Base Area] (Guangdong: Renmin, 1993).

94. See, for example, Jiang Hongye, ed., *Zhongguo difang yinhangshi* [A History of Local Banks in China] (Changsha: Hunan, 1991). The Bank of China also commissioned a history of its Beijing branch based on the archives housed at the Beijing Municipal Archives. See Zhongguo yinhang Beijing fenhang et al., *Beijing de Zhongguo yinhang, 1914–1949* [The Bank of China in Beijing] (Beijing: Zhongguo jinrong, 1989).

95. Zhejiangsheng gongxiao hezuoshe shizhi bianjishi, comp., *Zhejiangsheng gongxiao hezuoshe shiliao xuanbian* [Selected Historical Materials on Supply and Marketing Co-operatives in Zhejiang] (Hangzhou: Renmin, 1990).

96. Sun Guoda, *Minzu gongye daqianxi* [The Great Migration of National Bourgeoisie Industries] (Beijing: Zhongguo wenshi, 1991); and Jindai Zhongguo diandangye bianweihui, ed., *Jindai Zhongguo diandangye* [A History of Pawnshops in Modern China] (Beijing: Zhongguo wenshi, 1996), both under the series title "Jindai Zhongguo gongshang jingji congshu" [Anthology on Commerce and Industry in Modern China].

97. Wu Chengming, "Yao zhongshi shangpin liutong zai chuantong jingji xiang shichang jingji zhuanhuanzhong de zuoyong" [Focus on the Role of Commodity Circulation in the Transition of China's Traditional Economy to a Market Economy], *JJS* 2 (1995), p. 2. From a theoretical perspective, the concept has been dismissed by Huang Songying in "Lüelun Zhongguo zibenzhuyi mengya de lilun neirong" [Theoretical Issues of the Sprouts of Capitalism], *SHJJ* 1 (1993), pp. 93–99.

98. Long Denggao, "Songdai chengxiang shichang dengji wangluo fenxi" [An Analysis of Song Hierarchial Rural–Urban Market Networks], in Wu Xiaoliang, ed., *Songdai jingjishi yanjiu* [Studies in the Economic History of the Song Period] (Kunming: Yunnan daxue, 1994), pp. 368–411.

99. Liu Kexiang, ed., *Qingdai quanshi* [A Comprehensive History of the Qing Dynasty], 10 vols. (Shenyang: Renmin, 1993), vol. 10, pp. 502–9.

100. Liu Xiusheng, "Qingdai zhongqi de sanji shichang jiegou" [The Tripartite Market Structure of Mid-Qing], *SHJJ* 1 (1991), pp. 91–99.

101. Li Wenzi, *Ming Qing shidai fengjian tudi guanxi de songiie* [The Relaxing of Feudal Land Relationship During the Ming and the Qing] (Beijing: Zhongguo shehui kexue, 1993), pp. 568–79. Li further elaborated on this issue by differentiating among four types of peasant households, each relating to the market in distinctive ways. See his "Lun Ming Qing shidai nongmin jingji shangpinlü" [Commercialization Rates of Farming Households During the Ming and the Qing], *JJS* 1 (1993), pp. 21–42.

102. See, for example, Wang Shui, "Ping Bojinshi guanyu Zhongguo guonei maoyiliang de guji" [A Review of Perkins's Estimate of China's Domestic Trade], *Zhongguo shehui kexue* [Social Science in China] 3 (1988), pp. 37–47.

103. Jiang Jianping, *Qingdai qianqi migu maoyi yanjiu* [A Study of the Rice and Grain Trade in Early Qing] (Beijing: Beijing daxue, 1992); and Lu Manping and Jia Xiuyan, *Minguo jiageshi* [A History of Price During the Republican Period] (Beijing: Zhongguo wujia, 1992).

104. Chen Chunsheng, *Shichang jizhi yu shehui bianqian* [Market Mechanism and Social Change] (Guangzhou: Zhongshan daxue, 1992), pp. 101–2.

105. Xiao Guoliang, "Qingdai qianqi fengjian guojia dui shangye jingji de ganyu" [Interference in the Commercial Economy by the Feudal State in Early Qing] (Ph.D. dissertation, Chinese Academy of Social Sciences, 1989).

106. Liang Miaotai, *Ming Qing Jingdezhen chengshi jingji yanjiu* [Studies of Jingdezhen's Urban Economy During the Ming and the Qing Period] (Nanchang: Renmin, 1991), pp. 149–87.

107. Xie Jun, *Zhonghua shangfa jianshi* [A concise history of commercial law in China] (Beijing: Zhongguo shangye chubanshe, 1989); Ye Xiaoxin, *Zhongguo minfashi* [A History of Chinese Civil Law] (Shanghai: Renmin chubanshe, 1993); Zhang Chuanxi et al., comp., *Zhongguo lidai qiyue huibian kaoshi* [Annotated Collection of Contracts in Chinese History] (Beijing: Beijing daxue chubanshe, 1995).

108. Li Zhimin, *Zhongguo minfashi* [A History of Civil Law in Ancient China] (N.p.: Falü chubanshe, 1988), p. 1; Zhang Jinfan, ed., *Zhongguo fazhishi yanjiu zongshu* [Studies on Chinese Legal History] (Beijing: Zhongguo renmin gong'an daxue chubanshe, 1990), pp. 383–84.

109. Zigongshi dang'anguan, et al., comp., *Zigong yanye qiyue dang'an xuanji* [Selected Contracts on the Zigong Salt Industry] (Beijing: Zhongguo shehui kexue chubanshe, 1985); Peng Jiusong, *Zhongguo qiyue gufanzhi* [Contracts and Joint-stock System in China] (Chengdu: Chengdu keji daxue chubanshe, 1995).

110. On the debate regarding whether unlimited-term contracts represent an evolution and improvement upon fixed-term contracts, see Peng Jiusong, "Zigong yanye qiyue kaoshi" [Annotated contracts from Zigong], *Yanyeshi yanjiu* [Studies on the Salt Industry] 1 (1986); and Wu Tianying, "Qingdai Sichuan Furong yanye gufen 'fendeng' shuo bianxi" [On the "Graded" Shareholding System of the Furong Salt Industry], *SHJJ* 4 (1992).

111. Luo Yixing, *Ming Qing Foshan jingji fazhan yu shehui bianqian* [Economic Development and Social Change in Foshan During the Ming and the Qing] (Guangzhou: Renmin, 1994), pp. 57–63. In contrast, Ye Xian'en and Tan Dihua considered the control of these "feudalistic" elements an obstacle to the development of the town and its industries. See their "Fengjian zongfa shili dui Foshan de kongzhi jiqi chansheng de yingxiang" [The Control of Foshan by Feudalistic Kinship Forces and Its Effects], in Guangdongsheng shixuehui, ed., *Ming Qing Guangdong shehui jingji xingtai yanjiu*

[Social and Economic Formations of Guangdong During the Ming and the Qing] (Guangzhou: Renmin, 1985), pp. 144–64.

112. Yao Yuming, "Jindai 'Ningbobang' wenhua xintai chutan" [The Cultural Psychology of Modern Ningbo Merchants], *SHJJ* 2 (1990), pp. 72–78.

113. Ma Min, *Guodu xingtai: Zhongguo zaoqi zichanjieji goucheng zhi mi* [Transitional Formation: The Mystery of Early Capitalists in China] (Beijing: Zhongguo shehui kexue, 1994), pp. 191–221. See also his earlier work "Zhongguo jindai shangren xinli jiegou chutan" [A Preliminary Study of the Psychology of Modern Chinese Merchants], *Zhongguo shehui kexue* 5 (1986), pp. 99–108; and Xu Dingxin, "Jindai Shanghai xinjiu liangdai minzu zibenjia shenceng jiegou de toushi" [Penetrating the Deep Structure of Two Generations of Modern Shanghai National Bourgeoisie], *Shanghai shehui kexueyuan xueshu jikan* [Academic Quarterly of the Shanghai Academy of Social Sciences] 3 (1988), pp. 39–50.

114. Wang Zhenzhong, "Ming Qing Yangzhou yanshang shequ wenhua jiqi yingxiang" [The Community of Yangzhou's Salt Merchants and Its Impact on the Culture of Yangzhou], *ZGS* 2 (1992), pp. 104–16; and idem, *Ming Qing Huishang yu Huaiyang shehui bianqian* [Social Change in Huaiyang and the Huizhou Merchants During the Ming–Qing Period] (Beijing: Sanlian, 1996). For a contrasting perspective, see Xiao Guoliang, "Ming Qing Lianghuai yanshang de shechixing xiaofei jiqi jingji yingxiang" [The Extravagant Spending of Lianghuai Salt Merchants and Its Economic Impact During the Ming and the Qing], *LS* 4 (1982).

115. Tang Lixing, "Ming Qing Huishang xinli yanjiu" [The Psychology of Huizhou Merchants During the Ming and Qing Periods], in Tang Mingsui and Wang Qichen, eds., *Jinnian Liang Fangzhong jiaoshou xueshu taolunhui wenji* [Commemorative Essays in Honor of Liang Fangzhong] (Guangzhou: Zhongshan daxue, 1990), pp. 268–91.

116. Du Xuncheng, *Zhongguo chuantong lunli yu jindai ziben zhuyi* [Traditional Chinese Ethics and Modern Capitalism] (Shanghai: Shanghai shehui kexueyuan, 1993).

117. Unraveling the secret of the Asian miracle is an industry by itself, and the literature influenced by Weber is too abundant to cite here. See, for example, Wang Shaolin, ed., *Zhongguo zongjiao lunli yu xiandaihua* [Chinese Religious Ethics and Modernization] (Hong Kong: Shangwu yinshuguan, 1991).

118. Wo Bojun, "Gongyehua chuqi chuyi ziben de xingcheng" [Regional capital formation and early industrialization], *JJS* 2 (1993), pp. 22–30. On the Wushi networks, see Zhao Yongliang, "Gaishu Wushi Yang Xie Rong Zhou deng liuge ziben jituan de xingcheng yu fazhan" [The Formation and Development of the Six Capitalist Groups Headed by the Yangs, Xies, the Rongs and the Zhous of Wushi], in *1982 nian Jiangsusheng xueshu taolunhui lunwenji* [Proceedings of the Jiangsu Provincial Academy, 1982], pp. 8–16; and Gao Jingyue, "Wushi saosi gongye de fazhan he qiye guanli de yanbian" [The Development of Wushi's Silk-reeling Industry and the Evolution of Their Management], *SHJJ* 1 (1983), pp. 102–10.

119. Chen Qingde, "Zhongguo jindai shangpin jingji yanjiu" [A Study of the Commodity Economy in Modern China], in Peng Zeyi et al., eds., *Zhongguo shehui jingji bianqian* [Social and Economic Change in China] (Beijing: Zhongguo caizheng jingji, 1990), pp. 650–52.

120. Wu Chengming, *Jiuminzhu zhuyi geming shiqi,* pp. 1055–75; idem, *Xinminzhu zhuyi geming shiqi,* pp. 746–72.

121. Wang Di, "Wanqing zhongshang zhuyi yu jingji biange" [Mercantilism and Economic Reforms During the Late Qing], *Shanghai shehui kexueyuan jikan* [Journal of the Shanghai Academy of Social Sciences] 4 (1989), pp. 63–70; Tang Lixing, *Shangren yu Zhongguo jinshi shehui* [Merchants and Modern Chinese Society] (Hangzhou: Renmin, 1993); and Ma Min, *Guanshang zhijian* [Between Official and Merchant] (Tianjin: Renmin, 1995).

122. See Zhang Haipeng et al., *Zhongguo shida shangbang* [Ten Great Merchant Guilds in China] (Hefei: Huangshan shushe, 1993), and a ten-volume expanded edition of the work published by the Hong Kong branch of Zhonghua shuju in 1995.

123. Zhao Yunxing et al., *Zhongguo dazibenjia chuan* [Biographies of Major Chinese Capitalists], 10 vols. (Changchun: Shidai wenyi, 1994).

124. Xu Dixin, ed., *Zhongguo qiyejia liechuan* [Biographies of Chinese Entrepreneurs], 3 vols. (Beijing: Jingji ribao, 1988–89).

125. Mo Yanjun, ed., *Zhonghua dazibenjia fajilu* [The Rise of Chinese Industrial Magnates] (Beijing: Hongqi, 1993).

126. Li Yamei et al., *Haomen wenhua toushi* [Insights into the Corporate Culture of the Rich and Powerful Corporation] (Beijing: Qiye guanli, 1994). A photograph of its senior executives taken with Bill Clinton was prominently displayed outside the Beijing Hotel in the summer of 1995, a testimony to the efficacy of political fund-raising.

127. Zhang Haipeng and Wang Tingyuan, eds., *Huishang yanjiu* [A Study of the Huizhou Merchants] (Hefei: Anhui renmin, 1995).

128. On this latest genre of business history literature, see Rong Jingben et al., *Liangxi Rongshi jiazushi* [A History of the Rongs of Liangxi] (Beijing: Zhongyang bianyi chubanshe, 1995); Ma Hong et al., *Zhongguo jingying dashi* [Chinese Great Masters of Management] (Beijing: Zhongguo fazhan, 1994).

129. The China Merchants' Steamship Navigation Company underwrote both the publication of proceedings and the conference on its history. See Tang Zhaolian, ed., *Zhaoshangju yu Zhongguo jinxiandaihua* [The China Merchants' Steamship Navigation Company and China's Modernization] (Guangzhou: Renmin, 1994), pp. 459–67. The *Pingzhun xuekan* is sponsored by the Beijing Dong'an Group and Shenzhen Yunxing Group. On the other hand, the selected archives of the Kailan Mining Administration, which took researchers over a decade to prepare, remain unpublished because of a lack of funding.

Chinese Studies in History, vol. 31, nos. 3–4, Spring–Summer 1998, pp. 65–94.
ISSN 0009–4633/1998 $9.50 + 0.00.

MAN-HOUNG LIN

Interpretative Trends in Taiwan's Scholarship on Chinese Business History: 1600 to the Present

Institutional Basis for Taiwan's Scholarship on Chinese Business History

This essay focuses on business history as the human dimension of commercial history, that is, how mercantile activity has been perceived by society; how merchants accumulate their capital; the relations among merchants and between merchants and government; how merchants manage their enterprises; and their rise or fall. Transportation, currency, and market structure will not be included. I will cover Taiwan studies of the Chinese mainland from 1600 to 1949, studies of Taiwan from 1600 to the present, and some studies of overseas Chinese.

Taiwanese studies of Chinese business history, as defined above, come mainly from the fields of history, sociology, business administration, and political science. Most such studies are university degree theses, which are available through Taiwan's Central Library or the Social Science

---

From a paper presented at the workshop on Scholarly Research on Chinese Business History: Interpretative Trends and Priorities for the Future, University of Akron, October 27–29, 1995.

Man-houng Lin is a Research Fellow at Academia Sinica, Institute of Modern History, Nangang, Taiwan.

A note on romanization: The Wade–Giles system is used for the names of authors and universities. As this system is standard in Taiwan, several names will already be known to readers in the Wade–Giles form. However, the pinyin system is used for place names, titles and publishers, which is in keeping with the romanization that is used elsewhere in this volume.—Ed.

This author thanks Professors Bob Gardella, Andrea McElderry, Jane Leonard, and Philip A. Kuhn for their editorial comments.

Material Center of National Cheng-chih University (Cheng-chih). CD-ROM abstracts of the theses written between 1960 and 1990 are available at the Central Library. Some of these theses have been published as books or articles.

In addition to degree theses, Academia Sinica researchers and university instructors have produced a number of works related to Chinese business history. The National Science Council (NSC) has been the most important sponsor for Taiwan's academic research. For example, 72.7 percent of the historical research projects from 1988 to 1992 were supported by the NSC.[1] Whether scholars are recipients of NSC research project grants or not, they can use their research results to apply for the NSC's annual research-outcome grants, which are equivalent to as much as one-sixth of a college teacher's regular salary. Project or research outcome summaries from the NSC's network and databases may be obtained by applying for an account on the network or by paying a staff member to look up the references at the NSC's Science Material Center on Hoping East Road.

Most books on Chinese business history are published by Academia Sinica's Institute of Modern History (IMH), Institute of Economics (IEAS), and Sun Yat-sen Institute of Social Science and Philosophy (ISSP), and by United Daily News in its historical studies series. Contemporary studies have been published by Renjian, Daoxiang, Yeqiang, Wunan, and by the Academia Sinica's Institute of Ethnology.

Theses written on Chinese business history tend to be concentrated at certain universities. In the field of sociology, the Graduate Institute of Sociology of Tung-hai University (Tung-hai) has had a series of projects on contemporary Taiwan enterprises influenced by Kao Cheng-shu and Gary Hamilton. Studies from the Department of Sociology of Tsing-hua University are an offshoot of the Tung-hai studies. Similar series have come from the Graduate Institute of Business Administration at National Taiwan University (NTU), Taiwan's Institute of Technology (TIT), and National Chung-shan University (NCU). With regard to historical studies, good theses have been produced at the Graduate Institute of History of National Taiwan Normal University (NTNU), NTU, Cheng-chih, Tung-hai, and National Chung-cheng University (Chung-cheng).

Several theses may explore a common theme or center on a particular period. For example, Man-houng Lin's master's thesis exploring the socioeconomic impact of the opening of treaty ports in Taiwan (1860–1895) was followed by similar studies on Jiujiang (1861–1911), Shantou (Swatow) (1867–1931), Chongqing (1873–1919), Qifu (1867–1919), Tianjin (1867–1931), and Dalian (late Qing–1931).[2] This series was made possible by the IMH's interest in the modernization of China. Liu Tsui-jung's work on Hankow's foreign trade was also crucial for these studies.[3] At NTU, Hsu Hong supervised related theses on the late Ming and early Qing periods. Theses on Qing China and on colonial and postwar Taiwan have been completed under the direction of Li Kuo-chi, Chang Yu-fa, and Chen San-chin at NTU, and Man-houng Lin at NTNU and Chongcheng. Theses on the Republican period, based on the archives of the National Historic Bureau and the Institute of Modern History, Academia Sinica, have been guided by Wang Shu-huai at Tung-hai and NTNU, by Liu Tsui-jung at NTU, and by Ch'en Tzu-yu at National Cheng-chih University. In addition, the scholars at IMH have produced a series of works on the self-strengthening industries, including telegraph, steamship, and mining.

The IMH studies and related theses on late Qing and pre-1949 government enterprises are primarily descriptive works dealing with the establishment, organization, and history of these enterprises, and Ch'en Tzu-yu has written bibliographic notes on these studies.[4] Hence, I shall focus on the interpretive trends of other Taiwanese studies of Chinese business history, essentially merchant history.

Positive Influence of Chinese Religious Ethics on Chinese Mercantile Activities

Yu Ying-shih's well-known book *Zhongguo jinshi zhongjiao lunli yu shang-ren jingshen* [Religious Ethics and the Merchant Spirit in Modern China], published in 1987, explores the intellectual background for the growing justification for commercial activities in Chinese society.[5] The secular elements in ancient Chinese ideas were obscured during the Six Dynasties, when big clans dominated the society's intellectual life and stressed classical scholarship as well as ritual studies. The concept of re-ordering society was revived in the mid-Tang by Zen Buddhists who sought to communicate with the common people. Such interpenetration of religious ethics and worldly affairs was continued by Confucian thinkers, especially those of the Wang Yangming school, and by the Daoists. The secularization of knowledge also facilitated the printing of commercial handbooks in the Ming and Qing dynasties. The religious ethics shared by these three religions, diligence, honesty, and charitable works were thereby spread to the common people. Religious ethics shared by the boss and the clerks bolstered the strict training of the clerks. Family relations stressed by all of these religions bolstered Chinese business organizations. Merchants could perform beneficent works to gain religious merit and to command social respect. Big merchants, such as those from Shanxi and Anhui, even embraced the ambition to build their own commercial empire to compete with the imperial empire. Before the Ming dynasty, the concept of the social significance of merchants appeared mainly in the works of scholar-officials. From Ming times onward, more and more merchants spoke for themselves about their own significance.

Cho Ke-hua's 1990 book on Taiwan's guild merchants in the Qing period reveals their close connection with religion. The guild head was called the head of the incense burner; the guild members were called the legs of the incense burner. Although guilds were usually controlled by a few big merchants, on the birthday of the sea goddess, all of the guild members gathered for a banquet to discuss guild affairs. The lists of member's names were called *yuanbu*, meaning a record of people brought together by luck or fate. The guild head was chosen by drawing lots in front of the deity, and he had to provide incense or a drama for entertaining and honoring the deity. Guild offices were often located in temples, and scales were placed in the temples to monitor measurements. Only a few written guild regulations, recorded on the eve of the Japanese occupation, remain in the private laws collected by the Japanese government. Legal sanctions were not relied upon as much as religious force.[6]

In Japanese colonial Taiwan, religious festivals were used for commercial promotions as pointed out by Sung Kuang-yu (1989).[7] Huang Yun-lung and Hsu Mu-lan (1992) have found religious ethics to be favorable even for modern enterprise management. The religious commitment of the leaders of an enterprise, whether Christian, Buddhist, or Daoist, influences an enterprise to develop an honest, upright, and law-abiding spirit. Such enterprises also tend to have more social concern for staff, which enhances the staff's dedication to the firm and the internal harmony of the enterprise.[8]

By pointing out these studies, I am by no means trying to invalidate Max Weber's assertion that Chinese religious values hindered the rise of capitalism since capitalism is not equivalent to mercantile activities. But these studies do suggest a trend among scholars in Taiwan that takes note of the positive influence of Chinese religion on the development of Chinese business.

The Symbiotic Relationship Between Traditional Chinese Merchants and the Imperial Government

Yu Ying-shih has also noted that in the Ming–Qing period more and more scholars came from or were supported by merchant families.[9] Lin Li-yue (1980) has discussed scholar-officials' cooperation with medium- and small-scale merchants in the maritime smuggling trade during the period between 1522 and 1566.[10] In her 1993 study of top guild merchants in Taiwan who came from Fujian during the Qing period, Man-houng Lin found that some were from Fujian bureaucratic families who had family members serving in such high posts as governor-general of Sichuan and governor-general of Guangdong and Guangxi. When native products were gathered by sea, in small boats, carrying twenty to thirty piculs, or on land, the merchants might be molested by the rascal offspring of certain strong lineages. Hence, merchants had to be powerful as well.[11]

Evidence of officials' private investment in business can be seen in long distance trade and elsewhere. As discovered by Hsieh Shi-fen (1977), in the late Qing in Nanchang, Jiangxi, finance capital came mainly from officials' private investment.[12] According to the study of Fan I-chun (1981), around 1870 investment in a rich merchant house in Shantou came partially or primarily from local bureaucrats, including the lieutenant governor-general.[13]

Sung Hui-chung's 1995 study of the remittance merchants (piaoshang) in the late nineteenth century further reveals the informal and formal relationship between traditional merchants and Qing officialdom.[14] The remittance merchants included the Shanxi merchants and the families or private secretaries of Qing high officials, such as Li Hongzhang and Zuo Zongtang. The rise of the Shanxi merchants was related to military provisioning for the Qing state during its conquest of China and during the Ten Campaigns in the Qianlong period. Many remittance banks opened by officials had close relations with the Shanxi merchants. In the late nineteenth century, the officials often paid their contributions for academic degrees or official titles through the remittance banks, and they also used the banks for savings and remittance of their personal wealth.

From the initial years of the Taiping Rebellion onward, the remittance banks started to distribute the state's revenue among the provinces. In addition to remitting funds, the remittance merchants sometimes took charge of the collection and disbursement of revenues. The state revenues that passed through the hands of the remittance merchants tended to be newly created revenues supervised by the governors or governor-generals. These included customs revenues, lijin, opium taxes, and levies for indemnities, which were supervised by the governors or governor-generals. Remittance merchants even took charge of the maritime customs banks in Fujian, Zhejiang, and Guangdong. The land taxes, salt taxes, and native custom revenues were still forwarded in cash and supervised by the financial commissioners, who were appointed by the Board of Official Appointment in the central government. It was not until 1903 that the Board of Revenue placed its revenues in the remittance banks to earn interest.

This symbiotic relationship between the Qing bureaucracy and merchants differentiates China's traditional merchants from Henri Pirenne's autonomous city merchants who arose in the course of European expansion. And this Chinese phenomenon was connected to China's crucial method of capital accumulation: partnership (*hehuo* or *hegu*). As Lei Hui-erh's thesis reveals, Japanese South Manchurian Railway investigations show that through this form of capital accumulation, the exact names of the investors could be hidden and hence it was especially favored by officials.[15]

Partnership as the Crucial and Enduring Method of Capital Accumulation for Chinese Business

Partnerships prevailed in China in the late nineteenth and twentieth centuries. According to Lei Hui-erh's study (1980), 67 percent of the stores in Jilin, Jingzhou, and Yingkou in the 1930s accumulated capital through forming partnerships.[16] This method of capital accumulation was not limited to family members, contrary to what Max Weber wrote.[17] Many of the native banks in Shantou were capitalized by joint investment from the people of the same native place.[18] In Taiwan, people from different provinces in China or from different families formed business partnerships.[19] Liaison stores (*lianhao*) in which the same investors had several stores engaged in the same or different business in Manchuria were organized among siblings as well as people of different surnames and different places.[20]

One pitfall for the partnership system was the insecure nature of this kind of investment, since the running of the business was entirely entrusted to managers. Investors tended to have shares in many enterprises. When an enterprise appeared to become risky, the investor might capriciously withdraw his shares and precipitate bankruptcy. The formula for profit sharing was also unfavorable to reinvestment. An investigation conducted in 1930 of thirty-three businesses in Jilin, Jingzhou, and Yingkou, shows that the average interest rate for current capital was seven times that for fixed capital; 82 percent of the profit was taken by the investors; and only 18 percent remained in the enterprises.[21] This suggests that the nature of the partnership arrangement was unfavorable with regard to long-term and large-scale investment.

But the fact that the above investigation was conducted in 1930 when China was hit by world depression may have had a negative influence on firm stability. Li Ho-cheng's study of liaison stores in Manchuria (1991) and the separate studies by Ichiro Numasaki (1992) and Hsieh Kuo-hsing (1995) of contemporary Taiwan's Tainan conglomerates reveal partnerships with provisions for ongoing capital accumulation.[22] In Manchuria's liaison stores, written contracts specified profit sharing among investors and managers according to their contribution in terms of capital or labor. When the business was booming, the investor or the manager might unite with other stores' investors or managers to set up new stores. These branch stores might engage in other lines of business or be located in other places. A rice store owner might risk investment in soy bean oil stores, grocery stores, or native banks. The branch store might or might not be a part of the same accounting unit as the main store. When a branch failed, capital would be diverted to other branches. Turnover could be as high as fifty-six times that of invested capital. The liaison stores were not only networks for the flow of goods but financial networks as well. Their credit systems functioned to enable them to purchase goods at lower prices.

The liaison stores in Manchuria can be traced back to 1644. A silk store named Tianheli, set up in Shenyang (Mukden) in 1644, established grocery stores in the Faku district in 1744, another silk store in Shenyang, two grocery stores in Changchun in the Guangxu period, a grocery store in Jilin in 1880, a grocery store in Suihua in 1897, and a grocery store in Harbin in 1901. According to South Manchuria Railway investigations, by 1925, there were 597 similar types of liaison units in Manchuria.

The Tainan conglomerate in present-day Taiwan developed in a pattern similar to the liaison system of Manchuria over a period extending from the seventeenth into the twentieth centuries. The Tainan group started as a partnership, and its partners continued to cooperate to develop new enterprises. Even when a partner left to open his own enterprise, he did not leave the original enterprise. The head manager of each enterprise enjoyed more and more autonomy in personnel matters and accounting. The Board of Directors made decisions about the general direction for further development. The Tainan conglomerate is now one of the big ten conglomerates in Taiwan.

Since the other nine conglomerates in Taiwan are dominated by one family, the Tainan group's reliance on partnership caused me to raise a question regarding whether partnership in contemporary commercial cooperation was related to landownership patterns initiated during the settlement period in the seventeenth century. Tainan had fewer big landlords than other parts of Taiwan from the settlement period onward. In 1977, I observed that the capital accumulation pattern for the sugar cane mills in southern Tainan (in the northern part of southern Taiwan) was different from Gaoxiong (in the southern part of the southern Taiwan). In Gaoxiong, one big capitalist or landlord provided capital, while the peasants were merely laborers. In Tainan, two to five medium-scale to rich farmers or twenty not so well-off farmers formed partnerships.[23] Tainan's partnership pattern of capital accumulation also applies to the financing of irrigation works during the Japanese period.[24] Significantly, the single ownership pattern is more common in regions where land distribution was less equal during the settlement period, while the partnership is more likely to be found in regions with more equal land distribution.

Thus, partnerships may not only serve to perpetuate enterprises over several centuries, as in the Manchuria and Tainan cases, they may also sustain a very modern conglomerate that operates textile, cement, construction, and investment companies, banks, and twenty-four hour neighborhood convenience stores in contemporary Taiwan. The Tainan example further suggests that long-lasting partnerships could stem from more equal land distribution in the initial settlement period.

Smaller Firms Flourished at Local, Interregional, and International Levels

Chao Yu-chih's study (1995) of the Chamber of Commerce in colonial Taiwan reveals the strength of Chinese merchants under Japanese rule in comparison with Korean merchants who were also subject to Japanese colonial rule. Japanese merchants penetrated to the local level in colonial Korea, while in colonial Taiwan medium- and small-scale Chinese merchants were more powerful than the medium- and small-scale Japanese merchants at the local level.[25]

Medium- and small-scale traders also participated in China's long distance trade as noted by Liu Kwang-ching in his study of *huiguan*. Since *huiguan* were associations set up by merchants from the same province outside of their home province, their members were likely to be agents for long-distance trade. In one of Liu's examples, 15 merchants in one *huiguan* in Suzhou around 1729 donated 6 to 66 taels for repair of the guild's building, and 210 merchants donated 1 to 5 taels. From reading stele inscriptions of the Qing dynasty *huiguan*, Liu perceived that in the early and middle Qing period, *huiguan* for medium- and small-scale merchants multiplied.[26]

Medium- and small-scale merchants were involved in international trade as well. Since the archives of the Taiyi Hao have been donated to the Nagasaki City Museum, Taiwan's Chu Te-lan has joined with Japanese scholars to study this Fujian merchant family that settled in Nagasaki in 1850 and traded throughout Japan, Taiwan, and China. Like its parent store, Taichang Hao, Taiyi Hao was engaged in international trade, but Taiyi Hao itself had only a small amount of capital, about 7,000 Mexican dollars accumulated through a partnership of six to seven investors. The firm had about ten employees.[27] During the Japanese colonial period, when Taiyi Hao traded with wholesale merchants in Jilong (Keelung), it traded more with Taiwanese merchants, especially medium- and small-scale merchants, than with Japanese merchants.[28] Such a phenomenon parallels Liu Shih-chi's finding (1978) that, in Ming–Qing China, market towns were more prosperous than administrative centers, partially because of their links with national and international trade.[29]

These patterns call to mind Man-houng Lin's "Characteristics of China's Traditional Economy" (1992), in which she describes the predominance of medium- and small-scale economic organizations in China. Even though earlier scholars describe north China during the Han and Six dynasties as having a manorial economy, the average size of a farm was about 1.5 hectares, and the number of tillers five or six. Certainly, there were large landlords in Chinese history, but their land was scattered here and there. Thus, the size of each farming unit was small. The total area of land owned by China's landowners, as much as a thousand hectares, could not compare with the several tens of thousands of hectares owned by European manors. China did, however, have large-scale economic organizations. Using water-driven wheels for irrigating land, spinning cotton, grinding wheat, and drilling for petroleum could entail large-scale operations. Cotton fields in the Ming–Qing period could be over one million acres, and cotton spinning operations could spin as much as 100 kilograms daily.

Moreover, China developed extensive shipping networks on interconnected canal, riverine, and coastal shipping routes. Over long periods, China's capital cities were the world's largest cities. Nonetheless, about 93 percent of China's resources were allocated within the vicinity of local market towns. The long-standing and preponderant use of copper cash, a currency of low value in world monetary history, was a reflection of the predominance of medium- and small-scale economic organizations in China.[30] And in postwar Taiwan from 1945 to the 1970s, around 80 percent of Taiwan's private enterprises were medium- and small-scale.[31] These enterprises were the chief movers of Taiwan's export industry during the take-off period. These examples illustrate another long-standing feature of Chinese economic organization.

The Resilience of Traditional Merchants in the Face of the Western Impact

Previous scholarship, especially on the mainland, tends to claim that China's traditional merchants declined after the Western impact. Recent studies in Taiwan on traditional merchants show more growth than decline. For the intra-Asian trade, Chang Pin-tsun's study (1989) shows the advantages of Chinese merchants between the sixteenth and eighteenth centuries based on: (1) the greater need of Europe for goods from Asia than vice versa; (2) the closed nature of the Chinese market; (3) the diaspora of Chinese scattered around East Asia, which suited the needs of navigation technology at this time for island-by-island transport; and (4) the efficiency of the Chinese small-scale organization.[32] Chang's further comments on the loss of the above advantages for the Chinese in the nineteenth century are congruent with the findings of other Taiwan scholars.

In the nineteenth century, although foreign trade was dominated by foreign merchants, China's interregional trade was, for the most part, dominated by domestic merchants.[33] Among the foreign merchants, only Russian and Japanese merchants could, to some extent, do without compradors. This was because of their effort to learn Chinese languages and customs. Russian merchants purchased brick tea directly in Jiangxi;[34] Japanese merchants beat Chinese merchants in the competition to sell Japanese cotton textiles in Manchuria, Tianjin, and Sichuan.[35]

The lack of a standard measurement system and medium of exchange, as well as commission rates, which differed depending on the commodity, inhibited foreign merchants from entering China's interregional trade.[36] Strict guild sanctions were another hindrance. In Shantou and Qifu, local merchants who had contact with foreign merchants without the consent of the merchant guild were boycotted until they became bankrupt.[37] Chinese merchants tended to advance credit to peasant producers while foreign merchants dared not do so because of lack of information.[38] After the arrival of Western competition in Manchuria, guild cohesion was not sufficient to sustain small- and medium-size businesses, but liaison businesses with a parent company and branches organized into a hierarchy were successful. Liaison business also benefited from a wider market and more convenient transportation. They extended their business to Osaka, Yokohama, Shanghai, Guangzhou, and Taiwan. With less expensive means of capital accumulation, the liaison stores were competitive with the British when Manchuria's treaty ports were opened in the late nineteenth century. The liaison store owners also invested heavily in modern enterprises, such as railroads, modern banks, and water companies.[39]

Rhoads Murphey used the dual-economy model to describe the relationship between the treaty ports and China's hinterland after 1840. He argued that imported foreign goods were, by and large, used only in the treaty port areas and that the treaty ports constituted a kind of enclave economy. Unlike China's traditional cities, the treaty ports had little connection with rural China.[40] But evidence from the period of the late 1870s to 1906 does not support Murphey's thesis. Indeed, the littoral area continued to grow and formed a stark contrast to the hinterland. Central and southern China were responsible for more than 95 percent of China's foreign trade in 1889–93.[41] The prosperous cities of the littoral region were more likely to have modern facilities, quicker to adopt advanced technology,[42] and consumed more luxury goods.[43] But, at the same time, the economy of the hinterland grew and the connection between treaty ports and hinterland was actually very much reinforced. According to Wu Chengming's estimate, interregional trade was about 387 million taels. According to Man-houng Lin's adjustment of Dwight Perkins's figures, it grew to 730 million by 1908.[44]

The series of studies in Taiwan about the impact of opening the treaty ports in the hinterland reveal crucial information about the potential for profits when the interregional trade of traditional merchants and compradors was linked to foreign trade. Most Chinese economic life was localized in the standard market system and little influenced by the international market. However, the merchant who gained access to information about the international market could make very high profits. In the tea trade of Jiangxi, the middlemen earned profits of 45–55 percent.[45] The profit in the soybean trade in Manchuria was 50 percent.[46] A sugar merchant in southern Taiwan made 55 percent profit on the final selling price for export goods in addition to some profit earned on the exchange between silver and copper cash.[47] These profits help account for the rise of comprador merchants in modern China. About 90 percent of the official-supervised and merchant-managed enterprises were financed by the compradors.[48] The Shanxi Bankers involved in interregional trade increased their capital by tenfold between 1840 and 1905.[49] The native banks in Shanghai, a substitute for small-scale modern banks, also prospered.[50]

Using the British East India Company's archives, Ch'en Kuo-tung (1990) reconstructed the history of the Cantonese hong merchants. They went from prosperity between 1760 and the 1810s to bankruptcy between 1820 and 1843, with the Pan family as a rare exception. Their prosperity was due to favorable trade conditions while their failure can be attributed chiefly to their mutual loan system and to official exactions.[51] In her Harvard doctoral thesis, written about the same time, Man-houng Lin shows that China's economy was connected to the world economy. And China relied heavily on Latin America's silver from the eighteenth century onward. China's economy grew in the eighteenth century when the silver supply was abundant, but it declined in the early nineteenth century when Latin American silver production dropped. The income of both the imperial government and merchants went up when the economy boomed and declined during recession years. In boom years, merchants did not feel that their large contributions to the government were particularly burdensome; in recession years, even though contributions were smaller, their sense of burden increased.[52]

Man-houng Lin (1994) applied the same concept to explain the fluctuation of guild merchant trading between Taiwan and mainland China between 1820 and 1895. Previous scholarship had concluded that these merchants declined in this period due to Western competition. However, Lin found that most of these studies were based on observations made in the early nineteenth century when both Taiwan and mainland China were hit seriously by a worldwide recession. The late nineteenth century was marked by an economic boom, particularly from the late 1850s to the 1880s, and the guild merchants prospered even with Western competition. They increased their stores, trade volume, junk numbers, and modernized some of their commercial practices. In addition to some dependency on Western capital after Western penetration of the Asian world, these Taiwan guild merchants actually relied more on Chinese capital provided by Shanxi Banks and Chinese native banks, developing a kind of dual-dependency.

Japanese scholars, such as Hamashita Takeshi, Sugihara Kaoru and others, have stressed how intra-Asian trade expanded after the Western impact and how Chinese merchants were very dominant in this trade. The strength of Chinese merchants in the late nineteenth century provides another example. However, the Taiwan studies on the fluctuation of trade in accord with world economic cycles may have some implications for the whole intra-Asian trade.[53]

More Justification of Commerce, yet More Intervention in Enterprises by a Weak State in the Late Qing Republican Period

Lin Hui-jun (1988) has pointed out that merchants were criticized in novels of late Qing China.[54] Nonetheless, many studies done in Taiwan in the 1970s described the rise of ideas that stressed the positive role of the businessman in the late nineteenth century. Wang Erh-min, Wu Chang-chuan, and Chen Li Shun-yen have all dealt with this issue. Merchants who had been perceived as being of lowly status historically became heroes to save the country. Their modern industries would save the country's foreign exchange and help to defend the country by paying more taxes than the agricultural sector.[55] Since these studies were done before Yu Ying-shih's 1987 book, they did not take into account the emphasis on commerce in the early modern period that he describes. Also the emphasis on commerce in the late Qing period was different from that in China's early modern period. As discussed by Lin Li-yue (1989) for the Ming–Qing transition period and by Man-houng Lin (1991) for the early nineteenth century, the emphasis on commerce was coupled with an emphasis on agriculture.[56] The change in the tax structure was crucial in changing the balance. Beginning in the late Qing, the Chinese government relied more on commercial taxes than on agricultural taxes. As Man-houng Lin (1989) pointed out, although all developing countries tend to place more emphasis on the rapid development of modern industries, some also develop modern agriculture as well. China's development of modern agriculture was inhibited by incessant foreign threats, which required an emphasis on weapons and wealth to achieve security. Another reason was the great distance between the cities and the countryside with respect to information.[57]

While previous studies emphasized late Qing China's stress upon commerce, Man-houng Lin (1989) has drawn attention to the shift from noninterventionist to interventionist economic policies effected from the late Daoguang era to the self-strengthening period.[58] There seems to be some congruence between these phenomena. Actually, the emphasis upon commerce stressed mercantile activities compared with agricultural activities. Whether merchants would, in fact, have autonomy in their commercial activities was affected by the time and the particular case involved. For example, in Fan Cheng-ch'ien's study of the China Merchants' Company, he points out that since the government needed the merchants, they had collective powers to put some pressure on the government (which was still situated in a dominant position).[59] Huang Wang-ming's study of the Bank of China and the Jiaotong Bank noted that both banks were often used by politicians for their temporary needs in the late Qing and Yuan Shikai periods. Between 1916 and 1927, the two banks gained more autonomy.[60]

As described by Juan Chung-ren, the Board of Commercial Affairs set up by the Qing government in 1903 was the first formal modern institution to protect and encourage merchants. (The Board of Revenue and Board of Works were not concerned with modern commerce, and the Tsungli yamen was mainly preoccupied with industry and transportation.) Contrary to previous scholars' emphasis on the conflicts among the central government, the local government, and the merchants, Juan argued that the three were bound by common interests. The failure to implement beneficial policies was due to inadequate ability, not mutual hostility.[61]

Economic nationalism was the main reason for the cooperation between the state and private enterprise. Ku Wei-yin's study of Chinese participation in international exhibitions shows this trend increasing in the early twentieth century. China's participation in the Liège Fair in Belgium in 1905 marked a turning point. Before that event, the foreign-management Inspectorate of Chinese Maritime Customs supervised such participation; after Liège, new statutes directed Chinese involvement.[62] Commercial ports were opened one by one by the Qing government itself to secure domestic commercial competitiveness.[63]

The problem was the weakness of successive Chinese governments. For example, the Qing had a treaty with Korea to provide that China's telegraph bureau would cooperate with Korea to build a Korean telegraph system. The ensuing Japanese threat, however, made the treaty futile.[64] China's government was also too weak to set up a more reasonable tax system for China. The export tax on Taiwan's coal, for example, was thirteen times the tax on imported coal.[65] Meanwhile the Japanese government was able to lower the taxes at the port of Dalian, which diverted trade from Yingkou.[66] To cite a final example, the hyperinflation of 1935–48 has been found to have been more affected by China's loss of control over foreign exchange (due to British and American policies and control of supplies) than by the issuance of currency.[67]

Transformation of Merchants' Associations

In eighteenth- and nineteenth-century Suzhou, many merchant associations, such as *huiguan, gongsuo, gongtang, gongsu,* and *gongju,* were established. In contrast with merchant organizations founded during the sixteenth century, these new ones were spontaneously formed, ongoing, legally recognized organizations. Earlier literature tended to stress these associations' limitations on free competition. Chiu Peng-sheng (1988) finds that, although there were some limitations on the recruitment of apprentices, there were no serious restrictions on the expansion of capital or the improvement of technology.[68]

As Lei shows, Japanese observations in Manchuria stated that, especially after the arrival of Western competitors, cohesion within guilds was insufficient to sustain their businesses.[69] While guilds had been relatively egalitarian, liaison businesses with more paternalistic forms of organization thrived in their stead. This "democratic" description of guilds may be verified by examining Taiwan's guilds in the Qing period. Guild members drew lots in front of the deities to select the guild executives. Fees were paid yearly or monthly and varied according to the size of the business. The guild's account book could be kept by one staff member and checked by others. The guild also provided a place for the townfolk's assembly to meet.[70]

Mainland studies of Shanghai's General Chamber of Commerce have focused on the relationship between the General Chamber of Commerce under various regimes and the imperialist Western powers. Chan Huanchung (1994), however, focused on the chamber's internal organization and the way in which socioeconomic changes in Shanghai affected it. After 1915, committees were set up to implement an organizational form of governance to replace the personal form of governance characteristic of the period between 1902 and 1915. In that period, the chamber was more concerned with its internal affairs, while after 1915, it devoted more effort to providing commercial service. This included opening an extension school, establishing a publishing house and libraries to promote commercial knowledge, and organizing and participating in commercial exhibitions. These changes were connected with the growth in membership and the message of change in Shanghai's society that the new members brought to the chamber.[71] From 1909 to 1924, nonguild members correspondingly increased from 25.2 percent to 76.6 percent. Those from Ningbo remained dominant in this chamber, and they increasingly fought over commericial issues rather than for their native-place interests. Also the average age of the chamber's membership consistently decreased.[72] This all shows the weakening of native-place bonds and age hierarchy.

More State Intervention and More Development of Taiwanese Merchants Under Japanese Rule

Contrary to the hostile relationship between the Taiwanese people and the Japanese government as described by earlier scholars, Chao Yu-chih's study of Taiwanese chambers of commerce in the Japanese colonial period (1995) reveals more penetration from the Japanese government and more participation of these Taiwanese merchants than under the previous regime.

It is not until the period of Taisho democracy in the 1920s that Taiwan's merchants established their chambers of commerce. Although the governor-general rejected many petitions from these organizations, there were close ties between them and Japanese local government officials. These local officials frequently attended the Taiwanese chambers' meetings and were appointed as honorary presidents, advisers, and consultants. The chamber and Japanese officials jointly petitioned the governor-general on behalf of local development projects. Local officials sponsored and administratively assisted many of the chamber's activities. Some were even appointed to its staff. The lowest ranks of the colonial administration were fully intertwined with these Taiwanese commercial associations.

The Taiwanese chambers were quite democratic. Since there was an average ratio of 1 executive per 6.8 members, there was not much of an organizational hierarchy. Executives were directly elected to one-year terms of service, and members were constantly rotated into executive offices. Small merchants were also able to participate in the chamber, since membership fees were low. The organization set no restrictions on the kind of businesses in which its members were engaged, hence it was very open. By 1938, there were 93 chambers of commerce on Taiwan, with a total membership of 13,500. The average membership of each chamber was 145, but the largest one had more than 800 members. There were three island-wide associations. Sixty percent of the chambers were located in towns with less than 20,000 people and more than 80 percent of Taiwan's towns had set up chambers of commerce.

Most of the merchants in the Taiwanese chambers were grain or fertilizer merchants, revealing the grassroots nature of Taiwan's newly established merchant class. The predominance of merchants over manufacturers during the colonial period is evident in the names of these associations. Most of them were then known as associations of merchants and manufacturers (*shanggong hui*), whereas after 1945 the use of associations for promoting manufacturers and merchants (*gongshang xiejin hui*) was more common. Executives of the Taiwanese chambers came less and less from distinguished families decorated by the Japanese government and more and more from the ranks of the merchant members, which is evidence of greater upward mobility among the members at large. Most of the members were elementary school graduates or had studied with classical Chinese tutors. However, some were graduates of normal or professional schools or had studied abroad. Many of the leading executives of the Japanese colonial era continued to serve in the post-1945 Taiwanese chambers.[73]

In general, Chinese merchants were very responsive to market conditions. In 1890, British merchants introduced the iron mill for grinding sugar cane into southern Taiwan. The average total cost of using the iron mill was lower than the average variable cost of using traditional stone mills. Taiwanese were reluctant to adopt the iron mill, which, if we apply Joseph A. Schumpeter's principle of technology transfer, indicates a lack of entrepreneurship with regard to technology transfer among Chinese merchants. However, if we compare the Taiwan example to an analogous case of technology transfer in Manchuria, it is clear that the decision was market-driven. When high output steam-powered soybean mills were introduced in Manchuria in 1861, they were not accepted because they would displace the existing workforce and traditional technology. When the Japanese and German markets were increasingly opened to Manchurian soybean exports, however, the technology of the soybean mills was upgraded three times. By contrast, the southern Taiwan sugar market in 1890 was dwindling because of competition from Javanese sugar.[74] When the Japanese ruled both Taiwan and Korea, they found Taiwan Chinese much more responsive to market factors than the Koreans.[75]

The Taiwanese responsiveness to market was enhanced during the Japanese colonial period. Enhanced promotion techniques include sales held at the end of the year, in the summer, and during religious festivals. The merchants added display windows to their shops, sponsored lectures, and sent investigators overseas. On pilgrimage marches, they used decorated vehicles and costumed figures to advertise. More precise accounting methods were developed to calculate the outcome of "price-cutting, volume sales" policies. The concept of brand names was spread through competitive exhibitions of products. In 1936, there was even a special festival for merchants (*shanggongji*) that symbolized their rise in Taiwan's society.[76]

The above discussion relates to the domestic market in Taiwan. Another dimension is foreign trade. Man-houng Lin (1993) has studied Taiwanese merchant trading between Taiwan and China between 1895 and 1937.[77] Prior to 1895, when Taiwan was ceded to Japan, Taiwanese merchants rarely had experience in direct foreign trade. In the trade with China during the Japanese colonial period, they gained significant experience in direct investment and marketing abroad as well as in the financing of foreign trade. Following the example of Japanese merchants, Taiwanese merchants also adopted several new business practices. These included accumulation of capital by selling stocks, the realization that a company's life can extend beyond the investing families' interests, and novel methods of advertising. Taiwan's merchant families also developed greater solidarity among themselves during this period through formal and informal associations. This experience paved the way for Taiwan's dramatic foreign trade expansion after 1945. Moreover, these Taiwanese merchants also reversed the two century old historical trend of capital and technology flowing from mainland China into Taiwan, thus prefiguring the flow of capital and technology from Taiwan into China today.

Private Enterprises' Ways of Capital Accumulation in Postwar Taiwan

Taiwan's postwar private enterprises accumulated capital in various ways. By 1953, textile companies were the main private enterprises. There were eleven textile companies in Taiwan, three of which were public companies. Of the remaining eight private textile companies, seven originated on the Chinese mainland and enjoyed a 34.1 percent exchange rate discount in the export trade.[78] The government developed a surrogate spinning and weaving policy, under which manufacturers with inadequate capital were prompted to spin and weave by being supplied with cotton provided by U.S. aid as well as receiving abundant processing rewards.[79]

Between 1949 and 1952, land reform transformed much existing agricultural capital into industrial capital by exchanging land ownership rights for stocks. The stock market practices introduced by mainland entrepreneurs also caused much private capital to flow into the stock market.[80] Private foreign capital came to Taiwan mainly after the 1960s. Before that era, American aid comprised a third of Taiwan's capital formation.[81] American and Japanese companies tended to form joint companies with local entrepreneurs; they focused on investing in manufacturers, especially in electronics companies encouraged by the government. Overseas Chinese tended to invest in the service sectors such as trading companies.

American aid encouraged the establishment of commercial banks to assist medium- and small-scale enterprises. In general, the initial capitalization of such enterprises came from relatives or friends. Taking 1980 as an example, medium- and small-scale enterprises shared only 32.75 percent of the total loans from Taiwan's banks, while the island's large enterprises enjoyed the lion's share of bank loans. Banks for medium- and small-scale enterprises were established to avoid having these businesses resort to "underground" banks. They charged interest rates lower than 20 percent, had lower mortgage requirements, fewer requirements for companies to sell stocks, and tried to publicize banking services for the common people.[82]

Loosening Blood Ties: The Nature and Transformation of Family Enterprises in Postwar Taiwan

Family enterprises constituted the lion's share of postwar Taiwan's firms. In 1973, 82 percent of the medium- and small-scale enterprises involved in exports were family businesses whose property was more than half-owned by one family.[83] Of the island's 97 conglomerates, 86.6 percent had both their president and chief managers belonging to the same family.[84] Family enterprise prevailed as well in Japan, Korea, Germany, England, and the United States.[85] Among them were famous firms, such as DuPont, Ford, Krober, Mitsui, Mitsubishi, and Samsung. The basic difference between Taiwan's family enterprises and those of other developed countries was the separation of ownership and management. Taiwan's owners often filled upper- and middle-rank management positions, while in other developed countries business owners relied upon salaried managers at these levels.[86]

Such differences were related to China's particular concept of the family extension. The Japanese were concerned with family extension, but the content of this concern was different from China's. In Japan, the continuation and enhancement of the ancestors' prestige and material prosperity, such as property and business, were stressed, while in China more importance was placed on the continuation and expansion of blood ties.[87] As Japan's concept of family (*ie*) emphasized the extension of business rather than the extension of blood ties, nonfamily employees could be more loyal to the enterprise. Such employees were often deemed outsiders in Chinese enterprises, and they were correspondingly not as loyal as Japanese employees. As a result, Chinese enterprises tended to have shorter lifespans than Japanese or American enterprises, and medium- and small-scale enterprises tended to be preponderant.[88]

To face these problems, Taiwan's enterprises have paid serious attention to the education and training of the successors, who often obtain Ph.D. or M.B.A. degrees and return to their family businesses to start from an elementary level. Sons-in-law have also received more attention as business managers. Employment of professional managers increased from 10 percent to 24 percent between 1978 and 1985. (In Japan, the proportion of professional managers rose—from 20 percent in 1900 to 25 percent in 1930 and 94 percent in 1965.)[89] Taiwan's conglomerates introduced profit incentives for each branch enterprise. Computerization of market investigation, accounting advances, and development of research also helped to replace personal management.[90]

From Dominance to Cooperation: The State and Business Enterprises in Postwar Taiwan

Chen Jin-man's study of fertilizer industries reveals that intervention was greater in early postwar Taiwan than under the Nationalist government in pre-1949 mainland China or under the Japanese colonial government in Taiwan. During the Japanese colonial period, fertilizer companies were owned by Japanese *zaibatsu*, while in the early postwar period (before the 1970s) the Nationalist government owned them. Up to the 1980s, government-controlled fertilizer companies still produced 86 percent of Taiwan's fertilizer. In pre-1949 mainland China, the fertilizer industry had been established by the government during the Anti-Japanese War (1937–45), but its scale was small due to the war and scarcity of capital. As a consequence, the fertilizer used in China was mainly imported by foreign merchants and distributed by Chinese private merchants. In postwar Taiwan, the Nationalist government not only owned the fertilizer companies, but also used the peasant association system set up by the Japanese government for distribution. During the Japanese colonial period, private merchants could also purchase imported fertilizer to supply the market and peasants could purchase fertilizer with cash. In the early postwar period, however, peasants were required to exchange fertilizer for their grains. The Japanese colonial government, on the other hand, used coercion to promote the use of fertilizer, while the Nationalist government (with American aid) used more persuasive means for such promotion.[91]

According to Cheng Yueh-sui's 1993 study, at the time of the Nationalist government's takeover of Taiwan, Taiwanese enterprises only owned

9 percent of the total share value of enterprises capitalized at over 200,000 yuan, while 91 percent of such businesses were owned by the Japanese government and Japanese merchants. These Japanese-owned enterprises, although somewhat damaged in World War II, were transferred to the Nationalist government. The government also relocated some state-owned businesses from the mainland, such as the Central Bank, the Central Trust Bureau, China Textiles, and the China Merchant Company.[92]

Using these resources, together with American aid, which commenced in 1951, the Nationalist government set up its authoritarian rule over Taiwan from 1953 to the early 1980s. At this time, technocrats in the government and the party held themselves aloof from Taiwanese private entrepreneurs. As Chu Yun-han showed in 1992, with its unquestioned anti-Communist mission and substantial international recognition, the government in early postwar Taiwan did not need to resort to private enterprise for help.[93] Hsueh Yi-shu's 1986 study shows that merchants relied on government for support with respect to such policies as import-substitution, the maintainence of favorable exchange rates and low interest rates, the encouragement of export expansion, and the establishment of a scientific park to upgrade industrial technologies. Government-owned enterprises under the Ministry of Economic Affairs also had larger backward or inward linkage-effect ratios than the average of all industries. Meanwhile, government-owned enterprises cushioned many setbacks caused by economic recessions. For example, in the 1973 Oil Crisis, the China Petroleum Company had to sell oil at a price lower than the imported cost to ease the burden of the private enterprises.[94]

As private enterprises grew, they became increasingly impatient with government-owned enterprises that monopolized raw materials or energy, such as oil and electricity, needed for production.[95] Wu Jo-yu's 1992 study shows that in 1978 the efficiency of government-owned enterprises was about half that of private enterprises in terms of capital-output ratio, turnover of capital, or turnover of commodities. There were several factors contributing to such inefficiency—improper management by the nonprofessional retired bureaucrats chosen as enterprise heads, selection of employees on the basis of civil service examinations rather than technical skills, misallocation of funds to purchase expensive capital equipment, and the red tape that accompanied official supervision of government enterprises. This inefficiency was increasingly questioned after the 1980s. Privatization accompanied the opening of markets and changes of ownership. Markets have been opened in the banking and airlines sectors, and the sale of public enterprises to private owners has been successfully achieved by large firms, such as China Chemical Industry and China Engineering Company. Other

major public enterprises involved in oil production and electricity generation have begun partial privatization.[96]

Chu Yun-han (1992) further shows that, as authoritarianism faded away,
rapid democratization made Taiwan's Legislative Yuan the basic arena for
reallocating political resources. Private enterprises could now support legisla-
tors favorable to them in costly elections. The Nationalist government turned to
buying relations with the enterprises by awarding them party positions. However, as each enterprise seeks its individual advantage, there has been no coordination of efforts. Enterprises also lack sufficient academic staff to evaluate
the governments' overall policies, including macroeconomic policies.[97] But,
according to Wang Cheng-huan's study of 1992, the Nationalist party did
not lose its control. Rather, through some reorganization, it formed alliances
with private enterprises.[98]

Political Vicissitudes and Chinese Merchants' Adaptation

Cheng Jui-ming has studied how Koxinga's regime in Taiwan, 1661–1682,
developed a trade with Southeast Asia that was about as important as its
trade with Japan.[99] Chu Te-lan has worked on Taiwanese merchants trading
between Japan and Siam under Koxinga's (Cheng Ch'eng-kung's) regime
by examining two examples.[100] Based on this relationship, when the Qing
conquered the Koxinga regime on Taiwan, some of the latter regime's
subordinates migrated to southern Vietnam. While settling there, they
helped the Nguyen regime to restore sovereignty and served as its officials.[101]
Lu Shi-peng has studied the Sino–Vietnamese trade during the high Qing.
At this time, Vietnam was divided between the northern and the southern
regimes. Although the Qing government conducted tribute trade with the
northern regime, this could not compete with private trade between people
of both regimes and China. Private trade with the northern regime was often
interrupted by internal turmoil and was dwarfed by private trade with the
southern regime. Due to the efforts of some of the Koxinga regime's left-
over followers, the southern regime became more prosperous than the northern regime.[102]

Chen Yin-i (1976) describes the influence of imperial taste on the rise
and fall of the jade trade from Xinjiang to Beijing. It rose because of the
Qianlong emperor's interest and fell because of the Jiaqing emperor's disin-
terest in jade.[103] Chang Chun-wu (1978) has pointed out how the Sino–
Korean tribute trade reinforced Sino–Korean diplomatic relationships.[104]

It is still an open question as to whether the maritime traders intertwined with the Koxinga regime on Taiwan were also closely linked to
the Qing government. By comparison to Zhejiang merchants, Fujian mer-

chants were still dominant in the early Qing period as they pressed the government to loosen the construction regulations on shipping. Firms that had close official connections naturally tended to decline with the fall of the Qing dynasty. Examples are the Shanxi banks that absorbed bureaucratic capital. With the competition from the newly established modern government and foreign banks, the flow of remittances handled by the Shanxi banks decreased. The decline of trade with Mongolia and Russia accelerated the decline of the Shanxi Banks.[105] Guild merchants trading with Taiwan also failed with the demise of the Qing.[106]

Liu Kwang-ching has discussed the transformation of merchants into intellectuals. Zheng Guanying's promotion of self-strengthening and government reform paved the way, to some extent, for the 1911 Revolution, as Sun Yat-sen was very much influenced by Zheng.[107] Yet, according to a study by Chang Huan-chung, merchants in Shanghai had not explicitly supported the revolutionaries until the Republican government replaced the Qing in 1911. Before 1911, Shanghai merchants gave greater support to the Constitutionalists. An examination of the structure of Shanghai's Chamber of Commerce reveals that from 1915 to 1929, the public relations committee overshadowed other committees, reflecting the fact that the insecure political situation forced the merchants to spend heavily on buying influence.[108]

The 1911 Revolution combined with Japanese discriminatory policies against Taiwan's guild merchants dealt those merchants a fatal blow. The same was true for the liaison stores in Manchuria. In the early twentieth century, they were progressively squeezed by Japanese and Russian capitalists who controlled railroads and modern banking. But it was not until the establishment of Manchukuo in 1932–45 that they almost completely disappeared. In the early Republican period, 39.1 percent of the investors in liaison stores came from Shandong; 30 percent, from Manchuria; 23.8 percent, from Hebei; 3.2 percent, from Shanxi; and 2.3 percent, from Guangdong. Higher tariffs after 1932 limited further capital flows from China's interior.[109]

Taiwanese merchant reaction to the Japanese colonial government reveals their pragmatic approach to national identity. The Japanese colonial government adopted a carrot and stick policy in dealing with Taiwanese merchants. Sometimes it united with the Japanese chambers of commerce to oppress the Taiwanese chambers of commerce. But Japanese colonial authorities also appointed three-fourths of the leaders of the Taiwanese chambers of commerce to be political heads of grass-roots public offices. In addition, one-half of the Taiwanese merchants were appointed as staff in local credit cooperatives, and one-quarter were designated as owners of monopoly rights. As a result, not only were anti-Japanese sentiments mitigated, but Taiwanese merchants became very much identified with the Japanese government. In fact, Taiwanese merchants in the 1930s were more enthusiastic about the "Southern Advance" policy than the Japanese merchants in Taiwan. The Taiwanese chambers of commerce also appointed more Japanese local officials as presidents and advisers than did the Japanese merchants' chamber of commerce in Taiwan. Encouraged by the Japanese government, Taiwanese merchants led the way in purchasing stocks issued by the Taiwan Developmental Company. Despite the presence of some cadres who led an anti-Japanese movement, the Taipei Chamber of Commerce, when holding its meetings, routinely sang the Japanese national anthem, hung the Japanese national flag, and declared "Long live the Japanese empire." Especially after the Mukden Incident (1931), the Taiwanese chambers of commerce were turned into tools for Japan's expansionist policies.[110]

According to the Treaty of Shimonoseki, Taiwanese who did not leave Taiwan prior to the 1897 deadline were to be considered Japanese nationals, and some Taiwanese did go to the Chinese mainland to preserve their national identity. Yet, the Boxer Movement, the 1911 Revolution, and warlordism made these Taiwanese feel that China was less secure than Taiwan. Some Taiwanese who had relocated to the mainland to maintain their Chinese nationality returned to Taiwan. Later, about 400 Taiwanese went to China to fight against the Japanese between 1937 and 1945, but about 20,000 Taiwanese were involved in supplying goods to Japan for its war in China. Taiwanese "rascals" sold opium and opened brothels in the Xiamen area, and provided intelligence to the Japanese Army as it advanced toward Xiamen. Taiwanese merchants in Shanghai who claimed to be Chinese before the Japanese occupation, afterward claimed to be Japanese. In Manchuria, even Taiwanese notables, such as the Lins of Banqiao and the Lins of Wufeng, were recruited by the Japanese government to invest in the Manchuria Opium Company. When Taiwan's green tea could not be sold in Southeast Asia because of the overseas Chinese anti-Japanese movement, it was instead sold in Manchuria. Taiwan's tea growers and merchants, who were now able to market their tea in Manchuria, described the Sino–Japanese war as a "Holy war."[111]

Wu Chien-hsiung has studied the effect of U.S. discrimination policies on Chinese immigrants in New York in the late nineteenth century. Echoing American workers' demands, these policies confined Chinese immigrants to a socially marginal status as proprietors of laundries, restaurants, and grocery stores. This was quite different from the treatment Chinese received from Southeast Asian political regimes, which at the time welcomed Chinese immigrants as a minority middle-class.[112]

Other than the foregoing interpretive trends, Taiwan's studies of Chinese business history also reveal that, in addition to the work of the established or professional scholars, junior and independent scholars have contributed a great deal to the whole field. Similar to the dominance of small- and medium-sized enterprises in Chinese business, academic activity also reveals the flourishing of the small managing unit in Chinese culture.

Notes

1. Liang Chi-tzu, "Lishixue xuemen jenli zhiyuan xiankuang jianjie" [A Brief Introduction to the Allocation of Manpower], in *Lishixue xuemen xiankuang yu fazhan yantaohui* [Workshop on the current condition of manpower allocation in the field of the history and development of historical studies], sponsored by the Branch of Humanities and Social Science, National Science Council, and the Institute of History and Philology, Academia Sinica, June 11, 1995.

2. Lin Man-houng, "Cha tang zhangnao ye yu wan Qing Taiwan" [The Industry of Tea, Sugar, and Camphor and Taiwan in the Late Qing Period], *Research Series of the Bank of Taiwan*, no. 115 (1976); Hsieh Shi-fen, "Jiujiang maoyi yanjiu" [Research on Jiujiang's Trade] (master's thesis, NTU, 1977); Lei Hui-erh, "Dongbei de douhuo maoyi, 1907–1931" [Manchurian Soybean Trade, 1907–1931] (master's thesis, NTNU, 1980); Fan I-jun, "Duiwai maoyi yu Hanjiang liuyu de jingji bianqian, 1867–1931" [Foreign Trade and the Economic Change of the Han River Valley, 1867–1931] (master's thesis, NTNU, 1981); Liu Su-fen, "Yantai maoyi yanjiu, 1867–1919" [A Study of Yentai Trade, 1867–1919] (master's thesis, NTU, 1982); Yeh Shu-chen, "Tianjingang di maoyi dui qi fudi jingji zhi yingxiang" [Trade of Tientsin Ports and Its Impact on the Hinterland] (master's thesis, NTU Graduate Institute of Economics, 1983); Chang Shu-fen, "Jindai Sichuan pendi duiwai maoyi yu gongshang ye bianqian" [Foreign Trade Industry and Commercial Change in the Modern Szechwan Basin] (master's thesis, NTNU, 1982).

3. Liu Ts'ui-jung, *Trade on the Han River and Its Impact on Economic Development, c. 1800–1911*, Monograph Series, no. 16 (IEAS, 1980).

4. Ch'en Tzu-yu, "Jindai Zhongguo gongkuangye shi de yanjiu" [Studies on the Industries and Mining of Modern China], *Liu-shinian lai de Zhongguo jindaishi yanjiu* [Studies on Modern Chinese History] (IMH, 1989).

5. Yu Ying-shih, *Zhongguo jinshi zhongjiao lunli yu shangren jingshen* [Religious Ethics and the Merchant Spirit in Modern China] (Taipei: Lian-jing, 1987).

6. Cho Ke-hua, *Qingdai Taiwan de shangzhan jituan* [Mercantile Groups of Taiwan in the Qing Dynasty] (Taipei: Tai-yuan, 1990), pp. 58–86; 144–52.

7. Sung Kuang-yu, "Xiahai chenghuang qidian yu Taibei da daochen shangye fazhan de guanxi" [The City God and the Commercial Development of Tataotia], *Zhongyang yanjiuyuan lishi yuyan yanjiuso jikan* [Bulletin of the Institute of History and Philology] 63, no. 2 (1993).

8. Huang Yun-lung and Hsu Mu-lan, "Qiye gaojie zhuguan zongjiao xinyang dui jingying guanli shiwu de yingxiang" [The Influence of Enterprises' Higher Rank Leaders' Religious Beliefs on Management]. Paper presented at *Qiye zhuzi, shehui guanxi yu wenhua guanxing: Huaren shehui zhi bijiao yanjiu xueshu yantao hui* [Workshop on enterprise organization, social relations, and cultural practice: A comparative study

among Chinese societies]) (Nangang: Institute of Ethnology, Academia Sinica, September 15–17, 1992).

9. Yu Ying-Shih, *Zhongguo jinshi zhongjiao lunli yu shangren jingshen*, pp. 97–121.

10. Lin Li-yue, "Minnan shishen yu jiajing nianjian de haishang zousi maoyi" [Scholar-Officials and the Smuggling Maritime Trade in Southern Fujian], *Shida lishi xuebao* [Bulletin of the Graduate Institute of History, NTNU], no. 8 (May 1980), pp. 91–112.

11. "Prosperity or Decline?—Mainland China's Merchants Trading Across the Taiwan Straits," Paper presented at the Workshop on Commercial Networks in Asia, during the 11th International Economic History Congress held in Milan, September 11–16, 1994 (preworkshop held at Keio University, Japan, March 17–19, 1994).

12. Hsieh Shi-fen, "Jiujiang maoyi yanjiu," p. 184.

13. Fan I-chun, "Duiwai maoyi yu Hanjiang liuyu de jingji bianqian, 1867–1931," p. 39.

14. Sung Hui-tsung, *Piaoshang yu wan Qing de guanliao tixi* [Remittance Merchants and the Late Qing Bureaucracy] (master's thesis, Chung-cheng, 1995).

15. Lei Hui-erh, "Dongbei de douhuo maoyi, 1907–1931," pp. 83–84.

16. Ibid, p. 83.

17. Max Weber, *The Religion of China* (New York: Free Press, 1951), p. 95.

18. Fan I-chun, "Duiwai maoyi yu Hanjiang liuyu de jingji bianqian, 1867–1931," p. 41.

19. Wen Cheng-hua, "Qingdai Taibei pengdi jingji shehui de yanbian" [Socioeconomic Change in the Taibei Basin During the Qing Dynasty] (master's thesis, NTNU, 1978), pp. 66–67.

20. Li Ho-cheng, *Qingmo minchu dongbei minzhu ziben zhong lianhao de yanjiu (1860–1931)* [National Capital in the Liason Stores System of Manchuria in the Late Qing to Early Republican Period] (master's thesis, NTNU, May 1992), pp. 71–73.

21. Lei Hui-erh, "Dongbei de douhuo maoyi, 1907–1931," p. 84.

22. Ichiro Numazaki, "Networks and Partnership: The Social Organization of the Chinese Business Elite in Taiwan" (Ph.D. dissertation., Michigan State University, 1992); Hsieh Kuo-hsing, *Qiye fazhan yu Taiwan jingyan Tainanbang de ge'an yanjiu* [Enterprise Development and the Taiwan Experience: A Case Study of the Tainan Group) (IMH, 1994), chap. 2 and 5.

23. Lin Man-houng, "Cha tang zhanghao ye yu wan Qing Taiwan," pp. 55–56.

24. Kuo Yun-ping, "Guojia yu shehui zhijian de Jianan dajun, 1920–1945" [The Jianan Irrigation Work Between the State and the Society, 1920–1945] (master's thesis, Chung-cheng, July 1994), pp. 124–25.

25. Chao Yu-chi, "Riju shiqi Taiwan shanggong hui de fazhan" [The Development of Taiwan's Chamber of Commerce] (master's thesis, NTNU, 1995), pp. 57–72.

26. Liu Kwang-ching, "Jinshi zhidu yu shangren" [Institutions and Merchants of Early Modern China], in *Jingshi sixiang yu xinxing shiye* [Statecraft Ideas and the Newly Arisen Enterprises] (Taipei: Lian-jing, 1990), p. 317.

27. Chu Te-lan, "Mingzhi shiqi Changqi huashang Taichanghao han Taiyihao guoji maoyi wangluo zhi zhankai," [The Extension of the International Trade Network of Two Nagasaki Chinese Merchant Houses, Taichanghao and Taiyihao], *Renwen ji shehui kexue jikan* [Bulletin of the ISSP] 7, no. 2, pp. (1995) 53–75.

28. Chu Te-lan, "Rijushiqi Changqi huashang Taiyihao yu Jilong pifa hangzhijian de maoyi" [The Wholesale Trade Between Taiyihao in Nagasaki and Keelung's Wholesale Traders in Japanese Colonial Taiwan], *Zhongguo haiyangshi lunwenji* [Essays in Chinese Maritime History], ISSP 5, (February 1993), pp. 427–65.

29. Liu Shih-chi, "MingQing shidai Jiangnan diqu de zhuanye shizhen" [Market Towns for Special Products in the Lower Yangtze Area], *Shihuo Monthly* 8, nos. 6, 7, and 8 (September–November 1978).

30. Lin Man-houng, "Zhongguo chuantong jingji de tezheng" [Characteristics of China's Traditional Economy], *Renwen ji shehui kexue tongxun* [Newsletter for Humanities and Social Science], Ministry of Education (February 1992).

31. Huang Kuang-kuo, "Tan jiazhu qiye de zhuzhi xingtai" [The Organization Pattern of Family Enterprises], *Zhongguo luntan* [China Forum] 13, no. 7 (January 1982), p. 21.

32. Chang Pin-tsun, "Shiliu shiba shiji huaren zai dongya shuiyu de maoyi youshi" [The Advantages of Chinese in the Maritime Areas of East Asia], *Symposium on Chinese Maritime History*, ISSP, no. 3 (March 1989).

33. Lin Man-houng, "Kouan maoyi yu jindai Zhongguo" [Trade of the Treaty Ports and Modern China], *Jindai Zhongguo quyushi huiyi lunwen ji* [Symposium on Regional History of Modern China], IMH (December 1986), pp. 892–95.

34. Hsieh Shi-fen, "Jiujiang maoyi yanjiu," p. 106.

35. Lei Hui-erh, "Dongbei de douhuo maoyi, 1907–1931," p. 158; Liu Su-fen, "Yantai maoyi yanjiu, 1867–1919," p. 129.

36. Chang Shu-fen, "Jindai Sichuan pendi duiwai maoyi yu gongshang ye bianqian," p. 94.

37. Fan I-jun, "Duiwai maoyi yu Hanjiang liuyu de jingji bianqian, 1867–1931," p. 53; Liu Su-fen, "Yantai maoyi yanjiu, 1867–1919," p. 122.

38. Fan I-jun, "Duiwai maoyi yu Hanjiang liuyu de jingji bianqian, 1867–1931," p. 39; Chang Shu-fen, "Jindai Sichuan pendi duiwai maoyi yu gongshang ye bianqian," p. 94.

39. Li Ho-cheng, *Qingmo minchu dongbei minzhu ziben zhong lianhao de yanjiu (1860–1931)*, p. 60.

40. Rhoads Murphey, *The Treaty Ports and China's Modernization: What Went Wrong?* (Ann Arbor, MI: University of Michigan, Center for Chinese Studies, 1970), pp. 52–57.

41. Yen Chung-p'ing et al., *Zhongguo jindai jingji shi tongji ziliao xuanyi* [Selected Statistical Materials on China's Modern Economic History] (Kexue chubanshe, 1955), pp. 67–68.

42. Lei Hui-erh, "Dongbei de douhuo maoyi, 1907–1931," p. 78.

43. Lin Man-houng, "Qingmo shehui liuxing xishi yapian yanjiu—gongji mian zhi fenxi, 1773–1906" [A Supply-side Analysis of Opium Prevalence in Late Qing China, 1773–1906] (Ph.D. dissertation, NTNU, 1985), p. 105. It is pointed out that imported opium was mainly used by Jiangsu, Fujian, and Guangdong.

44. Ibid., p. 435.

45. Hsieh Shi-fen, "Jiujiang maoyi yanjiu," p. 148.

46. Lei Hui-erh, "Dongbei de douhuo maoyi, 1907–1931," p. 155.

47. Lin Man-houng, "Cha tang zhanghao ye yu wan Qing Taiwan," pp. 123–26.

48. Ibid., p. 16.

49. Wang Yeh-chien, *Zhongguo jindai huobi yu yinhang de yanjiu* [The Development of Money and Banking in China, 1644–1937], IEAS (1981), pp. 64–71.

50. Cheng I-fung, *Shanghai qianzhuang de xingshuai (1843–1937)* [The Rise and Fall of the Shanghai Bank], ISSP (July 1981).

51. Kuo-tung Ch'en, *The Insolvency of the Chinese Hong Merchants, 1760–1843*, Monograph Series, no. 45, IEAS (June 1990), Chinese abstract, see *Xinshixue* [New History], 1, no. 4 (December 1990); Ch'en Kuo-tung, "PanYoudu: Yiwei chenggong de yanghang shangren" [A Successful Hong Merchant: Pan Youdu), Chang Pin-tsun, ed., *Zhongguo haiyang fazhanshi lunwenji* [Symposium on Chinese Maritime History], 5, ISSP (1992), pp. 245–300.

52. Man-houng Lin, "Currency and Society: The Monetary Crisis and Political-

Economic Ideology of Early Nineteenth-Century China" (Ph.D. dissertation, Harvard University, 1989).

53. Man-houng Lin, "Prosperity or Decline?—Mainland China's Merchants Trading Across the Taiwan Strait."

54. Lin Hui-jun, "Wan Qing xiaoshuo zhong fanying de shangye jie" [The Commercial Circle as Reflected in the Novels of Late Qing China) (master's thesis, Cheng-chih University, 1988).

55. Wang Erh-min, "Shangchan kuannien yu Zhongshang sixiang" [Ideas for mercantile struggle and for the stress on commerce], *Zhongguo jindai sixiang shilun* [Intellectual History of Modern China] (Taipei: Wang Erh-min, 1977), p. 235. Wu Chang-chuan, "Yangwu yundong zhong de shangwu sixiangyi Li Hungzhang wei zhangxin de tantao" [The Mercantile Thought of the Self-Strengthening Movement: A Case Study of Li Hungzhang], *Jindai Zhongguo zhishi fenzi yu ziqiang yundong* [Chinese Intellectuals and the Self-Strengthening Movement], *Shih-huo Monthly* (March 1972); Chen Li Hsun-yan, "Wan Qing de Zhongshang zhuyi yundong" [The Mercantile Movement in the Late Qing Period], *Bulletin of the Institute of Modern History* 1, no. 3 (March 1972).

56. Lin Li-yueh, *Shilun Ming Qing zhiji shangye sixiang de jige wenti* [A Preliminary Discussion on the Commercial Thought in the Ming–Qing Transition], *Jindai Zhongguo zhaoqi lishi yantaohui lunwenji* [Proceedings of the Conference on the History of Early Modern China], IMH (April 1989), pp. 711–33; Man-houng Lin, "Two Social Theories Revealed: Statecraft Controversies over China's Monetary Crisis, 1808–1854," *Late Imperial China* 12, no. 2 (December 1991), pp. 15–17.

57. Lin Man-houng, "Wan Qing de yapianshui" [Opium Taxes in the Late Ch'ing Period, 1858–1906], *Si yu yan* [Ideas and Words], 16, no. 5 (1979), p. 49; Lin Man-houng and Lu Shi-chiang, "Xiandai jingji de qibu" [The Beginnings of a Modern Economy in China], in Ch'in Hsiao-i, ed., *Zhonghua Minguo jingji fazhanshi* [The Economic Development of Republican China], series 1, chapter 1, section 1 (Taipei: Jindai Zhongguo chubanshe, 1983); Lin Man-houng, "Zhanhou fuyuan yu tonghuo pengzhang" [Reconstruction and Inflation After the Sino–Japanese War], ibid., series 2, chapter 2 (with Sun Chen and Liang Chi-yuan as co-authors).

58. Man-houng Lin, "Currency and Society."

59. Fan Cheng-chien, "Qingji zhi guandu shangban qiye ji qi guanshang guanxi (1873–1911)—Zhao shangju yu dian baoju zhi yanjiu" [The Official-Supervised and Merchant-managed Enterprises and Their Official-Merchant Relations—A Case Study of the China Merchants' Company and the Telegram Bureau] (Ph.D dissertation, NTU, 1985).

60. Huang Wang-ming, "Zhongguo Jiaotong liang yinhang de fazhan yu zhengfu de guanxi 1896–1927" [The Development of the Bank of China and the Bank of Communications] (master's thesis, Tung-hai University, 1983).

61. Juan Chung-jen, "Qingmo minchu nonggongshang jigou de sheli—Zhengfu yu jingji xiandaihua guanxi zhi jiantao" [The Establishment of the Board of Agriculture, Industry, and Commerce in the Late Qing Period: Goverment and Economic Modernization] (master's thesis, NTNU, June 1987), Monograph Series, no. 19, NTNU (1988).

62. Ku Wei-ying, "Cong xuanqi, saizhen dao jiaoliu, shangzhan: Zhongguo jindai duiwai guanxi de yige cemian" [From "Showing-off of the Exotic" and "Competing for the Rarities" to "Friendly Exchange" and the "Commerce War": A Perspective on the Foreign Relations of Modern China], *Si yu yan* [Ideas and Words] 24, no. 3 (September 1986), pp. 249–66.

63. Chang Chien-chiu, "Qingmo zikai shangfu zhi yanjiu 1898–1911" [A Study of the Self-Opened Ports] (master's thesis, NTNU, June 1991).

64. Hsin Tai-jia, "Zhongguo yu Chaoxian zaoqi dianxian zhi jingyin" [The Early

Stage of Telegraph Management in China and Korea] (master's thesis, NTU, 1986).

65. Tai Pao-tsun, "Qingji Danshui kaigang zhi yanjiu" [A Study of the Opening of Tamsui as a Treaty Port] (master's thesis, NTNU, 1983), p. 95; also cf. Monograph Series, no. 11, NTNU.

66. Lei Hui-erh, "Dongbei de douhuo maoyi, 1907–1931," p. 126.

67. Liu Wen-pin, "Guomin zhengfu de fabi zhengce ji qi shishi" [The Nationalist Government's Fabi Policy and Its Implementation] (master's thesis, Chengchih, 1987).

68. Chiu Peng-sheng, "Shiba shijiu shiji Suzhoucheng de xinxing gongshangye tuanti" [The Newly Arisen Handicraft and Commercial Organizations in the Township of Suzhou] (master's thesis, NTU, 1988).

69. Li Ho-cheng, *Qingmo minchu dongbei minzhu ziben zhong lianhao de yanjiu (1860–1931)*, pp. 135–36.

70. Cho Ke-hua, *Qingdai Taiwan de shangzhan jituan*, pp. 111–15.

71. Chang Huan-chung, "Shanghai Zhongshanghui yanjiu" [A Study of Shanghai's Chamber of Commerce] (master's thesis, NTNU, 1994), pp. 65–66, 106–15.

72. Ibid., pp. 47–87.

73. Lin Man-houng, "Riju shidai Taiwan jingjishi yanjiu zhi zhonghe pingjie" [Economic History of Japanese Colonial Taiwan: State of the Field], *Shixue pinglun* [Chinese Historical Review], no. 1 (July 1979), p. 171.

74. Lin Man-houng, "Kou'an maoyi," p. 903.

75. Lin Man-houng, "Riju shidai Taiwan jingjishi yanjiu zhi zhonghe pingjie," p. 171.

76. Ibid.

77. Lin Man-houng, "The Taiwanese Merchants in the Trade Between Taiwan and China, 1895–1937." Paper presented at the Workshop on China in Asian International Economic History c. 1850–1945, Osaka University, Japan, May 22–23, 1993, 42 pp.

78. Lin Pang-chung, "Taiwan mianfangzhi gongye fazhan zhi yanjiu" [A Study of the Development of Taiwan's Textile Industry], *Taiwan yinhang jikan* [Taiwan Bank's Quarterly] 20, no. 2, p. 82.

79. Liu Chin-ching, *Taiwan zhanhou jingji fenxi* [An Analysis of Postwar Taiwan's Economy] (Taipei: Renjian, June 1992), pp. 214–15.

80. Liu Chin-ching, *Zhanhou Taiwan jingji zhi fenxi*, pp. 232–33.

81. Chao Chi-chang, *Meiyuan de yunyong* [The Application of American Aid] (Taipei: Lian-jing, June 1985), pp. 13–14.

82. Chen Chieh-hsuan, *Xieli wangluo de shehui jiegou—Taiwan zhongxiao qiye de shehui jingji fenxi* [A Life Structure Woven by Cooperation—Social–Economic Analysis of Taiwan's Medium- and Small-Scale Enterprises] (Taipei: Lian-jing, 1994), pp. 78–96; I am grateful to my student Wang Hui-ying, who did preliminary research on postwar Taiwan's capital accumulation for private enterprises.

83. Lin Hsiu-hung and Chen Ts'ui-ying, "Jiazhu qiye de huolu zai nali?" [Where Has Family Enterprise Gone?], *Xiandai guanli yuekan* [Modern Management Monthly] (July 1987), p. 27.

84. Chen Hui-er, "Taiwan jiazhu qiye chuancheng leixing zhi yanjiu" [A Study of the Inheritance Pattern of the Family Enterprise in Taiwan] (M.B.A. thesis, Chung-yuan University, June 1993), p. 29.

85. Hsu Ching-yun, "Chiazhu qiye de jiceng wenti—Guonei jiazu qiye jichengren de peiyu" [The Inheritance Problem in Taiwan's Family Enterprise—The Cultivation of Successors] (master's thesis, NTU Graduate Institute of Commerce, June 1992), p. 2; Fan Yang-fu, "Jiazhu qiye guanli chengxu zhi yanjiu" [A Study of the Management Succession of Family Enterprises] (master's thesis, Taiwan Industrial Technology Institute, June 1986), p. 3; Chi Tao, "Cong jiben kan jiazhu yu qiye jingying" [Families and

the Management of Enterprises from the Perspective of Japan], *Tianxia zhazhi* [Tianxia Monthly] (January 1983), p. 59.

86. Chen Ming-chang, "Jiazu wenhua yu guanli" [Family Culture and the Management of Enterprises], *Qiyin jikan* [Qiyin Quarterly] 8, no. 1 (July 1984), p. 33; Alfred Chandler, *The Visible Hand* [Chinese translation, Beijing: Zhongwu Press, 1987), pp. 580, 590.

87. Man-houng Lin, "The Perpetuation of Bloodline Versus Family Property: A Crucial Factor for the Different Demographic Dynamics of Pre-industrial China and Japan," Symposium on Modernization in China, IMH, March 1991.

88. Fan Yang-fu, "Jiazhu qiye guanli chengxu zhi yanjiu," pp. 88–91; Editorial Board, "Zhong-Ri jiceng guanxi bijiao" [A Comparison of Inheritance Systems in China and Japan], *Tianxia zazhi* [Tianxia Monthly] (August 1985), p. 35; "Riben qiye jiazhu zhuyi" [The Familism of Japan's Family Enterprises], "Do Ta Jun," trans., *Laogong zhiyou zhazhi* [A Magazine for the Labor Friends], nos. 457–458 (January–February 1987), pp. 24–27, 30–31.

89. Liu Hsiang-ren, "Jiazhu qiye maixiang zhuanyehua jingyin zhi yanjiu" [The Professionalization of Family Enterprises] (master's thesis, Taiwan Industrial Technology Institute, n.d.), p. 122.

90. Wang Yen-ren, "Qiye chengzhang yanbian celue—Taisuo qiye zhi tantao" [The Change of the Strategy for an Enterprise to Grow: A Case Study of a Formosan Company] (master's thesis, Graduate Institute of Commerce, NTU, June 1994), pp. 68–70, 82–83; Chang Hsien-cheng, "Taisou qiye jingying fenxi zuoye moshi zhi yanjiu" [A Study of the Analytical Process Pattern of Formosan Company Management] (May 29, 1994), pp. 1, 4. I am grateful to my student Chang Hsiang-lin, who did preliminary research on postwar Taiwan's family enterprises for me.

91. Chen Jin-man, "Taiwan feiliao de zhengfu guanli yu peixiao 1945–1953— Guojia yu shehui guanxi zhi yi tantao" [The Governmental Management and Distributiom of Fertilizer in Taiwan 1945–1953: An Investigation of State–Society Relations] (master's thesis, NTNU, June 1995).

92. Cheng Yueh-sui, "Xianjieduan gongying shiye minyinghua tupoxing de zuofa" [The Breakthrough Approach for the Privatization of Public Enterprise], *Jinri heku* [Today's Cooperative Unions] 19, no. 9 (September 1993), pp. 58–59.

93. Chu Yun-han, trans. Chi Ling-ling, "Taiwan zhengquan zhuanxing qi zhengshang guanxi de zai jiemeng" [The Realliance of Politicians and Merchants in a Political Transformation Period], *Zhongshan shehui kexue jikan* [Quarterly of Social Sciences of Chung-shan University] 7, no. 4 (December 1992), p. 63.

94. Hsueh Yi-shu, "Woguo guoying shiye qiyehua jingying zhi tujing" [Approaches to Managing Government-owned Enterprises as Private Enterprises], *Zhengzhi pinglun* [Political Review] 44, no. 4 (April 1986), p. 207.

95. Liao I-hsing, "Taiwan diqu zhengshang guanxi de yanbian" [The Transformation of Taiwan's State–Business Relationship], *Guojia zhengce shuanzhou–kan* [Biweekly for State Policies], no. 103 (1995), p. 2.

96. Wu Jo-yu, *Zhanhou Taiwan gongying shiye zhi zhengjing fenxi* [Political– Economic Analysis of Postwar Taiwan's Public Enterprises] (Taipei: Yeqiang, December 1992).

97. Chu Yun-han, "Taiwan zhengquan zhuanxing qi zhengshang guanxi de zai jiemeng," p. 69.

98. Wang Cheng-huan, "Taiwan xin zhengshang guanxi de xingcheng yu zhengzhi zhuanxing" [Formation of New Political–Economic Relations and the Transformation of Politics in Taiwan], *Taiwan minzuhua zhong de guojia yu shehui* [State and Society in the Process of Democratization in Taiwan] (Hsinchu: Ching-hua Univer-

sity, March 1992). I am grateful to my students Liu Shu-tien, Hsu Li-hui, and Li Min-fang for doing preliminary research on postwar Taiwan's political-economic relation.

99. Cheng Rui-ming, "Taiwan Mingzheng yu dongnanya zhi maoyi guanxi chutan—Fazhan dongnanya maoyi zhi dongji shiwu ji waishang zhi qianlai" [A Preliminary Study of the Trade Relations Between the Koxinga Regime and Southeast Asia—Motivation, Real Development, and the Visit of the Foreign Merchants], *Shida lishi xuebao* [Bulletin for Historical Studies, NTNU], no. 14 (June 1986), pp. 57–108.

100. Chu Te-lan, "Ming Zheng shiqi Taiwan haishang jingying rixian maoyi yu guonei shangpin liutong guanxi" [Trade with Japan and Thailand and Its Relationship with China's International Trade During the Koxinga Regime], *Donghai xuebao* [Bulletin of Tung-hai University], 28, (1987) pp. 91–97.

101. Cheng Rui-ming, *Qingdai Yuenan de huaqiao* [Overseas Chinese in Vietnam During the Qing Period], NTNU, Monograph of the Graduate Institute of History, no. 1 (Taipei, 1976).

102. Lu Shih-peng, "Shengqing shiqi de Zhong–Yue jingji guanxi—Jianshu huaren dui nan qi de kaifa" [The Sino–Vietnamese Economic Relationship in the High Qing—Chinese Development of Southern Vietnam], *Jindai Zhongguo chuqi lishi yantaohui lunwenji* [Proceedings of the Symposium on the Early History of Modern China], IMH (August 1988).

103. Chen Yin-i, "Qingdai Qian-Jia shiqi xinjiang gongyu zhidu zhi yanjiu" [A Study of the Tribute Jade System in the Qianlong and Jiaqing Period of the Qing Dynasty] (master's thesis, Cheng-chih University, Institute of Ethnology, June 1992).

104. Chang Chun-wu, *Qing Congfan maoyi* [Tribute Trade Between the Qing Reign and Korea] (monograph, no. 39, IMH, June 1978).

105. Sung Hui-chung, *Piaoshang yu wan Qing de guanliao tixi*, pp. 153–60.

106. Man-houng Lin, "Prosperity or Decline?"

107. Liu Kwang-ching, "Jinshi zhidu yu shangren," pp. 419–521.

108. Chang Huan-chung, "Shanghai Zhongshanghui yanjiu," pp. 66, 207–23.

109. Li Ho-cheng, *Qingmo minchu dongbei minzhu ziben zhong lianhao de yanjiu (1860–1931)*, pp. 71–75, 144.

110. Chao Yu-chih, "Riju shiqi Taiwan shanggong hui de fazhan," pp. 478–79.

111. Lin Man-houng, "Taiwan yu dongbei jian de maoyi, 1932–1941" [Trade Between Taiwan and Manchuria, 1932–1941], *Bulletin of the IMH* 2, no. 24; Lin Man-houng, "Yijiu saner zhi yijiu siyi nian jian Taiwan yu dongbei maoyi jiaqiang de shehui yihan" [Societal Implications for the Reinforcement of the Trade Between Taiwan and Manchuria During the Period 1932–1941], *Symposium on Sino–Japanese Relations in the Last Century*, IMH (March 1996).

112. Wu Chien-hsiung, "Niuyueshi huaren de hangye yu shiye bianqian (1855–1965)—Yi huafu wei zhongxin de yanjiu" [Trade and Occupational Change of Chinese in New York—A Study of Chinatown], *Zhongguo haiyang fazhanshi* [Essays in Chinese Maritime History], vol. 4, ISSP (1991).

Chinese Studies in History, vol. 31, nos. 3–4, Spring–Summer 1998, pp. 95–105.
ISSN 0009–4633/1998 $9.50 + 0.00.

MADELEINE ZELIN

Critique of Scholarship on Chinese Business in the People's Republic of China and Taiwan

Professor Kwan's and Professor Lin's articles on business history in the People's Republic of China (PRC) and Taiwan, published in this issue, are meticulously researched historiographic essays; these two pieces provide a much needed road map to the diverse scholarship on Chinese business now being produced in Chinese. At the same time, both provide an impressive glimpse at the role of political and economic change in the transformation of analytical frameworks.

Among scholars in the PRC the connection between scholarship and current politics is particularly strong. This is not simply a result of political repression and ideological constraints imposed by the state. Equally important is the set of institutional relationships within which scholars have been able to do their work under the current regime. Scholarly associations, research institutes, and even academic departments have set research agendas and these agendas most often followed and did not establish the political line of the day. Thus, throughout the almost fifty-year history of communist rule in China, we have seen a direct link between the direction of research and changes in the political climate.

Immediately after the founding of the PRC, the need to justify communist revolution required the discovery of a capitalist foundation in China. This led to a series of publications of materials on China's modern industries and modern economy. Joining this project were studies that grew out of the debate over the

---

From a paper presented at the workshop on Scholarly Research on Chinese Business History: Interpretative Trends and Priorities for the Future, University of Akron, October 27–29, 1995.
Madeleine Zelin is on the faculty of Columbia University's East Asia Institute.

sprouts of capitalism in China. However, while the search for capitalist foundations had its roots in the analysis of the revolutionary situation, "sprouts of capitalism" fed a different obsession, the quest for a reason for China's failure to modernize. Here the goal was not to determine whether China had progressed sufficiently along the road to capitalism to warrant a revolution by the proletariat. Rather, it was to demonstrate that, had the imperialist powers not placed a stranglehold on China's economy, the progress of capitalism in China would have been much greater than it already was. In the end, both political stances produced similar products, although the sprouts of capitalism debate focused more attention on examples of rural division of labor, commercialization of agriculture, and handicraft production, a major force in Chinese economic development that was of somewhat less interest to those in search of an industrial base.

Of course, there is a contradiction inherent in such research, between the political imperative to denigrate capitalists and the desire to elevate their contribution as a way to elevate China's national self-esteem in a capitalist world system. During the early to mid-1950s, the nationalization of private enterprises and a series of political campaigns that specifically targeted factory and business managers and capitalists who remained in China after liberation made the documentation of capitalist enterprise more difficult for scholars. Scholarship began to focus on the class struggle between workers and capitalists and on examples of capitalist enterprises that had successfully made the transition from private to socialist management.

The net result of these sponsored projects was a large number of volumes of collected materials on important commercial and industrial enterprises, compiled and edited under both national and local auspices. As Professor Kwan points out, the biases built into the selection of case studies, as well as the materials selected to illustrate these case studies, necessitate extreme care when using them to engage in scholarly research on business history. Nevertheless, because management practices were often viewed as ammunition in the class war against the bourgeoisie, these studies often brought together a wealth of data of value to the scholar of Chinese business.

Following the dry years of the Cultural Revolution, the study of Chinese business reemerged, but once again subsumed under the search for China's capitalist foundations. Thus, although the positive role of capitalists is acknowledged, the nature of the questions being posed by scholars, even those Professor Kwan sees as moving away from the established line, is not that dissimilar from the questions posed by scholars during the period before the Cultural Revolution. Many scholars continue to devote their energy to dating the sprouts of capitalism. Should their emergence be linked to the rise of handicraft workshops in the Ming, or were the "sprouts" the result of what in the West might be called "protoindustrialization" during the Qing? Was handicraft workshop production an important stage in the evolution of industrial production or did China develop what might be called a dual economy in which industrial production imitated Western practice, leaving handicraft production to contribute to the perpetuation of the small peasant economy? Indeed, did foreign investment contribute to or hinder Chinese economic development and the rise of native capitalism?

For much of the twentieth century the orthodox Marxist view that the rise of commercial capital had an inhibiting, rather than a stimulating, effect on the rise of industrial capital dominated Chinese scholarship. Efforts to counter this line have led to a number of detailed studies of commercial capital, examining its role in the development of workshop as opposed to household production, and documenting the growth of interprovincial and intraregional trade. In the process, a fair amount of data on the management of commercial enterprises has been collected, but as I note below, this has not resulted in systematic studies of Chinese business practices and management strategies.

The debate over the role of foreign investment has also moved in new directions as economic reform in contemporary China has begun to encourage not only joint ventures but independent foreign investment as well. However, most studies in the PRC continue to focus on the exploitative role of foreigners. In this vein, the most interesting of the new literature is that which begins to identify the Chinese role in firms that existed under the shield of foreign capitalism because of the trade, tax, and credit benefits this would bring to such a firm.

Two other themes have influenced studies of Chinese business, one that is firmly based in Marxist historiography and one that results from China's own historical experience. Ironically, the dominance of class analysis in the study of Chinese business history has resulted in neglect of some of the most important factors contributing to enterprise development. Scholars have found it difficult to deal with the labor practices of firms. Even in the case of successful firms, politics has dictated that scholarship condemn their owners for exploiting their workers, instead of investigating their approaches to worker training and transmission of skills, management of labor, and the development of human capital resources. At the same time, in the case of twentieth century firms, there has been a tendency to identify most instances of labor unrest with the activities of the Communist Party. This has resulted in scholarly neglect of the role of long-standing institutions and alliances within the laboring community and their contribution to the ability of workers to negotiate in their own interest.

An obsession with class labeling has also tended to obscure the actual activities of business people and the fact that people have played many roles in their lifetimes, often simultaneously. Thus, the economic activities of compradors become "negative" factors in Chinese business history, and whole generations of twentieth century historians have wasted their time trying to determine who was and was not a member of the "national bourgeoisie." Even Professor Kwan gets caught in this paradigm when he notes that not all members of the "national bourgeoisie" were noble—that many of them exploited their workers, dumped products to drive out competitors, took kickbacks and engaged in price-fixing behavior. While this is certainly true and reflects a much more realistic appraisal of capitalists in China's early modern period, such distinctions contribute little to our understanding of Chinese business history. They are premised on the existence of an ideal type of capitalist whose activities bring about the transition from feudalism to capitalism. They also reflect popular Chinese ambivalence about the role that profit-taking plays in capitalist economics.

Rather than framing their work as a quest for an ideal type that does not exist, historians of Chinese business would do well to look at the conditions under which these practices emerged. How important were they to the survival of firms? What role did government play in their regulation? Many such practices emerged because conditions of competition were imperfect and, to survive, firms had to stake out their advantage other than in the quality of the product, efficiencies of production, and so on. The important thing is not to establish class labels but to determine the way in which networks, connections, and institutions of various kinds contributed to how enterprises were established, financed, and managed. At the same time, we still have a long way to go in our efforts to understand the concrete social, economic, and political conditions under which these practices evolved.

The role played by state enterprise investment in China has had a profound effect, both on the writing of Chinese enterprise history and on Chinese attitudes toward the relationship between state and business in contemporary China. State regulation and taxation of business in the late imperial period was unpredictable, but on the whole low. State investment in salt and tea production was virtually nonexistent by the Qing. State investment in silver and copper mining varied, with "merchant investment and merchant management" dominating during the eighteenth century, only to be reversed in the nineteenth. However, by the early nineteenth century state-run silk and porcelain manufactories had largely given way to a system of contracting out to private workshops. Thus, by the eve of the Opium War, the most important role affecting businesses that the state played was in upholding guild regulations and privileges and in providing a legal framework that upheld the enforceability of contracts.

The issue of state investment in enterprise development became a major focus of PRC historians when they begin to examine that period in Chinese history known as the self-strengthening period, roughly the 1860s–1890s. Until recently, the main criteria by which an enterprise during this period was judged was the class designation of its investors. The search for a national bourgeoisie, free of ties to a supposedly feudal state and free of ties to imperialists was a major focus of historians of China's nineteenth-century economy. Professor Kwan sees a new trend in the call by some scholars to forget the class of the investor and look to whether the funds invested are private or public/state funds. In fact, this approach is not very different from the approach that preceded it. For one thing, it is not always possible to distinguish between private and state funds, particularly because many of China's most important investors and entrepreneurs had both public and private positions. At the same time, it drives scholars to continue to base their analyses of enterprises not on economic criteria, but on arbitrary moral judgments that, by their very nature, preempt the determination of value based on economic criteria.

The moral judgment that state involvement, either through control of the management structure or through investment, is detrimental to enterprise development and to China's overall capitalist development is a theme that gained increasing currency during the 1980s. My own first encounter with this argument was in a monograph by Wei Qingyuan on Qing mining, in which he points to the rapid development of mining in the southwest during the mid-eighteenth century when the state experimented with "merchant management and merchant investment" and the rapid decline in output when the state moved back in. While the veiled glorification of private enterprise in the postreform period lies behind much of this scholarship, in recent years its focus has come to reflect a growing concern with corruption, nepotism, and other evils of bureaucratic capitalism.

My own work is on small-scale private industry. What I have found most interesting in the literature on these firms is its radically laissez-faire approach to economic issues. Particularly in *wenshi ziliao*, local publications that reflect the attitudes of the thinking public even more than do scholarly journals, a major theme is the destructive role of the state whenever it gets involved in business. The state is often seen to be at fault in the collapse of businesses, either as the agent of excessive taxation, through its distribution of privileges, or as a contributor to the destabilization of the business environment through weak governance or warfare. Nowhere do we see an acknowledgment of the need for a strong state presence in the regulation of business practices, in standardization and quality control, in the creation of a fair trading environment, in the enforcement of labor standards, or in the upholding of business agreements. This ambivalence toward the state is manifested in today's economic environment, which in many respects has all of the worst features of capitalism and none of the benefits of socialism.

The focus on macrolevel issues, particularly the factors that either inhibit or contribute to the development of capitalism in China leads to a serious neglect of microeconomic issues, even in studies of individual enterprises. What I would like to suggest to PRC scholars of Chinese business is that they step back from the issues raised above and ask smaller questions: How did business work? What mechanisms, institutions, and patterns of interaction were used to solve what problems, and to what new problems did they give rise? In this vein, let me raise three broad areas of inquiry of particular interest to me.

1. How did the Chinese legal system affect business practices? This was a system with no written civil code, no independent system of courts, and no concept of individual liability for individual people, much less a conceptual framework in which a firm could be viewed as a legal individual. Does this mean that the Chinese could not deal rationally with the disputes that emerged within the business community? Does it mean that firms could have no legal identity? The answer to both questions is no.

First, we now know that there was a highly developed customary law that governed the behavior of businesses in China. Both the circulation of goods and merchants and the circulation of elites and officials guaranteed that customary law had a national character and could be relied upon by businessmen wherever they went in China. The fact that the state did not intervene in setting standards and practices for businessmen meant that much more had to be spelled out by the businessmen themselves. In some places we have records of "the customs of the trade" in written form. Guilds and later trade associations all had written trade regulations. More important, written contracts establishing agreements over partnership and investment, the redistribution of assets, as well as sales, were extremely detailed as to the steps to be taken in transactions, the nature of the goods to be exchanged (including the money), and the management structures to be used to govern them.

Second, disputes among merchants and businessmen were handled in a fairly routine manner, by guild arbitration or by the magistrates' courts in the Qing and by trade associations and chambers of commerce mediation boards in the twentieth century. The records of these boards and courts, which have been preserved in a number of archives in China, provide an extraordinary resource for the study of local business practices.

Third, the primary basis upon which disputes were settled was the written agreement between the parties. In certain cases the intent of the parties was superseded. While this has been seen by some as evidence of the irrationality of traditional Chinese law, in fact the principles followed are principles now quite popular among Western legal reformers. Most notable is the principle that in the handling of a bankruptcy case, every effort be made to settle the case such that the defaulting party not be destroyed, but be allowed the wherewithal to rebuild. In the Chinese case the damage to the community in terms of lost jobs, lost future earnings, and future taxes were all explicit in the exercise of this principle.

Fourth, the problem of liability and the protection of assets was probably the most difficult for Chinese business. Almost no work has been done on this issue. From my own work I can see a number of elements of importance to the study of Chinese rights of property. (1) Rather than a sign of backwardness, the use of lineage institutions, especially the lineage trust or *tang* as a means to consolidate and protect assets was a critical step in the development of modern corporate institutions in China. It allowed great flexibility in management, could accommodate nonfamily managers, and could act as a framework for the establishment of both horizontally and vertically integrated businesses. And, most important, it could protect assets from division by relatives. (2) *Tang* incorporation also encountered enormous problems that the Chinese business community did not entirely overcome. Liability is never divorced from the liability that inheres in traditional family law. Thus, for example, debts were inherited, and debts in one firm could be dunned to other firms sharing partners. (3) Given these problems we might ask why so few firms chose to use the modern incorporation law once it was promulgated in the twentieth century. Were they simply afraid of being taxed? What effect did this have on the structures of credit, notions of ownership and property, and the development of investment and management practices?

2. Next to management structures, the issue least understood and most critical to our understanding of the development of Chinese business is that of credit. The Chinese literature has now paid homage to the existence of remittance banks (*piaohao*) and native banks (*qianzhuang*). But what real role did they play in the financing of business? If, indeed, their role was largely that of a clearinghouse and mover of funds, then we need to look elsewhere to understand the capitalization of business. A number of questions come to mind: (1) What role did family, native place, and other forms of face-to-face ties play in the assembling of capital for business ventures? (2) Were there specialists whose role it was to bring investors together, and what role did they play in the business once it was underway? An example of such specialists were the *chengshouren*, who brought landowners and investors together in the drilling of salt wells at the Furong salt yards during the Qing and Republic. (3) What role did nonmonetary investment play in the establishment of firms in China? We have very provocative evidence of labor investment and investment comprised of property or tools. At Furong, artisans are known to have become partners by investing their expertise and tools, and Wei Qingyuan's study of coal mining contains evidence of laborers

who became investors by deferring their wages. (4) If, indeed, undercapitalization was a chronic problem among Chinese businesses, what impact did it have on the conduct of business and on management choices? What mechanisms were built into partnership agreements to deal with issues of capitalization? In my own work, investors were required to make periodic infusions until a salt well came in. Partnership contracts included regular mechanisms for buyouts and share redistribution if a partner defaulted. Professor Kwan mentions in his article that people preferred to rent out their factories rather than accept the risk of running them themselves. However, if we look at industries in which this was common, such as textiles, rental of factories was often a response to capital shortage. Investors who built factories often found themselves without the startup costs needed to buy raw materials, and hire and pay labor. Therefore, the physical plant was leased to a second group of investors who had not incurred the first group's capital costs.

3. Finally, the focus on macroeconomic issues has deflected attention away from the internal workings of businesses once they were founded. Robert Gardella's excellent study of accounting demonstrates the kind of work that can be done in this area and, indeed, has begun among a small group of Chinese scholars. Accounting practices provide an excellent example of change in business practices as the business environment becomes more complex. They also provide an excellent example of how business structures, and not ideology or cultural biases, play a key role in the evolution of business. For example, the impact of Chinese accounting methods on the ability to determine profit streams was a serious handicap in Chinese business planning that had nothing to do with attitudes toward family, profit, or the state.

Professor Kwan notes a number of studies that examine the business practices of Shanxi merchants and *piaohao*. The Dashengkui gave their managers an incentive by giving them shares in the firm. Of even greater significance is the fact that each share was limited to 10,000 taels in dividends. The rest of the profits were plowed back into the firm. As Professor Kwan notes, this allowed them to invest in native banks and subsidiaries specializing in raw materials such as camel hair, grain, silk, tea, livestock, and wool. These then become the basis for workshops producing blankets and rugs. What Professor Kwan does not highlight is that their presence as a major force in interregional trade contributed to the circulation of capital in China. Shanxi merchant and *piaohao* management practices became a model for businesses throughout China and contributed to a national standard in the formation of partnerships, accounting techniques, and so on.

Professor Kwan ends by noting the recent popular interest in business history in China, producing both a new genre of Chinese business hagiography and new opportunities for scholars to free themselves from dependence on state funding for research and conferences. I was heartened by these comments not only because they promise a flood of future work on Chinese business history; but also because they offer hope of reversing a disturbing tendency among Chinese bureaucrats to totally discount the relevance of Chinese business history to the contemporary task of economic reform. In a recent meeting with the man in charge of the team drafting the new Chinese company law, I was told that the nature of the contemporary business environment was so different as to make the experience of late Qing and Republican businessmen and the drafters of their commercial and company laws irrelevant to today's business community. While he was certainly correct to insist that large scale enterprises, and particularly those engaged in international trade, needed to conform to certain international standards, he completely ignored that vast sea of small-scale, local businesses for which something that can only be called "Chinese" business practices were the foundation of contemporary growth. This man, a leading Chinese legal expert, was caught in the same epistemological trap that reigns in much of Chinese scholarship. Western patterns of business management, like Western patterns of development, are taken to be the universal model against which all Chinese activity is to be judged. Chinese practice, if no longer stigmatized as feudal, is now seen as primitive. Not only do such analysts fail to recognize that even in the developed West, the vast majority of firms are small-scale individual proprietorships and partnerships from whose experience China might have much to learn. They also ignore the vast store of Chinese customary practice, with its deep historical roots, upon which the explosion of small-scale entrepreneurship in today's China is based.

Rather than trace a genealogy of Chinese writing about business history, Man-houng Lin's article outlines a large number of themes that have been important to the study of Chinese business history in Taiwan. While she also pays close attention to Western paradigms and the issue of "modernization," Professor Lin's article demonstrates two important trends in scholarship in Taiwan. One is a revisionism that takes issue with some of the most firmly held assumptions about China's differences with the West. The other is an increasing empiricism that focuses on the structure of business management and the interaction of transportation, communications, resources, and culture in making Chinese firms what they were. Here I will only outline several of the most important themes raised.

Professor Lin notes a number of studies that take issue with Weber's critique of Chinese merchant culture. Among these are studies demonstrating that Chinese religion and the Chinese family system encouraged the spread of values highlighted by Weber as embodying the "spirit of capitalism." These include diligence, honesty, and charity. Scholars in Taiwan have also addressed the stereotype that all Chinese sought to be officials and Confucian scholars and that merchants lacked a sense of pride and an identification with their own occupation. Both of these approaches have found adherents in work in the West that has examined Chinese language and literature for evidence of a growing merchant self-identification and confidence. The work of Richard Lufrano, which focuses on merchant petitions and merchant handbooks, is particularly significant in this regard.

The second major theme, which is closely related to the first, is the interpenetration of merchant and official activity. Professor Lin notes that despite the evidence of growing merchant identity, this blurring of the lines between groups is seen by some scholars as preventing the rise of an independent bourgeoisie. The relationship between merchants and the state is an issue given considerable attention in both Taiwan and the mainland. An important focus of such studies is tax policies. Mainland scholars tend to focus on exploitation by the state. Professor Lin points to many studies in Taiwan that show how the increasing importance of commercial taxation in late Qing led some bureaucrats to promote commercial enterprise. Economic nationalism was also a key issue inspiring state encouragement of native industry and commerce. Research in this area provides an important counter to the emphasis on foreign privilege and imperialist dominance.

A key problem in this regard is the weakness of the state and its inability to carry out many of its programs. Professor Lin gives examples taken from the records of the Board of Commercial Affairs set up in 1903. This issue also finds a place in studies that focus on the degree to which business could operate autonomously. In Taiwan, as in mainland China, scholarly concern with the role of the state in enterprise management is strong. Professor Lin points to a number of studies of postwar Taiwan that portray state-run industries as less efficient than private enterprise.

Merchant organizations have also become an important focus of research in Taiwan. Professor Lin points to a number of studies arguing against the commonly held view that merchant guilds limited free competition. Chambers of commerce have garnered the attention of scholars in mainland China, Taiwan, and the United States. Professor Lin provides valuable insights into the increasingly democratic character of chambers in Taiwan—as evidenced by the following characteristics: (a) Chamber membership fees were set low so that small merchants could participate; (b) no limitations were placed on the kinds of businesses that could participate; (c) large numbers of chambers existed even at the local level; and (d) in most places the dominance of members of high-status families in chambers diminished over time. Research on chambers is also critical for an understanding of business practices. Among the functions of chambers that deserve further investigation are their role in (a) mediating merchant disputes, (b) setting standards, (c) upholding contracts, and (d) advocating merchant interests with the state.

Professor Lin also points to a number of studies that look at partnerships and capital accumulation. Scholars in Taiwan have now found that family or face-to-face ties were not essential in the pooling of investment resources. Professor Lin also cites studies showing that investors tended to spread their risk by joining many partnerships. High dividends have been thought to harm enterprise growth, but Professor Lin notes more recent studies of Manchurian and Tainan firms that used their profits to invest in new shops or enterprises.

Finally, Professor Lin notes a recognition among scholars in Taiwan of the dominance of small and medium-sized firms in China. Their survival into the Japanese colonial period in Taiwan is seen as testimony to their strength. Professor Lin's own work links this phenomenon to the scale of landownership throughout Chinese history. This approach is similar to what I have called the rural base of production to describe the predominantly rural and small market town location of most manufacturing and trade in pre-1949 China. While scholars have long recognized this phenomenon, it is only now that sufficient case studies are emerging to allow Chinese experience to contribute to debates over the nature and role of "protoindustrialization" in the development process. Lin links the rural base of production to the family system and the degree to which Chinese businesses, unlike Japanese, maintain family dominance not only in ownership but in management. As studies of individual regions and individual firms become available, we will be better equipped to judge the universality of this pattern in China and the conditions that bring it about. Of particular interest would be comparative work that focuses on the role of the second layer of management, those managers who were most engaged in the day-to-day operations of so-called family and lineage firms and who were not necessarily family members. A study of their training, recruitment, and career patterns would add considerably to our understanding of the evolution of Chinese businesses in the late imperial and Republican periods.

The most encouraging message of these two articles is that the difficult task of figuring out how business worked and the role that law, culture, environment, and government policy played in the evolution of practice is becoming the focus of ever greater numbers of scholars on both sides of the Taiwan strait. Professors Kwan and Lin have played a leading role in the promotion of such research, both in their own choice of research projects and in the role they themselves have played within the community of Chinese economic historians. We are, indeed, fortunate to have their contributions in the present issue.

Chinese Studies in History, vol. 31, nos. 3–4, Spring–Summer 1998, pp. 106–26.
ISSN 0009–4633/1998 $9.50 + 0.00.

YEN-P'ING HAO

Themes and Issues in Chinese Business History

This chapter examines the major themes and issues in Western literature on Chinese business history since the late Ming period. As an area of academic inquiry, Chinese business history is relatively new, being a subfield of America's postwar China studies, and less developed, reflecting the peripheral role of the bourgeoisie in Chinese history. There are limitations in doing research on this field, partly because of scarcity of materials in the official history, and partly because it does not have a clearly focused scope for study. Indeed, there is no generally accepted definition of business history, even in the United States, where this discipline started and has thrived. The amorphous nature of this field is further indicated by the fact that it does not have a counterpart on the Chinese side.

The study of Chinese business history can be traced back to its humble origin in 1949, when a brief survey of the modern Chinese business class was published. Kwang-Ching Liu's pioneering work on an American company in China and Albert Feuerwerker's important book on China's early industrialization represent the serious scholarship of the 1950s. Historiography grew in volume and sophistication in the following decades, reaching a milestone in 1980, when Sherman Cochran's book on China's big business was published as a volume in the Harvard Studies in Business History Series. Since then this field has developed further, as reflected by the *Business History Review*'s special issue on East Asia (1982), the formation of a

---

From a paper presented at the workshop on Scholarly Research on Chinese Business History: Interpretative Trends and Priorities for the Future, University of Akron, October 27–29, 1995.

Yen-p'ing Hao is on the faculty of the University of Tennessee, Knoxville, Department of History.

Chinese Business Research Group (in the 1980s), the publication of a news-letter (*Chinese Business History*, 1990–), and the international conferences on Chinese business history in London (1993), Akron, Ohio (1995), and Hong Kong (1996).[1]

The Business Firm and the Businessman

The Business Firm

Influenced by the postwar school of economic development in the West, China scholars in the 1950s and the 1960s began to examine the structure of the late Qing industrial firms in search of answers to China's "tardy" industrialization. Most of these enterprises were merchant endeavors under government super-vision (*guandu shangban*). Albert Feuerwerker argued that this type of hybrid business structure ended largely in failure because it was an attempt to make an industrial breakthrough while leaving the institutional frame-work essentially untouched.[2]

Large commercial firms received scholarly attention after the 1970s. Stimulated by the works of Alfred D. Chandler, Jr., Wellington Chan com-pared the structure and strategy of the Ruifuxiang of Beijing, a major tradi-tional mercantile establishment, and the Sincere Company, China's first modern department store. Robert Gardella recently examined the Dashengkui Company, a large trading company with branch offices extending through-out China. In contrast to the Chandlerian model of large, integrated corpora-tions in the West, this firm anticipated what is known today as a "network firm," based on contractual linkage and flexible modes of specialization. New research sheds light, too, on the nature of the associate companies. There has been little study, however, on the great majority of the business firms in Chinese history—the small, family firms, including the partner-ships, workshops, and stores. These countless households-cum-firms were in the main owned and managed by the family, and comprised of a work-force made up of family members, kin, and friends.[3]

One theme in the historiography of Chinese business firms concerns their compartmentalization. Their lack of vertical integration is reflected in the "cellular" form that existed in various industries. The production and distri-bution of salt, silk, and cotton textiles, for instance, were divided into vari-ous stages, each of which was undertaken by separate units. Another theme concerns the corporate nature of various business organizations, such as lineages, merchant guilds, joint-capital partnerships, and large commercial firms. In his recent study of China's company law in the twentieth century, William Kirby discussed the major organizational types of companies, the great extent to which Chinese firms remained unincorporated, and the reasons for the tenacity of these noncorporate firms.[4]

Historians, sociologists, and economists have recently examined a number of important aspects of the Chinese firm: on the organizational level, the flexibility of accounting by Robert Gardella, and the four-stage evolution of a family firm by Siulun Wong; on the functional level, business rationality by Linda Bell and Robert Gardella, and transaction costs by Fu-mei Chen and Ramon Myers, and Louis T. Sigel.[5]

The Businessman

As a rule, the term *shangren* has been translated as "merchant," which seems inappropriate. In English, "merchant" refers to a trader who engages in the purchase and sale of goods for profit. He is neither a manufacturer nor a financier. The Chinese term *shangren*, however, refers to persons who engage in various forms of commercial, financial, or industrial endeavors. It is, therefore, more appropriate to translate *shangren* as "businessman."

Scholars have shown great interest in China's important groups of businessmen. Of all the businessmen in the late imperial period, the most powerful were those who obtained monopolistic privileges from the government. The first group consisted of the salt businessmen of Lianghui, whose organization, operation, profits, and style of life were examined by the trail-blazing studies of Ping-ti Ho and Thomas Metzger. Next came the hong merchants, who had a monopoly over trade with Western merchants. While H.B. Morse and John Fairbank have discussed their general operations, new research by Kuo-tung Ch'en indicated that, given the precarious financial situation, these merchants were not as powerful as previously assumed.[6]

Another group of businessmen that received prominent attention was that of the commercial middlemen. Susan Mann showed the pivotal role of the *yahang*, the officially licensed brokers who proliferated rapidly after the seventeenth century. Prasenjit Duara suggested that the *yahang*, with their innovative ways of promoting transactions, might be considered as "entrepreneurial brokerages," in sharp contrast to the merchant guilds, which might be viewed as "protective brokerages." The comprador–merchants constituted another type of commercial middlemen. In my study of these Chinese managers employed by the foreign mercantile houses in China, I examined the role of the compradors as the middlemen between the foreign merchants and the Chinese business world.[7] The emphases on the monopolistic businessmen and the commercial middlemen reflect the importance of both government–business relations and networks in Chinese business history.

Entrepreneurship

Entrepreneurship is an important theme in Chinese business history. The old view of the 1950s and 1960s, associated mainly with Marion J. Levy, Jr., maintained that the reason for China's relative absence of entrepreneurial spirit was its particular social structure: Successful businessmen would waste their financial resources in helping their poor kin and in pursuing gentry status. For the official–industrialists, who led China's early industrialization, according to Albert Feuerwerker, the reason lay in China's political institutions, such as the civil service examinations and bureaucratic rigidity. In an interdisciplinary, highly analytical article on modern Chinese economic history, three leading scholars concluded in 1960 that the old order of the Qing was in favor of the middlemen instead of the entrepreneurs, that entrepreneurship was inhibited by officialdom, and that the whole prevailing structure of incentives discouraged risk taking or innovation.[8]

In 1970, I first challenged this view by demonstrating that many businessmen were in effect entrepreneurs. The comprador–merchants, for example, played a crucial role in China's early industrial enterprises. By being managers, fund raisers, innovators, and risk-takers, they were Schumpeterian entrepreneurs *par excellence.* Studies after the 1970s generally agreed with my view, and found numerous examples of Schumpeterian entrepreneurship in Chinese businesses: in the silk industry of the late Qing period, in the producer industries of the 1920s, in the officials who later became successful businessmen, and in those overseas Chinese who returned to China to start modern enterprises.[9]

In his recent field study of the Shanghai entrepreneurs in Hong Kong, the sociologist Siulun Wong made a major contribution to the study of Chinese entrepreneurship by suggesting that there are at least two types of entrepreneurs: the Schumpeterian type who is a risk-taker, experimenter, and profit-maximizer, and the McClellandian type who plans on the basis of steady rewards from long-term competition. According to Wong, these Shanghai industrialists, who dominated the cotton-spinning industry in Hong Kong after the 1950s, conform closely to the second type because of their emphases on the ability to handle people, dedication to the job, good market judgment, technical proficiency, honesty, and long-term perspective.[10]

These different interpretations of Chinese entrepreneurship are not necessarily irreconcilable for several reasons. First, entrepreneurship was more likely to develop in the private sector than in the officially related enterprises of the *guandu shangban* type. Second, those Chinese who were exposed to foreign influence tended to be more entrepreneurial than the ordinary businessmen. Third, entrepreneurship might be enhanced by personal ties because of business networking, or hindered by personal ties due to nepotism. Finally, the shift from the Schumpeterian to the McClellandian style of entrepreneurship in Chinese business history was a natural progression found in other parts of the world, which confirms Alexander Gerschenkron's model of the "modernization of entrepreneurship."

The Socioeconomic Institutions

The Family and Business

For a number of reasons the family has played a crucial role in Chinese business. For one thing, the Chinese business enterprise often operated according to principles, such as paternalism, that are identified with the family. Besides, Chinese businessmen have usually formed networks among themselves, making use of family connections in the process. Finally, families have owned and operated the great majority of all Chinese business enterprises. In this sense, the Chinese lineage was a form of familial business institution. David Faure showed that shareholding entitlements inherited from family and lineage trusts enabled Chinese family firms to act as corporations. The lineage appeared better equipped than any other contemporary institution to conduct business.[11]

Recent scholarship examined some of the distinguishing features of the family business organization: fluid business hierarchy, highly concentrated decision-making, and centrifugal force. New research has shed light, too, on the pattern of the long-term development of the family firm. The model of a four-stage life cycle postulated by Siulun Wong divided the evolution of Chinese family enterprises into emergent, centralized, segmented, and disintegration phases. Chi-cheung Choi, in his study of the history of a century-old firm, came to different conclusion. He observed that, due to competition among brothers, a Chinese family firm usually experienced a considerable restructuring process in which some brothers of the family would reinforce their status in the company while others were reduced to insignificance. Thus, the history of a Chinese family firm may be seen as a process of continuous integration and disintegration at the same time.[12]

Scholars have not agreed on whether the family benefited or hindered the Chinese business enterprises. The generally accepted interpretation in the 1950s and 1960s tended to emphasize its negative influences, such as nepotism and the drainage of capital. Writing on one of China's early industrial leaders, Albert Feuerwerker contended that Sheng Xuanhuai's loyalty to his family set limits to what he could do to his business enterprises. Recent research, however, has treated the family much more positively: Gary Hamilton on information sharing, Siulun Wong on its role in upholding the solidarity of the firm, and this writer on its role in mobilizing capital. Among the Shanghai industrialists in postwar Hong Kong, Wong found a "pervasive economic ethos," which he called "entrepreneurial familism," because the family not only was the basic unit of business competition, but also provided the impetus for innovation and risk-taking.[13]

The Guild

Since the late Ming period, Chinese businessmen have joined together to form various kinds of organizations such as occupational groups, native-place associations (*Landsmannschaften*), coalitions (*bang*), and chambers of commerce. Among these, scholars extensively studied the urban merchants' fraternal association (*gongsuo* or *huiguan*), known as the merchant "guilds" in Western literature. A perusal of this literature reveals that there were some major trends in the development of the Qing and early Republican guilds. First, the guilds evolved from simple to more complex organizations. Second, their goals shifted from general to specific ones. Finally, the common-place principle in the organization of guilds increasingly gave way to that of common trade.

Most of the writings on Chinese guilds tended to emphasize the functions of these corporate, self-governing organizations. Guilds played an important religious role in the eighteenth century, and assumed a wide range of civic responsibilities in the cities during the late Qing and early Republican periods. Politically, guilds acted as tax-farmers that produced lump sums for officials while lightening the burdens of individual businessmen.[14]

For merchants, the most important role of guilds was in terms of their economic functions, such as providing protection and information, adjudicating disputes, stabilizing prices, limiting competition, and setting trade standards. It is in these areas that we find some controversial issues. One issue concerns the way in which guilds affected the economy in general and the market mechanism in particular. Some scholars stressed the exclusive, protectionist, and monopolistic aspects of guilds, and, therefore, regarded them as having a pernicious influence on the economy. John Fei, on the other hand, took strong exception, arguing that collectivism of action on the part of guilds did not necessarily mean monopoly. Moreover, by contributing to cooperative finance and to a quick spreading of market information, guilds led to the lowering of transaction costs and to market perfection. The economy, therefore, benefited from enhanced organizational efficiency. In historical perspective, Fei concluded that the appearance of guilds "represented a Chinese quest for equity and proficiency."[15]

Business Networks

Historiography of the 1950s and 1960s tended to view Chinese business relationships as particularistic and dysfunctional. More recent studies have examined them from the perspective of networks and view them as a special Chinese style of business management. "Network" is a popular topic in a number of disciplines of the social sciences, and, through the work of some sociologists and anthropologists, has become a theme in Chinese business history.

These social scientists have delineated some salient features of Chinese business networks. According to them, the Chinese businessmen's highly personalistic traits are clearly observable in their emphasis on reciprocity and their social interaction. For them, business relationship precedes organization. They emphasize face-to-face contacts and nurture flexible, multi-stranded business relations. At the heart of Chinese business networks is *guanxi* or personal connection. Studies have demonstrated the importance of such personal connections based on kinship, place of origin, and schooling. Many observers regard the "unrenounceable kinship obligation" as the key to the success of Chinese business, but Siulun Wong differentiates its relative importance with regard to a firm's internal organization and its external relations. For Andrea McElderry, the "fiduciary community" of the Chinese bankers in nineteenth-century Shanghai can be visualized as a set of concentric circles. The innermost circle was the family, then, moving outward, were circles of kinship, place of origin, and guild.[16]

Based on field studies, a number of anthropologists have challenged the conventional view of the importance of kinship and ethnicity. Maurice Freeman, for instance, maintained that the crucial distinction between Chinese and Western business behavior is not the distinction between kin and non-kin, but between the personal and the impersonal. A crucial ingredient in this personal relation, according to Donald De Glopper, is *xinyong*, meaning trustworthiness or a businessman's willingness and ability to meet his business obligations. *Xinyong* is predicated on performance in business; it is not given or ascribed. Chinese businessmen, however, cannot afford to do business exclusively on the basis of *guanxi* or *xinyong*. They also use other means to expand their business activities, and one way to do this is through the institution of *bao* (guarantorship), which has long been an important feature of Chinese business transactions.[17]

The Market

Historical research on China's markets has flourished during the past two decades, and has concluded that markets were more sophisticated than was previously assumed. Compared to the West, the market was more important to Chinese business enterprises: The households-cum-firms depended heavily on the market for the exchange of goods and services, and the numerous small-scale enterprises relied on the market for reducing their transaction costs.

According to G. William Skinner, who published his influential analysis of China's traditional market structure in 1978, at the heart of the Chinese market hierarchy was the "standard market"—a rural hexagonal market that met all the normal trade needs of the peasant household. The central market town, where the officially regulated brokers (*yahang*) and exchange banks operated, had wholesaling functions. Ramon Myers recently proposed a bold interpretation of China's traditional market structure: China had a "reticular market system" in sharp contrast to the "plexus-type market system" of premodern Japan and early modern Europe.[18]

One issue in the study of the Chinese market concerns the degree to which interregional markets were integrated. Yeh-chien Wang's important study showed that in the Qing period grain prices across the five macroregions, as defined by William Skinner, moved essentially in a synchronic manner. This finding contradicted Skinner's hypothesis of regional autarky and asynchronic regional cycles, implying that China achieved considerable interregional market integration as early as the eighteenth century.[19] Another issue is market competitiveness. Although some disagreements remain, most researchers have now agreed that during the late imperial and early Republican periods, China had largely competitive markets.

To what extent were competitive markets beneficial to China? The postwar scholars of development economics, including those in China studies, assumed that a competitive market is good for economic development. Evelyn Rawski, however, argued in favor of the opposite: It was not underdevelopment but competitive markets that hindered economic development. The atomized, competitive market with numerous small firms was especially bad for China after the 1880s, because her competitors in the West experienced a managerial revolution that favored the large corporate enterprise. Questions were raised regarding this argument, for it is not clear whether atomized markets were necessarily competitive, and whether these markets had to be competitive to serve as an obstacle to economic development.[20]

Students of Chinese business history raised two issues that are closely related to the study of markets. The first concerned technology. In his now-classic study, Mark Elvin sought to answer the following question: From 1300 through 1800, why did China experience an economic expansion within a stagnant technology? He demonstrated that an efficient market mechanism prevented production and marketing from being integrated. The net result was the divorce of market and technology and substitution of commerce for management.[21] The second issue dealt with capitalism: Why did China, with its highly competitive markets, fail to develop a sophisticated capitalist system? Researchers focused on China's commercial capitalism and bureaucratic capitalism, a far cry from the emphasis on industrial capitalism in American business history.

The Political–Cultural Environment

State–Business Relations

The important role of the state in Chinese business history lies in the fact that it was engaged not only in regulating the market and allocating investment funds, but also in owning and operating a great number of business enterprises, especially in the twentieth century. While Andrea McElderry's fine study of the institution of *bao* (guarantorship) explored government–business relations in the traditional setting, Wellington Chan's emphasis concerned modern enterprises: the *guandu shangban* system, official–merchant partnerships, official–entrepreneur companies, and gentry–merchant cooperation in private business. Among them, the extensively studied *guandu shangban* system has generated controversial issues.[22]

Early historiography faulted these *guandu shangban* enterprises for their bureaucratism, corruption, and gross mismanagement. Newer research tends to stress their positive aspects, noting that they were unprecedented ventures in China and that their initial success was due to a balance between government financial support and enterprise autonomy. Evelyn Rawski recently made an even more positive assessment of the *guandu shangban* model, viewing it as part of a policy to protect "infant industries." She pointed out that the vertical integration characteristic of Li Hongzhang's enterprises represented one solution to the problem of finding a market for services and commodities that had no traditional precedents.[23]

How autonomous have businesses been in China vis-à-vis the state? The old view was that the all-powerful state hindered business development in traditional China, but gradually lost its control in the late Qing period due to political disintegration. Susan Mann has argued the opposite: The state tended to share power with the merchants in the market during the high Qing period, but became more intrusive after the mid-nineteenth century in a desperate effort to expand its income.[24]

Recently a number of scholars have begun to deemphasize the old stereotype of a businessman class oppressed by unsympathetic officials. They have shown that there were a multitude of symbiotic relations between the state and private businesses during the late imperial period, as evidenced by the absence of rebellions of urban merchants, by the relationship of "co-optation" in the salt industry, by the businessmen's role in "liturgical governance" in the local market, and by the Qing leadership's view of the state's resources and the people's livelihood (*guoji minsheng*). A parallel development in this government–business symbiosis was the rise of the businessmen as a social group after the mid-nineteenth century.[25]

It was generally assumed that Chinese businessmen enjoyed a high degree of autonomy under the Nanjing government, which—with a series of economic reforms—seemed to be pro-business. Parks Coble's recent publication, however, completely contradicted this view, showing that the Nanjing government, in its state-building effort, largely subdued the businessmen by the late 1920s.[16]

Culture and Business

Literature about Chinese culture's influence on business has witnessed changing perspectives: from an earlier emphasis on such negative influences as particularism and bureaucratism to the current positive evaluations of familial entrepreneurship and group cooperation.[27] Some have even suggested that, for the first time since the Industrial Revolution, the world may see a meaningful alternative to the rational model of the West, in that the Chinese have demonstrated that cultural collectivism and high economic achievement are compatible.

An obvious strength in Chinese culture, according to John Fei, lies in its emphasis on secularism. Ramon Myers was more specific, arguing that the strong preference of the Chinese for solo ownership–management by the household-cum-firm was based on Confucian tradition: a sense of personal evaluation of self and a strong propensity to glorify ancestors by achieving personal success. Others have maintained that Neo-Confucianism also helped not only by infusing officials with a moralistic "probationary ethic," but also by facilitating a harmonious relationship between management and labor.[28]

The influence of religion on business is a new research theme. In his Weberian, trail-blazing study on this subject, Ying-shih Yu concluded that the Confucian ethical principles as well as the religious teachings of Buddhism and Taoism in the late imperial period contributed substantially to the rise of the "businessman's spirit" (*shangren jingsheng*): self-consciousness, assertive attitudes, and a certain pride in their profession. Other recent research includes an examination of the relationship between folk religion and book-keeping practice in the Ming and Qing periods, and a study of the religious roots of entrepreneurship in postwar Taiwan.[29]

Family business and business networks, which have been examined earlier, constitute important ingredients in Chinese business culture. What other norms and attitudes did the Chinese businessmen have with regard to their occupational activities?

Chinese businessmen were considerably influenced by Confucian values, as evidenced by the "gentrification" of the rich salt merchants in the eighteenth century and of the coastal businessmen in the nineteenth century. In her field study of a Hong Kong factory in the 1960s, Barbara Ward stressed its "Chinese way of management," which included beliefs about the value of education, the virtue of hard work, and the self-evident goal of economic self-betterment. Siulun Wong similarly noticed the Confucian values among Hong Kong's postwar industrialists, who emphasized business harmony, peaceful persuasion, and social responsibility. The importance of family ties and personal relations among Chinese businessmen has led one scholar to declare that one distinguishing feature in Chinese business management is "weak organizations and strong linkages."[30]

Contemporary Chinese businessmen tend not to read the Confucian classics. Instead, they are more influenced by the popular literature on the knights errant and warriors. *The Romance of the Three Kingdoms* and Sunzi's *Art of War*, for instance, are being revived as models for handling business relationships and devising strategies for competition. They also share a strong desire to be owners of their own enterprises. This characteristic of "being one's own boss" (*dang laoban*) is true for the Chinese small businessmen in Taiwan and Southeast Asia as well as for the Hong Kong industrialists who are large employers.[31]

The Global Perspective

The Maritime Connection

Research on China's overseas business represents part of a larger trend toward the study of maritime China, which has lately received much scholarly attention. The junk trade was a flourishing business of maritime China during the Qing period, involving trade with three wings, at Nagasaki, Manila, and the ports of Malaya. One aspect of this trade, tribute relations, was examined by Sarasin Viraphol regarding Southeast Asia, by John Fairbank regarding coastal diplomacy, and by Takeshi Hamashita regarding the larger context of modern Asia.[32] Maritime China is currently experiencing an economic boom, and Chinese businessmen's vigorous activities are visible not only in Asia but throughout the world.

Chinese businessmen have been particularly successful in Southeast Asia where a large number of Chinese emigrated after the mid-Ming period. What accounted for the success of these overseas Chinese (*huaqiao*, "Chinese sojourners")? The orthodox view was that they were atypical of the Chinese population as a whole, because those who emigrated were the creative dynamic fringe. New research, however, offers different interpretations. The institutional school emphasizes that Chinese family ties and personal networks were conducive to business activities. The "statist" school, on the other hand, contends that the close relationship of Chinese businessmen with the host countries' governments was the key factor behind their success stories.[33]

A number of these overseas Chinese businessmen, with large funds and modern management skills, returned to China to start various kinds of businesses. These enterprises included a steam-powered silk filature in 1872, China's first privately owned modern enterprise; the Sincere Company in 1900, China's first modern department store; the Wing On Company in 1907, a large retailing firm; and the Nanyang Brothers Tobacco Company, a major manufacturing enterprise. Among these businessmen, Zhang Bishi was a most interesting figure. A multimillionaire from Java, he returned to China, where, from 1895 through 1910, he established various modern enterprises and built five railroads. He was honored even by America's Wall Street.[34]

Western Business in China

Given the strong presence of the West in modern China, Chinese business history would be incomplete without including Western enterprises. Indeed, the Chinese business enterprises were studied in the 1950s and 1960s as indices of "China's response to the West," which was the predominant paradigm of China studies at the time.

For many economic historians, it was the West that played the role of catalyst in modern China's economic development. For some business historians, a similar Western role may also be applied to the business world. The comprador–merchants, for instance, are known to have first introduced to China some modern business institutions such as insurance, joint-stock companies, and limited liability. Some aspects of China's company structure and management, too, were modernized by those overseas Chinese who had been exposed to Western influence.

With the notable exception of the general survey of Western business enterprises in China by Allen and Donnithorne, most writings on these enterprises have been company histories based on the companies' own records: the British East India Company, which virtually started the China trade; the two British conglomerates of Jardine, Matheson and Company and Butterfield and Swire; Hong Kong and Shanghai Banking Corporation, the most powerful Western financial institution in modern China; and the American commission house of Augustine Heard and Company.[35] Other writings have focused on the changing patterns of the major mercantile houses.

Western multinational corporations have also received some attention. Sherman Cochran, for instance, studied the British–American Tobacco Company's operations in China. Mira Wilkins examined several ways in which American multinational corporations, such as Standard Oil, General Electric, and Ford Motor Company, included China within their far-flung operations from the early nineteenth century to 1949. These multinationals often used their international connections to penetrate the China market: Singer Sewing Machine developed its China business through its London office, and Western Electric started its China operations through its Japanese affiliate, Nippon Electric.[36]

Sino–Foreign Business Relations

Some noticeable themes and issues emerge in China's business relations with the West—foreign trade and foreign investment. One theme is the cooperation between Chinese and foreign businessmen in China. I have previously examined the various ways in which this Sino–foreign symbiosis operated: the joint-account trade, the institution of Chinese investment in foreign enterprises (*fugu*), and the operation of Chinese businesses under foreign names (*maoming*). Furthermore, Robert Gardella has recently pointed out that Sino–foreign business collaboration was greatly effective in the process of institutionalizing the tea trade.[37]

Another theme of this relationship, competition, has received more scholarly attention. Various authors have examined the rivalry among foreign companies with a focus on specific topics: Kwang-ching Liu on the steamship business; this writer on imports and exports; Sherman Cochran on the cotton textiles industry; and Mira Wilkins on the marketing strategies of some multinational corporations.[38]

As for Sino–foreign business rivalry, in the long run China has not fared well on the world market in industries such as tea, silk, and tong oil. Literature on China's domestic market, however, has clearly demonstrated that Chinese businessmen competed vigorously and successfully with their foreign counterparts in imports and exports during the late Qing period, and in the match, textile, and machinery industries during the early Republican period. Sherman Cochran has masterfully analyzed the Chinese firm of

Nanyang Brothers Tobacco Company's intense competition with the Western multinational firm of British–American Tobacco.[39]

One issue concerning Sino–foreign business rivalry was whether or not it was an even competition. Some historians have argued that it was uneven because of foreign firms' advantages in capitalization, technology, management skills, and political leverage. In reply, other historians have contended that, on the contrary, Sino–foreign competition was even, because the Chinese firms had the advantage of local knowledge, nationalism, mobility, cheap labor costs, and greater labor intensity.[40]

Another issue was whether China's business relations with foreign countries benefited China. We have briefly mentioned the positive effects of such relations on Chinese business organizations, and recent analyses by Loren Brandt, Thomas Rawski, and Robert Gardella have shown that these relations improved the standard of living of many Chinese by creating commercial opportunities for farmers and handicraft producers.[41]

The neo-Marxists, on the other hand, blamed foreign trade and foreign investment for China's economic underdevelopment. The influx of cheap foreign imports, they argued, displaced the traditional Chinese handicrafts, while China's exports were skewed toward a few staples, exposing China to the instability of overseas market conditions. What commercialization brought China, they maintained, was not modern development but the intensification of peasant household subsistence production. According to Wallersteinian scholars, this was possible because foreign trade led to the commercialization of agriculture, which hastened China's process of proletarianization and "incorporation" in the exploitative world economy.[42]

Imperialism and Economic Nationalism

As the debate over Sino–foreign business relations developed, it was often conducted broadly in terms of two vigorously debated issues—imperialist exploitation and economic nationalism. To the nationalist-minded Chinese and the Marxist scholars, foreign business presence in China was exploitative and, therefore, imperialistic. On the other hand, from the perspective of neoclassical analysis, foreign presence gave impetus to Chinese economic nationalism, which was considerably effective in fighting against foreign economic intrusion.

According to Sherman Cochran, for a foreign company to exploit China, usually it would (1) drain wealth from China; (2) pay wages and prices lower than in a free market; (3) transform China's agrarian economy into monocultures dependent on the vicissitudes of foreign markets; (4) use its government's support to improperly promote its material interest; and

(5) engage in a monopoly to exploit customers and competitors. Cochran applied these criteria to the British–American Tobacco Company to test the degree to which it was imperialistic.[43] While the issue of economic imperialism is still being debated, it is probably safe to say that its beneficial and deleterious effects on the Chinese economy occurred concurrently and that, on balance, its effects were neither uniformly destructive nor wholly beneficial.

Scholars have not agreed on the effectiveness of Chinese economic nationalism vis-à-vis foreign economic intrusion, although recent literature has tended to emphasize its effectiveness. Major topics of research include the patriotic nature of the early *guandu shangban* enterprises, writings by officials and businessmen on the importance of *shangzhan* (business warfare) against foreigners, and Chinese participation in anti-foreign strikes, boycotts, and the "national goods movement." For example, in order to compete with the foreigners, a Chinese wine company continued to operate even after years of losing money. Chinese workers, too, were willing to go on strike more often against foreign companies than against Chinese companies, even though the former's wages were sometimes higher and never lower. On the diplomatic level, some prominent Chinese businessmen, motivated partly by patriotic sentiments, assumed crucial roles in convincing the government to adopt a new, more nationalistic approach to dealing with Japan and Korea in the late nineteenth century.[44] As economic historians have vigorously debated the issue of "moral economy," is it possible for students of Chinese business history to use "nationalistic business" as a category of analysis?

For a Chinese firm to be economically nationalistic, according to Sherman Cochran, usually it would: (1) be capitalized only by Chinese funds; (2) be identified with anti-foreign strikes, boycotts, and other popular demonstrations; (3) use raw materials from China for manufacturing; (4) form alliances with the Chinese government and benefit from the government's retaliation against foreign companies; and (5) compete directly with foreign rivals in the industry. Cochran applied these criteria to the Nanyang Brothers Tobacco Company to test the degree of its effectiveness in competing with the British–American Tobacco Company. Cochran concluded that just as the former did not completely embody nationalism, neither was the latter entirely imperialistic.[45] By delineating the whole spectrum of imperialism and economic nationalism, Cochran made a major contribution to these two controversial issues.

Comparative Approach

One can hardly find a major work in the literature of Chinese business history that does have a comparative perspective. One theme has been to compare Chinese business inside of China with that outside of China. Gungwu Wang's study on the culture of Chinese merchants is a good example. According to Wang, the Chinese merchants within China, with low social status and under official control, shared values and attitudes with other classes of people. They hardly had a distinguishing culture of their own. The situation greatly changed when they did business abroad, especially in Southeast Asia, where they had reached a dominant position by the fourteenth century. They became highly successful, and Western sources portrayed them as being not only thrifty and industrious but also adventurous, bold, ingenious, and highly entrepreneurial—a far cry from their typical counterparts within China.[46]

Another theme has been to compare China with Japan, including such topics as entrepreneurship, technological transfer, relations between government and business, early industrial enterprises, foreign trade, and urban–rural business integration. A third theme has been to compare China with the West, with special reference to business organization and strategy, technological innovations, market systems, business rationalism, and transaction costs. Comparative marketing, too, has been explored in a global perspective, especially with regard to the tea, silk, sugar, cotton, and cotton-textile industries.[47]

Susan Mann particularly emphasized the comparative approach in her study on the relationship between local merchants and officials in China from 1750 through 1950. She likened late nineteenth-century China to England on the eve of its civil war, France in the eighteenth century, the Ottomans in the sixteenth century, and Mughal India in the seventeenth century. She made comparisons, too, between China's socialist-market system in the twentieth century and those of the Soviet Union, Hungary, and Yugoslavia.[48]

Conclusion: Research Trends and Prospects

Several trends can be delineated in the study of Chinese business history during the past half century. First, in search of answers to China's "tardy" modernization, it began with an emphasis on the weaknesses of Chinese economic and business institutions, but gradually changed to more positive assessments, especially after the recent business boom in "Greater China." Second, it started under the general paradigm of "China's response to the West," was modified after the 1970s by the China-centered approach, and recently has paid increasingly more attention again to foreign factors. Third, it focused initially on industrial enterprises, then changed after the 1970s to commerce and finance, and has recently shifted to an emphasis on culture and institutions.

In spite of some weaknesses and problems in the study of Chinese business history,[49] this field is poised for a takeoff with the help of several favorable factors: a foundation of solid research, extensive newly available source material, a Chinese government friendly toward business, and the economic boom in "Greater China." What are the prospects for the future?

One question in this connection concerns the extent to which we apply to Chinese business history the models that are developed from Western experience. Alfred Chandler's emphasis on technology and big business organization, for instance, has worked wonders in the study of business history not only concerning the United States but also concerning Britain, Germany, and Japan. There are some considerable limitations, however, in applying it to China because of China's distinctive problems and historical contexts. To begin with, both the predominance of small-scale businesses in the nineteenth century and the importance of the official, bureaucratic enterprises in the twentieth century left little room for the Chinese manager's "visible hand" to maneuver. If American business history serves as a reminder of the power of economics and technology over culture, then we may say that Chinese business history provides an eloquent testimony to the importance of history over economics and technology. Indeed, since late imperial times, Chinese history has exhibited institutional features that, in their totality, constituted a distinctive framework for organizing business activities, such as networks, the family business, the reticular market structure, the co-optational relationship between the state and private enterprises, and "nationalistic business." These features, shaped by culture and history, constitute particular characteristics of Chinese business history, distinguishing themselves from the key features of other countries' business histories, such as managerial creativity in the United States and government policy toward business in Japan.

Particular characteristics such as these, that are the product of China's own unique history, thus deserve our special attention. A challenge to all students in this field lies in how to study Chinese business history by putting business enterprises and businessmen in proper historical context. I would like to argue, therefore, that the main business of Chinese business history is business in history.

Notes

1. Marion J. Levy, Jr., and Kuo-heng Shih, *The Rise of the Modern Chinese Business Class* (New York: Institute of Pacific Relations, 1949). Kwang-ching Liu published articles on the Shanghai Steam-Navigation Company in the *Business History Review* in 1954 and 1955; Albert Feuerwerker, *China's Early Industrialization* (Cambridge: Harvard University Press, 1958); Sherman Cochran, *Big Business in China: Sino–Foreign*

Rivalry in the Cigarette Industry, 1890–1930 (Cambridge: Harvard University Press, 1980); Given the short length of this article, it is not possible to cite all the works mentioned.

2. Feuerwerker, *China's Early Industrialization.*

3. Wellington K.K. Chan, " The Organizational Structure of the Tradition Chinese Firm and Its Modern Form," *Business History Review* 56, no. 2 (summer 1982), pp. 218–35; Robert Gardella, 'Perspectives on the Development of Accounting and China's Economic Transformation from Late Ming to the Early Republic," in Rajeswary A. Brown, ed., *Chinese Business Enterprise in Asia* (London: Routledge, 1995), pp. 45–59; Chi-cheung Choi, "Competition Among Brothers," in Brown, ed., *Chinese Business Enterprise in Asia*, pp. 96–114.

4. W.E. Willmott, ed., *Economic Organization in Chinese Society* (Stanford: Stanford University Press, 1972); David Faure, "The Lineage as Business Company," *The Second Conference on Modern Chinese Economic History* (Taipei: Institute of Economics, Academia Sinica, 1989), pp. 347–76; William C. Kirby, "China Unincorporated," *Journal of Asian Studies* 54, no. 1 (February 1995), pp. 43–63.

5. Robert Gardella, " Squaring Accounts: Commercial Bookkeeping Methods and Capitalist Rationalism in Late Qing and Republican China," *Journal of Asian Studies* 51, no. 2 (May 1992), pp. 317–39; Siulun Wong, "The Chinese Family Firm: A Model," *British Journal of Sociology* 36, no. 1 (1985), pp. 58–70; Fu-mei Chen and Ramon H. Myers, "Coping with Transaction Costs," *The Second Conference on Modern Chinese Economic History*, pp. 317–41; Louis T. Sigel, "Transaction Cost Economics and Chinese Business History," *Chinese Business History* 2, no. 2 (March 1992), pp. 1–3.

6. Ping-ti Ho, "The Salt Merchants of Yang-chou," *Harvard Journal of Asiatic Studies* 17 (June 1954), pp. 130–68; Thomas A. Metzger, "The Organizational Capabilities of the Ch'ing State in the Field of Commerce," in Willmott, ed., *Economic Organization in Chinese Society*; Kuo-tung Ch'en, *The Insolvency of the Chinese Hong Merchants, 1760–1843* (Taipei: Institute of Economics, Academia Sinica, 1990).

7. Susan Mann, *Local Merchants in the Chinese Bureaucracy, 1750–1950* (Stanford: Stanford University Press, 1987); Prasenjit Duara, *Culture, Power, and the State: Rural North China, 1900–1942* (Stanford: Stanford University Press, 1988); Yen-p'ing Hao, *The Comprador in Nineteenth Century China* (Cambridge: Harvard University Press, 1970).

8. John K. Fairbank, Alexander Eckstein, and Lien-sheng Yang, "Economic Change in Early Modern China," *Economic Development and Cultural Change* 9, no. 1 (October 1960), pp. 1–26.

9. Hao, *The Comprador in Nineteenth Century China*; Thomas G. Rawski, "The Growth of Producer Industries, 1900–1971," in Dwight H. Perkins, ed., *China's Modern Economy in Historical Perspective* (Stanford: Stanford University Press, 1975).

10. Siu-lun Wong, *Emigrant Entrepreneurs: Shanghai Industrialists in Hong Kong* (Hong Kong: Oxford University Press, 1988).

11. Faure, "The Lineage as Business Company."

12. Wong, "The Chinese Family Firm: A Model"; Chi-cheung Choi, "Competition Among Brothers."

13. Wong, *Emigrant Entrepreneurs: Shanghai Industrialists in Hong Kong.*

14. William Rowe, *Hankow: Commerce and Society in a Chinese City, 1796–1889* (Stanford: Stanford University Press, 1984).

15. Kwang-ching Liu, "Chinese Merchant Guilds: An Historical Inquiry," *Pacific Historical Review* 57, no. 1 (February 1988), pp. 1–23; John C.H. Fei, "The Chinese Market System in a Historical Perspective," *The Second Conference on Modern Chinese Economic History*, pp. 31–57.

16. Siulun Wong, "Business Networks, Cultural Values, and the State in Hong Kong and Singapore," in Brown, ed., *Chinese Business Enterprise in Asia*, pp. 136–53; Andrea McElderry, "Securing Trust and Stability," in Brown, ed., *Chinese Business Enterprise in Asia*, pp. 27–44.

17. Maurice Freedman, *Chinese Family and Marriage in Singapore* (London: Her Majesty's Stationery Office, 1957); Donald R. De Glopper, "Doing Business in Lukang," in Willmott, ed., *Economic Organization in Chinese Society*, pp. 297–326.

18. G. William Skinner, "Marketing and Social Structure in Rural China," *Journal of Asian Studies* 24, no. 1 (1964), pp. 3–43; no. 2 (1965), pp. 195–228; and no. 3 (1965), pp. 363–99; Ramon H. Myers, "State, Market, and Economic History," in San-ching Chen, ed., *Papers Commemorating the Ninetieth Birthday of Professor Kuo Ting-yee* (Taipei: Institute of Modern History, Academia Sinica, 1995), pp. 371–97.

19. Yeh-chien Wang, "Food Supply and Grain Prices in the Yangtze Delta in the Eighteenth Century," *The Second Conference on Chinese Economic History*, pp. 423–59.

20. Evelyn S. Rawski, "Competitive Markets as an Obstacle to Economic Development," *The Second Conference on Chinese Economic History*, pp. 289–311.

21. Mark Elvin, *The Pattern of the Chinese Past* (Stanford: Stanford University Press, 1973).

22. Andrea McElderry, "Guarantors and Guarantees in Qing Government–Business Relations," in Jane K. Leonard and John R. Watts, eds., *To Achieve Security and Wealth: The Qing Imperial State and the Economy, 1644–1911* (Ithaca, NY: East Asia Program, Cornell University, 1992), pp. 119–38; Wellington K.K. Chan, *Merchants, Mandarins, and Modern Enterprise in Late Ch'ing China* (Cambridge: Harvard University Press, 1977).

23. Rawski, "Competitive Markets as an Obstacle to Economic Development."

24. Mann, *Local Merchants in the Chinese Bureaucracy, 1750–1950*.

25. These scholars include Lien-sheng Yang, Thomas A. Metzger, Susan Mann, and Jane K. Leonard.

26. Parks M. Coble, Jr., *The Shanghai Capitalists and the Nationalist Government, 1927–1937* (Cambridge: Harvard University Press, 1980).

27. S. Gordon Redding, *The Spirit of Chinese Capitalism* (Berlin and New York: Walter de Gruyter, 1990), emphasizes the role of culture in Chinese business.

28. Ramon H. Myers, "Confucianism and Economic Development," in Chung-hua Institute for Economic Research, ed., *Conference on Confucianism and Economic Development in East Asia* (Taipei: Chung-hua Institute for Economic Research, 1989); Wen-hsin Yeh, "Corporate Space, Communal Time: Everyday Life in Shanghai's Bank of China," *American Historical Review* 100, no. 1 (1995), pp. 97–122.

29. Ying-shih Yu is currently writing an English version of his Chinese book (1987) on this subject; Gardella, "Perspectives on the Development of Accounting and China's Economic Transformation from Late Ming to the Early Republic"; Ian Skoggard, *The Indigenous Dynamic in Taiwan's Postwar Development* (Armonk, NY: M.E. Sharpe, 1996).

30. Barbara E. Ward, "A Small Factory in Hong Kong," in Willmott, ed., *Economic Organization in Chinese Society*; Wong, *Emigrant Entrepreneurs: Shanghai Industrialists in Hong Kong*; S. Gordon Redding, "Weak Organizations and Strong Linkages," in Gary Hamilton, ed., *Business Networks and Economic Development in East and Southeast Asia* (Hong Kong: Centre of Asian Studies, University of Hong Kong, 1991).

31. Wong, *Emigrant Entrepreneurs: Shanghai Industrialists in Hong Kong*.

32. Sarasin Viraphol, *Tribute and Profit* (Cambridge: Council on East Asian Studies, Harvard University, 1977); John K. Fairbank, *Trade and Diplomacy on the China Coast: The Opening of the Treaty Ports 1842–1854*. (Cambridge: Harvard University

Press, 1953 [reprint 1963]); Takeshi Hamashita, "The Tribute Trade System and Modern Asia," in A.J.H. Latham and Heita Kawakatsu, eds., *Japanese Industrialization and the Asian Economy* (London: Routledge, 1994), pp. 91–107.

33. Chan Kwok Bun and Claire Chiang. See Ngoh, *Stepping Out: The Making of Chinese Entrepreneurs* (Singapore: Prentice-Hall, 1994); Michael R. Godley, "Nanyang Perspectives on Chinese Business," *Chinese Business History* 4, no. 1 (fall 1993), pp. 1–3; Hamilton, *Business Networks and Economic Development in East and Southeast Asia*; Brown, ed., *Chinese Business Enterprise in Asia*.

34. Wellington K.K. Chan, "The Organizational Structure of the Traditional Chinese Firm and Its Modern Form"; Cochran, *Big Business in China*; Michael R. Godley, *The Mandarin-Capitalists from Nanyang* (Cambridge and New York: Cambridge University Press, 1981).

35. H.B. Morse, *The Chronicles of the East India Company Trading to China* (Oxford, Oxford University Press, 1926–1929); Margaret Keswick, ed., *The Thistle and the Jade* (London: Octopus, 1982); Frank King, *The History of the Hong Kong and Shanghai Banking Corporation* (New York: Cambridge University Press, 1987–1991); Stephen C. Lockwood, *Augustine Heard and Company* (Cambridge: Council on East Asian Studies, Harvard University, 1971).

36. Mira Wilkins, "The Impact of American Multinational Enterprise on American–Chinese Economic Relations, 1786–1949," in Ernest R. May and John K. Fairbank, eds., *America's China Trade in Historical Perspective: The Chinese and American Performance* (Cambridge, MA: Committee on American–East Asian Relations of the Department of History in collaboration with the Council on East Asian Studies, Harvard University, distributed by Harvard University Press, 1986), pp. 283–92.

37. Louis Dermigny, *La Chine et l'occident: Le commerce à Canton au XVIIIe siècle, 1719–1833* (Paris: S.E.V.P.E.N., 1964); Yen-p'ing Hao, *The Commercial Revolution in Nineteenth Century China* (Berkeley: University of California Press, 1986); Robert Gardella, *Harvesting Mountains: Fujian and the China Tea Trade, 1757–1937* (Berkeley: University of California Press, 1994).

38. Cochran, "Japan's Capture of China's Market for Imported Cotton Textiles Before World War I," *The Second Conference on Modern Chinese Economic History*, pp. 809–41.

39. Cochran, *Big Business in China*.

40. Yu-kwei Cheng and Jean Chesneaux contended that the competition was uneven, but Chi-ming Hou and Robert Dernberger argued that the rivalry was even. See also Chi-ming Hou, *Foreign Investment and Economic Development in China, 1840–1937* (Cambridge: Harvard University Press, 1965).

41. Loren Brandt, *Commercialization and Agricultural Development* (Cambridge and New York: Cambridge University Press, 1990); Gardella, *Harvesting Mountains*.

42. Robert Y. Eng, *Economic Imperialism in China* (Berkeley: Institute of East Asian Studies, University of California, 1986); Philip C.C. Huang, *The Peasant Family and Rural Development in the Yanqzi Delta, 1350–1988* (Stanford: Stanford University Press, 1990); Frances Moulder, *Japan, China, and the Modern World Economy* (Cambridge: Cambridge University Press, 1979); Alvin Y. So, *The South China Silk District* (Albany: State University of New York Press, 1986).

43. Cochran, *Big Business in China*.

44. Michael R. Godley, "Bacchus in the East," *Business History Review* 60, no. 3 (1986), pp. 383–409: Louis T. Sigel, "The Treaty Port Community and Chinese Foreign Policy in the 1880's," *Papers on Far Eastern History* (Canberra) 11 (March 1975), pp. 79–105; Louis T. Sigel, "Business–Government Cooperation in Late Qing Korean Policy," in Leonard and Watt, *To Achieve Security and Wealth*, pp. 157–81.

45. Cochran, *Big Business in China.*

46. Gungwu Wang, *The Culture of Chinese Merchants* (Toronto: Toronto and York University Joint Centre for Asia Pacific Studies, 1989).

47. Lillian M. Li, "Silks by Sea: Trade, Technology, and Enterprise in China and Japan," *Business History Review* 56, no. 2 (summer 1982), pp. 192–217; Myers, "State, Market, and Economic History"; Rawski, "Competitive Markets as an Obstacle to Economic Development."

48. Mann, *Local Merchants in the Chinese Bureaucracy, 1750–1950.*

49. See Andrea McElderry's conference report, "Time and Space: Periodizing Chinese Business," *Chinese Business History* 6, no. 1 (spring 1996), pp. 5–6.

Chinese Studies in History, vol. 31, nos. 3–4, Spring–Summer 1998, pp. 127–44.
© 1998 M.E. Sharpe, Inc. All rights reserved.
ISSN 0009–4633/1998 $9.50 + 0.00.

WELLINGTON K.K. CHAN

Tradition and Change in the Chinese Business Enterprise

The Family Firm Past and Present

Introduction

Until the recent emergence of a thriving economy along the China coast and among communities of Chinese diaspora all over the Pacific Rim, the history of Chinese business and entrepreneurship had received scant scholarly attention. The new interest, however, has also generated a great deal of confusing interpretations because so many of the successful Chinese business organizations and practices in contemporary East Asia do not seem to conform to Western or Japanese models. Moreover, Chinese traditional business ideology and institutions are often considered unprogressively clannish, lacking in the transformative power of entrepreneurship as well as in the spirit of communal trust. This contrasts rather sharply with the state of the field of business history in the United States, where it is far more developed and recognized. Thus, the history of the rise of large-scale, multi-unit, and professionally managed corporations from modest beginnings, as well as their crucial impact on the American economy, are justly celebrated through the influential works of Alfred D. Chandler and others. And, in 1993, the Nobel Prize in economics went to two other senior practitioners in the field, Douglass C. North and Robert W. Fogel.[1]

The accomplishments of business history in the younger China field are still rather uneven and quite small by comparison. One important factor is the

---

From a paper presented at the workshop on Scholarly Research on Chinese Business History: Interpretative Trends and Priorities for the Future, University of Akron, October 27–29, 1995.

Wellington K.K. Chan is on the faculty of Occidental College, California, Department of History.

paucity of available company records. Not even the larger, long-lived corporations have kept archives consistently. And among those that tried to do so, very few could escape the disastrous effect inflicted upon their efforts by the political and social upheavals that have dominated Chinese life during much of the past two centuries. There is one other major factor: Until quite recently, scholars working in this field have had difficulty formulating the right questions, because they have tended to examine issues through Western models and their experiences.

Thus, on broad theoretical questions, such as the cause and effect between Chinese values and the rise of capitalism, Max Weber, who was among the first in the West to do a serious study on this subject, and who consciously tried to contrast Chinese cultural values against the West's Calvinist Protestant ethic, emphasized Chinese religion's ostensible absence of rationality and the Confucian this-world orientations as an explanation for China's failure to develop a modern economy. More recently, as Chinese business won kudos for its vibrant entrepreneurship, other scholars like S. Gordon Redding have concentrated on other aspects of Confucianism, such as diligence, frugality, and the love of education, as positive factors that have led to business success.[2]

The fact that relying solely or primarily on cultural values can lead to contradictory assessments only shows how inadequate such a form of analysis really is. At the very least, it would seem that value orientations of any culture must be considered in conjunction with specific sets of historical circumstances and related institutions if they are to be meaningful. But even studies that do so are not always helpful. For example, older studies on state–economy relations for the late imperial China period have been very critical of the state. According to their view, the latter marginalized commerce and placed severe limits on private enterprise, and its bureaucracy engaged in systematic corruption, nepotism, and unprincipled patronage.[3] Such an analysis seems to have been partially flawed by some preconceived notion that comparable institutions in China and the West would perform similar functions or do them similarly. In recent years, as scholars have gained a better understanding of the inner dynamics of China's traditional society, a range of more broadly based and internally generated views has emerged. Thus, one new perspective, as suggested by Jane Leonard, shows how the state understood the Mencian concern for assuring the people's livelihood, and how it organized public institutions and policies that facilitated positive fiscal, monetary, and legal actions in the economy.[4] Such a view is confirmed by Robert Gardella, who observes that the Qing government provided "a greatly expanded scope of operations for Chinese merchants and suppliers" in the domestic tea markets.[5] Likewise, thanks to recent works by G. William Skinner, William T. Rowe, and Linda C. Johnson, our view about urban organizations and business leadership in

Qing China's major cities, such as Hankou, Ningbo, and Shanghai, has changed from one of subordination to and exploitation by the state to one that emphasizes their partnership with the state, as well as their mutual contribution toward the urban community's social and economic integration.[6]

We are now inclined to believe that the professional roles of officials and merchants were not immovable categories, but interchangeable functional parts; that extended families and lineages consciously promoted the division of occupation strategies among sons and male members to provide credible mutual support from government positions and commercial wealth; and that Ming and Qing officials, especially at the local level, cooperated with businessmen far more than we usually give them credit for.[7] What is certain is that by the late nineteenth century, the functional divide between officials and merchants was so blurred that even conservative senior court officials like Grand Councilor Sun Yuwen, and middle-ranking Customs Taotai of Shanghai (and Governor-general Zeng Guofan's son-in-law) Nie Qikui, could quite openly, though never officially, acknowledge their ownership of the Yutang Company and the Huasheng Cotton Mill, respectively.[8]

This article will attempt to show why historians of Chinese business should first try to study past Chinese business on its own terms, and how that, in turn, will also inform our understanding of contemporary Chinese business institutions and practices. Indeed, by tracing these important linkages between the past and the present, I propose to show how contemporary Chinese business is already breaking loose from certain areas of the institutional, organizational, and cultural molds imposed by the past. This is not in agreement with one influential view, as espoused by scholars such as Gordon Redding and Francis Fukuyama, which argues that Chinese firms will continue to behave according to these historical forms and impulses.[9] In what follows, I propose to make the contrary argument that as institutions and cultural values in the larger society under which Chinese business operates have differed or changed over time, so also have those differences or changes generated forces that are allowing Chinese business to overcome forms that are no longer functional.

Some New Perspectives

Recent scholarship has indeed shed new light on how several areas and categories of the Chinese enterprise have been conducting business. They include the role of the family and lineage in business enterprise,[10] the structure and strategy of individual firms,[11] and several lines of business: Robert Gardella on the tea trade, Sherman Cochran on the cigarette industry, Andrea McElderry on the native banks, Madeleine Zelin on salt, and Wellington Chan on department stores.[12]

There are also studies that, by asking relevant questions about specific cultural and institutional contexts, provide new insights into certain unique characteristics of Chinese business. Thus, David Faure, Wellington Chan, and others have argued that practically all private businesses in late imperial China, except for the smallest, required state patronage, and that none could operate independently of official control or exactions. Faure has further pointed out that the traditional firm and its business operations were able to have a separate identity and some modicum of permanency only by the ingenuous use of religious sanctions and such cultural institutions as lineage. In the end, while Chinese business by the sixteenth century had become quite successful in developing thriving rural markets, artisan workshops, familial and lineage firms, it could not launch into a modern capitalist economy because the state failed to provide, at the very least, credit and banking institutions, public accountability in corporate management, or some working set of civil and commercial laws.[13]

Finally, for the more recent period during the Republican era, there is a similar updating of perspectives about the role the government plays in the nation's economy. The earlier views of a nonperforming economy under the Guomindang and of exploitative officials forcing unredeemed bonds and other forms of extortion on private entrepreneurs have been updated by newer studies suggesting that the state's overall impact on the economy has been minimal. Moreover, in sectors where the state had some control, for example, in modern industry, it contributed to modest and even respectable growth rates.[14] As for the post-1949 era, there is a major disjunction between mainland China's socialist economy, which until the early 1980s did not allow private enterprise, and the thriving Chinese-owned businesses outside China proper. Many of these enterprises, especially those from Hong Kong, Taiwan, and Southeast Asia, have become transnational enterprise groups, even while many aspects of their organization and strategy remain Chinese. They offer fertile ground for comparative studies to be done between them and their counterparts in Japan, Western Europe, and North America. Meanwhile, the complexity of the modern Chinese state's roles, from intents to results, is reflected by William Kirby in his recent article on the history of the late Qing and the Republican era governments' efforts at incorporating companies and establishing a functioning set of laws. Kirby shows how the state adopted several legal steps, between 1904 and 1944, to promote control and accountability. These efforts by and large failed, if only because Chinese merchants preferred using personal relations and networking instead of a legal code to reduce transaction costs. Most entrepreneurs stayed away from registration as companies with limited liabilities because they distrusted the extensive disclosures about ownership the process entailed.[15]

These varied perspectives on the state and the economy are most likely far less disparate than they appear because they pose somewhat different sets of questions or emphasize different aspects of the same relationships. In any event, broad macroeconomic issues involving the state and the economy properly belong to the economic historian's domain. The business historian's main preoccupation should be the nature of the business enterprise, and how the conduct of business in some institutional form, often thought of as a firm, is organized and managed. An understanding of the total environment in which it operates—not only the economic, but also the institutional and cultural—is obviously critical; that environment, however, is at once broader and more focused than the relationships between the state and the economy.

A central issue in Chinese business history, therefore, is to learn about the nature of the core structural and behavioral features of the Chinese firm that seems prevalent from late imperial times to the present, and how its different parts have changed or assumed different roles over time. In this regard, one is likely to agree on the following list as being representative of the Chinese firm's core features:[16]

1. small-scale, relatively simple organizational structure;

2. close overlap of ownership, control by individuals linked by family and kinship ties, or by partnerships among kin and family friends;

3. centralized decision-making;

4. personal and family networking that encourages opportunistic diversifications, cutting across regional and national boundaries to expand membership of affiliate firms and to reduce transaction costs in sourcing, capital acquisition, and contracts;

5. a high degree of strategic adaptability.

Given that we do not yet have a very large database of Chinese firms, some may argue that a great number of variations and exceptions can be added to such a list as new data become available. This is true; however, while the additional data will add richness and verisimilitude, we have attained a critical mass of information for the purpose of analysis. And the list above contains one common element that permeates all of its five characteristics. That common element is the family firm, if by it we mean that the ownership and effective control of the business is held by a single family, a single lineage, or several families or lineages joined as partners.[17] We shall now turn our attention to the family firm, and explore how each of those core features—ownership, control, size, structure, and strategy—interact with the environment of each period from the late imperial and republican periods to the present, and what changes occurred as a result of changing environments.

Ownership and Control

In Chinese society, family firms have generally established a close identity between ownership and control, and are reinforced by social values that make business an integral part of the whole fabric of communal life, from personal relationships and kinship obligations to civic functions. Networking of these types—family and communal—makes each of these enterprises far stronger than their nominally small to medium sizes would otherwise command. Moreover, within each family firm, cultural and institutional dynamics mirror those of the family. This means the primacy of paternalistic authority so that the father becomes both the head of the family (*jiachang*) and the head of the family enterprise (*dangjia*). And even after he retires from the latter position, he will continue to make ultimate decisions about the business unless he becomes senile. This is why ownership and control are practically inseparable in the Chinese family firm, and why professional management of the enterprise and its corollary, the separation between ownership and control, is seldom achieved among Chinese family firms.

Both aspects—interpersonal relations and paternal authority—of the family firm can become sources of weaknesses. First, the same priority on people and relationships makes the reliance on networking, loyalty, and trust indispensable to the success of the enterprise. It also means that the institutional structure of the firm, at least at the top, remains rather unstructured and informal. Even those firms that grow to large multi-unit sizes and require complex administrative coordination continue to have rather loose and flexible control groups that serve as advisers and senior managers to the owner. The latter in turn relies on networking and the interpersonal relations it generates to assure effective control. Such a structure and management style, therefore, are not in and of themselves a weakness. They become weaknesses only if the owner or his senior assistants abuse each other's trust. Yet, this is probably why Chandler and other historians of American business regard the family firm and personal management as traditional forms of business. From the Chinese perspective, however, one may argue that, compared to the modern West's formal and professional style of management, its informal structure and operations are neither traditional nor modern, just a different but equally efficient way for owners to make decisions and maintain control.

Second, there are also problems of changing family-firm ownership and the firm's ability to survive as each generation of father-owners dies or quarrels arise, causing the likelihood that the firm will be split up, reorganized, sold, or terminated. Siu-lun Wong has identified four phases of the family firm's developmental cycle over the generations—emergent, centralized, segmented, and disintegrative—and shows that family firms often start out as partnerships in order to better pool resources and talent. For those that succeed in growing and expanding into rather large establishments, there is likely to be a centralization of ownership. This is done when one of the partners assumes greater and greater control until the others are forced to sell out, or are shunted into the status of insignificant owners. Then, upon the death of the owner, because of the Chinese tradition of providing equal rights of inheritance among the male heirs, the firm is likely to develop into several divisions or centers of decision-making. This leads to breakups or asymmetrical growth in shareholding, as those brothers who manage successful parts of the business receive additional shares at the expense of the others. In all likelihood, even if the firm survives intact during this second generation, it is highly apt to disintegrate when the leadership is passed on to the third-generation children who, as first cousins, have even less reason to keep up the single family entity because of fewer emotional ties and smaller individual shareholdings among them.[18]

Wong's model helps explain why there are few Chinese firms of longevity. As a rule, many of those with claims going back several generations have gaps, as in the case of the Ruifuxiang of Beijing and Tianjin, which began in the eighteenth century, was dormant during much of the nineteenth century, then returned to activity and growth under a different branch of the Meng family from the late nineteenth through the early twentieth centuries. As for two long-lived family firms about which we have records, the Yutang Company (1770s through 1950s) of Jining, Anhui Province, and the Kin Tye Lung (since the 1850s) of Hong Kong, they show a consistent pattern of shifting branches of the family taking charge over the generations, some rising to prominence for a generation or two, only to fall into insignificance or disappearing altogether in another. The family as parts of a lineage may prevail, but the actual ownership and control would change from one family branch to another quite frequently.[19]

While close identity between ownership and control might be ideally suited for large numbers of family firms, it would also place heavy restraints on growth and diversification. An entrepreneurial owner would be expected to find ways to leverage his own ownership to control a larger pool of resources. In other instances, he may also relinquish control over what he owns in exchange for some other forms of benefits. In late imperial China, partnerships were quite commonly used as a means to achieve the latter goal. In this connection, Wong's observation (noted above) that partnerships are a highly transient kind of enterprise in the beginning phase of the life cycle of the family firm, needs some modification, for there are many partnerships that have lasted for long periods of time. Many successful owners of business are known to have small minority shares in other businesses, accepting the status of minority or even of undisclosed partners (*yinming hehuo*), with no involvement in the running of the enterprise. It appears that they do so in order to facilitate their networking with one another. Others see this as a means of spreading their risks. Since traditional China recognized no legal distinction between individuals or individual families and corporations, assets and liabilities of one became blended with those of the other, with no legal concept of limited liabilities separating one category from another. However, if a partnership failed and fell into debt, the law allowed a minority or undisclosed partner not involved in the business to limit his liabilities only to the full extent of his capital contributions.[20] Finally, there were those partners who concealed their identity because, as officials or as members of the upper scholar–gentry class, they were not supposed to own businesses. However, as noted earlier, it was widely known and quite openly accepted that officials or their families had family businesses. What the concealment did was to avoid disclosing the full extent of their business ownership. In this situation, as in the two others discussed above, control was purposely sacrificed in exchange for other benefits.

On the other hand, a successful owner is more anxious to leverage his ownership into larger spheres of control. And he has had greater opportunity to do so since 1904, when the Chinese government adopted into law the Western concept of limited liability for corporations, together with the registration and the public subscription of company stocks. The idea was to allow large corporations to be formed through the pooling of large amounts of capital from the public. However, until the 1950s, not many companies resorted to its use, because the registration required extensive disclosures that entrepreneurs were reluctant to provide to the government, while most Chinese with any savings were unwilling to invest in companies with which they had no personal relationships.[21]

However, there were many notable exceptions. The Wing On group of companies in Shanghai and Hong Kong, for example, made the corresponding registration with the Hong Kong authorities so that Guo Luo and Guo Quan, the two brothers who ran it as a tightly controlled family firm and as one of China's largest commercial establishments from the 1910s to the 1940s, were able to maintain effective control with just 5 percent of the total company stock. They did so with careful placement of interlocking directorships, and the use of old-fashioned networking with thousands of individually small shareholders, almost all of whom the two Guo brothers knew personally and with whom they shared overseas experiences in Australia or Hawaii.[22] In any event, since the 1960s, resorting to public subscriptions while retaining family control has become common among large corporate groups. This is especially true for Hong Kong and Singapore, where the presence of readily accessible financial markets and of competitive and huge multinational corporations is enhanced by minimal legal disclosure requirements regarding ownership.[23] Today, listing on the Hong Kong stock exchange is dominated by a small number of family-controlled enterprise groups, with each family exercising control through the ownership of an average 35–45 percent of the stocks of its primary companies. Among the Chinese-owned family firms of this stock exchange, the ten largest had individual market equity ranging from U.S. $3 to $16 billion in 1994. Since several families also control more than one firm each to form their enterprise groups, their size and capital resources are quite spectacular indeed.[24]

Size

The presence of these large family firms might suggest that this particular form of enterprise places no limits on size for the Chinese entrepreneur. The truth is far more complex. The great majority of Chinese-owned family firms remains small or relatively small. Even the large firms in Hong Kong and Singapore mentioned above, as well as comparable ones in Taiwan, are considerably smaller than their counterparts in the West, Japan, or South Korea. For example, in 1983 the total sales figures of the sixteen largest business groups (*keiretsu*) in Japan, at U.S. $871.3 billion, was over fifty times larger than the combined sales of U.S. $16.5 billion of the top ninety-six company groups (*jituan qiye*) in Taiwan.[25] And while Hong Kong's economy grew by leaps and bounds into a global center, the average size of firms in Hong Kong declined quite drastically, from 55.2 persons in 1950 to 18.4 persons in 1984.[26]

Indeed, many scholars argue that the relatively small size, which has been a consistent characteristic among Chinese business firms in the past, will continue unchanged into the future. The reasons given tend to be cultural and institutional. Gordon Redding expresses this view most forthrightly, arguing that the inherent nature of the family firm, with its reliance on networking and trust, would prevent its development into a large-scale, multi-unit professional organization. Both Rajeswary Brown and Karl Fields, looking at Chinese firms in Southeast Asia and Taiwan, respectively, decide that the primary reason for remaining small involves the way capital is acquired and utilized. Brown observes that Chinese entrepreneurs are primarily interested in achieving quick and high returns, and are unwilling to make large, long-term investments. For Fields, it is the limited sources of capital—from the lack of infrastructural linkages bringing savers and entrepreneurs together to the limited resources any family or groups of families can command.[27]

Examined by themselves, all the cultural and institutional reasons for the relatively small size of Chinese business firms suggested above sound reasonable and, on the whole, are supported by empirical evidence. However, if each of the cultural values and institutions is tested in interaction with the total environment, other explanations and different results can emerge.

Thus, with respect to cultural values, there is no cultural prohibition against largeness. On the other hand, in late imperial China, large-scale enterprises could be set up only as state monopolies or under official patronage. Then there was no consistent or dependable tradition of settling commercial disputes through the state's judicial process. Under this type of environment, the Chinese entrepreneur did what he thought was most expedient: He kept his business within the limits of a certain size in order not to attract excessive official attention, and made extensive use of networking, loyalty, and trust in order to lower the transaction costs of doing business. It stands to reason, therefore, that when the environment changes, networking and trust will change as well.

Such a change has been quite evident for Chinese entrepreneurs working in Hong Kong since the 1960s. As the territory's civil service bureaucracy, banking institutions, and legal establishments develop a consistently fair and efficient infrastructure that wins the trust and respect of those doing business there, networking takes on different roles, while the nature of trust is broadened to include other forms of trust. Business trust in late imperial China was particularistic and personal; it was based on familiarity such as kinship, friendship, and mutual interest. The new form of trust, according to Siu-lun Wong, who has borrowed the term from the German sociologist Niklas Luhmann, is called "system trust." It is built on an impersonal and generalized faith in a society that has an equitable and functioning system. Wong draws from the results of an extensive 1988 survey of social indicators conducted in Hong Kong to show how the new system trust has taken hold there. It appears that about two-thirds of the 1,662 representative respondents, among whom are business owners, express high faith in Hong Kong's judicial, governmental, and socioeconomic institutions.[28] In other words, a sizable majority of business owners in Hong Kong trusts the courts, the civil service, and the financial institutions to provide economic opportunities, enforce contracts, and settle disputes. It also explains how, with the newly acquired cultural and institutional tools, some of the Hong Kong family-owned enterprises have developed into large-scale corporations.

Similarly, other changes in the environment are likely to make Brown's quick-return-of-capital entrepreneurs more ready to build large-scale production facilities as long term investments. This seems to be taking place more and more often and across national boundaries as Chinese entrepreneurs in much of Southeast Asia acquire varying degrees of system trust and feel more integrated within their communities or have better collaboration with the indigenous political and military leaders. When system trust is combined with both traditional networking and the rising global economy, they become an increasingly powerful force for the integration of the region's economy. Finally, as for Fields's capital-scarce Taiwanese investors, as Taiwan's financial infrastructure goes through its reforms, and as the government now encourages companies to develop large-scale operations to better compete in the global market, more of them, like those in Hong Kong, are turning to public subscriptions to fund large projects while working out new corporate group structures (*jituan*) to grow into complex large enterprises.

Large-scale operations requiring intensive capitalization and complex coordination are therefore no longer strangers to the family firm, which seems to be quite adept at taking advantage of the new environment to develop new forms and practices. How this is carried out will be the subject of later discussion. Here, to continue our analysis on size and the family firm, it is critical to try to understand why most Chinese-owned firms continue to stay relatively small. First, there are limited sources of capital, as already noted. It seems that most Chinese entrepreneurs continue to rely on the financial resources of small circles of families and friends, on internally generated sources of funds, such as those resulting from the reinvestment of profits. Second, whenever the owner–entrepreneur of a family firm plans for the future, his plan is inevitably influenced by the traditional practice of equal inheritance among the sons, so that he is much more likely to start up, or financially help his sons to start up, several companies with related or unrelated lines of business, than to relentlessly enlarge existing ones.

Third, under certain conditions and for certain types of businesses, small-scale operations may simply be the most efficient and competitive. Francis Fukuyama observes that in recent years, countries dominated by relatively smaller firms such as Taiwan, Hong Kong, and Italy have achieved higher economic growth rates than their neighbors who have larger firms. It seems, when compared with very large corporations, that smaller, more informally structured firms enjoy greater flexibility and can make faster adjustments to changing product needs and market conditions. Joseph Bosco, an anthropologist who is intrigued by the fact that Taiwan's rapid industrialization has been led by small-scale family factories, argues along the same line, then goes on to point out that as existing socioeconomic conditions change, what constitutes useful and efficient size may also change. Thus, he shows how during the earlier phases of Taiwan's economic modernization, Taiwanese owners of small family enterprises and partnerships exploited the tightness of control, kept trade secrets, bypassed labor regulations, and minimized taxes, used informal networks for loans and contracts, and registered their businesses in their wives' names in order to limit liability. But, as Taiwan moves from the early stages of industrialization to capital- and knowledge-intensive industries, a different set of socioeconomic environmental factors will propel the same entrepreneurs to run operations with far larger scopes and scales. Similarly, Fukuyama also points out that the advantage of small size is likely to be limited to only some sectors of the economy. In a global economy that is increasingly interdependent and dominated by large multinational corporations, many vital high-tech sectors of the economy, such as the aerospace and aircraft industries, will continue to require complicated coordination and high technology systems of production under the control of large-scale, multitiered, and multi-unit enterprises.[29]

Structure and Strategy

By now it should be clear that as new environments emerge, Chinese entrepreneurs are able to successfully run operations of different organizational sizes. However, there seem to be several core values and practices that they have acquired over the centuries when the firm was small and simple, and that still endure. In the area of structure and strategy, what has endured includes family control and ownership, central decision-making, networking, a reliance on highly personal ties, and an informal chain of command at the top. There are also significant areas of changes, and these include a wider range of corporate sizes, a more inclusive sense of trust based on an infrastructure that provides a favorable climate to conduct business, and Western-style multi-unit organization, professional management, and the practice of integrated production. As for the firm's relationship with the government, the traditional practice was to work with government-appointed or -approved agencies, such as the guilds and trade associations on regulatory and communal matters, and to minimize direct contact with the government bureaus. There was a profound suspicion of government direction, because political authority was seen as capricious, hostile, and in need of careful manipulation. In contrast, firms today look to the state for infrastructural supports, for help in market access to other countries, and for favorable legislation. They also remain suspicious of excessive state control. A large part of Hong Kong's economic success is often credited to the noninterventionist policy of its government. Recently, the failure of government policies in both Taiwan and Singapore to slow the flow of capital by their own entrepreneurs to China and Southeast Asia, respectively, shows how difficult it is to restrain one's own companies.[30]

The following two examples of Chinese entrepreneurs, each of whom owns a large-scale family enterprise group, will illustrate how those traditions and changes are being carried out. The first is Thailand's Dhanin Chearavanont, whose father Chia Ekchor had started a family business in the production of vegetables and seeds some seventy-five years ago, first in Shantou, China, and then in Bangkok. As it added other farm goods and implements, the business grew rapidly, and by the early 1940s, it had become a large agribusiness with a large distribution network throughout Southeast Asia. From the 1950s through the 1970s it expanded further by forming close networking ties with political and military leaders not only in Thailand but also throughout Southeast Asia, and by entering into several joint ventures and franchises with American and Japanese companies, then using the acquired technology to go into modern mass production of chicken eggs, broilers, and animal feed. By the time Dhanin took over its leadership in the early 1980s, the family firm, by now known as the CP Group (for Charoen Pokphand), was developing into a multibillion dollar transnational business conglomerate of breweries and discount-retail chains, telecommunications, and high-tech electronic fabrication. Born in Thailand but educated in China, Dhanin was among the first to return to China when that country opened up for foreign investment in the late 1970s. With personal friendships extending to the highest ranks of the Chinese communist leadership, he quickly branched out into different operations by forming additional joint ventures with major Western and Japanese companies such as Heineken, Walmart, Ford, Honda, and Continental Grain. Today, with 250 companies in twenty countries and 100,000 employees, the Bangkok-based CP Group has invested $2 billion of its own funds in about 130 joint-venture projects in China to become its largest foreign investor. Dhanin's family fortune, estimated at $4.2 billion, makes him and his family among the world's wealthiest.[31]

Considerably larger than Dhanin in both personal wealth and the size of family-owned business operations is Hong Kong's Li Ka-shing. During the past ten years, he has expanded his two primary companies, Cheung Kong Holdings and Hutchison Whampoa, from about $20 billion to $50 billion in market capitalization (versus CP Group's $13.7 billion). Starting very modestly in synthetic-hair manufacturing during the early 1960s, he built his fortune on Hong Kong's rising property market, then expanded into a whole range of servicing, retailing, utilities, and telecommunications industries by taking over several premier British-owned companies in Hong Kong. His latest phase of expansion takes him into the Chinese market. There, he devotes the same amount of attention as Dhanin to networking, but uses different strategies to look for markets and capital. Thus, in concentrating on such infrastructural industries as real estate developments, toll roads, bridges, and power plants, Li returns to his core business. His joint-venture partners are mostly Chinese from China, while he makes use of Hong Kong's world-class financial resources and off-shore banking facilities, which are far richer than Bangkok's, to help fund his projects there.[32]

Yet, in spite of their enormous size and high complexity of operations, both Li and Dhanin insist on retaining family ownership and management control. They do not dispense with professional managers or a Western-style organizational format. Both rely on a large number of seasoned professionals from outside the kin and family circles to run their various companies. And they are quick to make use of modern technology such as database systems to raise efficiency and maximize the flow of information. This shows the effectiveness of having a professional staff and modern organization, and the deftness with which Li and Dhanin conclude transnational and crosscultural joint ventures and business projects. Indeed, many of Li Ka-shing's corporations are former British hongs steeped in English traditions and practices. And for many years, his closest and senior adviser was an Englishman by the name of Simon Murray.

But these new organizational patterns do not displace the traditional cultural preferences for loyalty, mutual trust, or keeping up one's good name (*xinyong*) in order to increase one's chances of running a successful operation with minimal transaction costs. Both systems are in place to complement each other. Dhanin, for example, quite openly exploits and extols his skillful business and political networking to open doors in China and elsewhere. World famous corporations court him and become his joint-venture partners precisely because of his extensive and well-placed connections (*guanxi*). Moreover, these old-fashioned values and tools of entrepreneurship are most evident in the planning of strategies and carrying out of major decisions among the owners. Even for large operators like Li and Dhanin, at their top management level, each one turns to a small, informal group of senior advisers, using a simple hub-and-spokes mechanism to maintain control and to help them make their final decisions. Both also take seriously the task of grooming their sons to take over their respective operations someday. Dhanin's eldest son is the chief executive officer of one of his major operations, the Thai cable-TV company. Li's son has recently been promoted to vice-chair and heir-apparent, and this took place soon after his long-time adviser Simon Murray was sent off into retirement.

Conclusion

The Chinese family firm, which still makes up the great majority of all Chinese business enterprises today, remains vigorous and profitable because it is both flexible and tenacious: flexible in adapting to the challenges of each new environment, yet tenacious in holding on to a set of core cultural values and institutional frameworks. Thus, to reiterate an example already discussed, Chinese entrepreneurs who had relied exclusively on personal trust to conduct business were able to broaden it to system trust when they realized that the modern state provided them with reliable legal, administrative, and economic institutions. At the same time, despite the family firm's many transformations, especially during the past century, there are certain essential forms and styles that remain constant—elements such as personal relationships, networking, ownership, and control.

The ability of the family firm to re-create itself into a new mix of various elements—cultural, institutional, and organizational—in order to optimize opportunities within each new environment is what makes it such a potent force in the reemerging economy of East and Southeast Asia. This refutes one major thesis advanced by Francis Fukuyama in his recent book, *Trust: The Social Virtues and the Creation of Prosperity*, where he argues that Confucianist China, with its low level of social trust, will fail to create a business organization large or flexible enough to compete in the global economy. There are others who express similar concerns but for different reasons, such as the continuing emphasis on family ownership and control. In all cases, it seems that these critics fail to take into account the entrepreneurs' flexibility in their responses. Thus, in the case involving allegedly insufficient social trust, we have seen how they have extended personal trust to system trust, which, as a form of universalistic trust, is closely related to social trust. In any event, there can be no question that entrepreneurs like Li Ka-shing and Dhanin Chearavanont are capably conducting large-scale business projects, often with parties in whom they have no personal trust, yet in a manner that is highly competitive in the world market. As for size, it is likely that none of the contemporary large-scale corporate groups owned and managed by Chinese entrepreneurs will ever reach the size of a Mitsui or a Hyundai. But this is due to the fact that capitalistic development among the Japanese, Koreans, and the Chinese has gone along different paths. What is critically more relevant is that those large-scale Chinese enterprises, with their own characteristics, have reached a size at which their economies of scale allow them to compete effectively.

And what of the future? No one can predict what forms and contents the Chinese firm will take. What is certain is that all its elements may change, including those parts that have remained constant, for neither culture nor institution is permanent. The Chinese firm has so far consistently held onto elements such as family ownership, personal relationships and networking. But this is partly because it has functioned largely in communities—even in those areas like Thailand and Indonesia in which ethnic Chinese are a minority—where these same values, based on emphasizing social bonds and not on individuals, are highly regarded. As more Chinese firms spread to North America and Europe, differences in the local environment will in due course likely bring changes to these elements that have endured up until now.

Notes

1. Alfred D. Chandler, Jr., *Strategy and Structure: Chapters in the History of the American Industrial Enterprise* (Cambridge: MIT Press, 1962); idem, *The Visible Hand: The Managerial Revolution in American Business* (Cambridge, MA: Belknap Press, 1977); Alfred D. Chandler, Jr., with Takashi Hikino, *Scape and Scope: The Dynamics of Industrial Capitalism* (Cambridge, MA: Belknap Press, 1990). See also William N. Parker, "A 'New' Business History? A Commentary on the 1993 Nobel Prize in Economics," *Business History Review* 67, no. 4 (winter 1993), pp. 623–36.
2. Max Weber, *The Religion of China: Confucianism and Taoism*, translated by Hans Gerth, ed. with an introduction by C.K. Yang (New York: Free Press, 1951); S. Gordon Redding, *The Spirit of Chinese Capitalism* (Berlin and New York: Walter de Gruyter, 1990).
3. Marion Levy, Jr., and Kuo-heng Shih, *The Rise of the Modern Chinese Business Class* (New York: Institute of Pacific Relations, 1949); Albert Feuerwerker, *China's Early Industrialization: Sheng Hsuan-huai (1844–1916) and Mandarin Enterprise* (Cambridge: Harvard University Press, 1958).
4. Jane Kate Leonard and John R. Watt, eds., *To Achieve Security and Wealth: The Qing Imperial State and the Economy, 1644–1911* (Ithaca, NY: East Asia Program, Cornell University, 1992).
5. Robert P. Gardella, "Qing Administration of the Tea Trade: Four Facets over Three Centuries," in Leonard and Watt, eds., *To Achieve Security and Wealth; pp. 97–118.*
6. G. William Skinner, ed., *The City in Late Imperial China* (Stanford: Stanford University Press, 1977); William T. Rowe, *Hankow: Commerce and Society in a Chinese City, 1796–1889* (Stanford: Stanford University Press, 1984); Linda C. Johnson, *Shanghai: From Market Town to Treaty Port, 1074–1858* (Stanford: Stanford University Press, 1995).
7. Susan Mann, *Local Merchants and the Chinese Bureaucracy* (Stanford: Stanford University Press, 1987).
8. Wellington K.K. Chan, *Merchants, Mandarins, and Modern Enterprise in Late Ch'ing China* (Cambridge: Harvard University Press, 1977); Kenneth Pomeranz, " 'Traditional' Chinese Business and Capitalist Rationality Revisited: Family, Firm, and Financing in the History of the Yutang Co. of Jining, 1779–1956," *Late Imperial China*, 18, no. 1 (June 1997), pp. 1–38.
9. Redding, *The Spirit of Chinese Capitalism*; Francis Fukuyama, *Trust: The Social Virtues and the Creation of Prosperity* (New York: Free Press, 1995).
10. David Faure, "A Note on the Lineage in Business," *Chinese Business History* 1, no. 2 (1991), pp. 1–3; Madeleine Zelin, "The Rise and Fall of the Fu-Rong Salt-Yard Elite: Merchant Dominance in Late Qing China," in Joseph Esherick and Mary Rankin, eds., *Chinese Local Elites and Patterns of Dominance* (Berkeley: University of California Press, 1990).
11. Chi-cheung Choi, "Competition Among Brothers: The Kin Tye Lung Company

SPRING–SUMMER 1998   143

and Its Associate Companies," in Rajeswary Brown, ed., *Chinese Business Enterprise in Asia* (London and New York: Routledge, 1995), pp. 97–114; Wellington K.K. Chan, "The Organizational Structure of the Traditional Chinese Firm and Its Modern Reform," *Business History Review* 56, no. 2 (summer 1982), pp. 218–35; Pomeranz, "'Traditional' Chinese Business and Capitalist Rationality Revisited."

12. Wellington K.K. Chan, "Personal Styles, Cultural Values, and Management: The Sincere and Wing On Companies in Shanghai and Hong Kong, 1900–1941," *Business History Review* 70, no. 2 (summer 1996), pp. 141–66; Sherman Cochran, *Big Business in China: Sino–Foreign Rivalry in the Cigarette Industry, 1890–1930* (Cambridge: Harvard University Press, 1980); Robert P. Gardella, *Harvesting Mountains: Fujian and the China Tea Trade, 1757–1937* (Berkeley: University of California Press, 1994); Andrea L. McElderry, *Shanghai Old-Style Banks (Ch'ien-chuang), 1800–1935* (Ann Arbor: University of Michigan, Center for Chinese Studies, 1976); Zelin, "Rise and Fall of the Fu-Rong Salt-Yard Elite."

13. Wellington K.K. Chan, "Chinese Business Networking and the Pacific Rim: The Family Firm's Roles Past and Present," *Journal of American–East Asian Relations* 1, no. 2 (summer 1992), pp. 171–87; David Faure, "Capitalism and the History of Chinese Business," unpublished paper presented at the Chinese Business History Conference, Centre of Asian Studies, University of Hong Kong, July 12–13, 1996.

14. Marie-Claire Bergère, *The Golden Age of the Chinese Bourgeoisie, 1911–1937* (Cambridge: Harvard University Press, 1989); Parks Coble, *The Shanghai Capitalists and the Nationalist Government, 1927–1937* (Cambridge: Harvard University Press, 1986); Lloyd Eastman, *The Abortive Revolution: China Under Nationalist Rule, 1927–1937* (Cambridge: Harvard University Press, 1974); Thomas G. Rawski, *Economic Growth in Prewar China* (Berkeley: University of California Press, 1989).

15. William C. Kirby, "China Unincorporated: Company Law and Business Enterprise in Twentieth-Century China," *Journal of Asian Studies* 54, no. 1 (February 1995), pp. 43–63.

16. Rajeswary A. Brown, *Capital and Entrepreneurship in Southeast Asia* (London: Macmillan, 1994); Gary Hamilton, ed., *Business Networks and Economic Development in East and Southeast Asia* (Hong Kong: Centre of Asian Studies, University of Hong Kong, 1991); S. Gordon Redding and R.D. Whitley, "Beyond Bureaucracy: Towards a Comparative Analysis of Forms of Economic Resource Coordination and Control," in Stewart Clegg and S. Gordon Redding, eds., *Capitalism in Contrasting Cultures* (Berlin and New York: Walter de Gruyter, 1990).

17. "Family" here refers to the fundamental social unit of association in Chinese society, each unit commonly living in one or several households and consisting of individuals who own common property and share kinship relationships either through blood or marriage. "Lineage" refers to a group of families whose male members claim descent from a common male ancestor.

18. Siu-lun Wong, "The Chinese Family Firm: A Model," *British Journal of Sociology* 36, no. 1 (March 1985), pp. 58–72.

19. Chan, "Traditional Chinese Firm and Its Modern Reform"; Pomenranz, "'Traditional' Chinese Business Forms Revisited"; Choi, "Kin Tye Lung Company and Its Associate Companies."

20. Kirby, "China Unincorporated," p. 46.

21. Chan, *Merchants, Mandarins, and Modern Enterprise*, pp. 180–83.

22. Chan, "Personal Styles, Cultural Values, and Management."

23. Tahirih V. Lee, "Coping with Shanghai: Means to Survival and Success in the Early Twentieth Century—A Symposium—Introduction," *Journal of Asian Studies* 54, no. 1 (February 1995), pp. 3–18.

24. Feng Bangyan, *Xianggang Yingzi caituan 1841–1996* (British Financial Conglomerates in Hong Kong, 1841–1996) (Hong Kong: Joint Publishing, 1996), p. 461.

25. Gary G. Hamilton and Marco Orru, "Organizational Structure of East Asian Companies," in Kae H. Chung and Hak Chong Lee, eds., *Korean Managerial Dynamics* (New York: Greenwood, 1989), p. 43.

26. Simon Tam, "Centrifugal Versus Centripetal Growth Processes: Contrasting Ideal Types for Conceptualizing the Developmental Patterns of Chinese and Japanese Firms," in Clegg and Redding, eds., *Capitalism in Contrasting Cultures*, pp. 153–84.

27. Rajeswary A. Brown, ed., *Chinese Business Enterprise in Asia* (London and New York: Routledge, 1995); Karl Fields, "Anatomy of a Financial Scandal: The Rise and Fall of the Cathay Business Group," unpublished paper presented at the Center for Chinese Studies Spring Regional Seminar, University of California, Berkeley, April 27, 1991; Redding, *Spirit of Chinese Capitalism*.

28. Siu-lun Wong, "Chinese Entrepreneurs and Business Trust," in Hamilton, ed., *Business Networks and Economic Development in East and Southeast Asia*, pp. 13–29.

29. Fukuyama, *Trust: The Social Virtues and the Creation of Prosperity*, p. 25; Joseph Bosco, "The Role of Culture in Taiwanese Family Enterprise," *Chinese Business History* 3, no. 1 (November 1992), pp. 1–4.

30. Gary G. Hamilton, "Overseas Chinese Capitalism," in Tu Wei-ming, ed., *Confucian Traditions in East Asian Modernity: Moral Education and Economic Culture in Japan and the Four Mini-Dragons* (Cambridge: Harvard University Press, 1997), pp. 340–41.

31. Paul Handley, "De-Mythologising Charoen Pokphand: An Interpretive Picture of the CP Group's Growth and Diversification," unpublished paper presented at the International Conference on Chinese Business in Southeast Asia, University of Malaya, Kuala Lumpur, June 23–25, 1997; *Far Eastern Economic Review*, January 23, 1997, pp. 38–45; East Asia Analytical Unit, Department of Foreign Affairs and Trade, Australia, ed., *Overseas Chinese Business Networks in Asia* (Canberra: AGPS Press, 1995), pp. 323–26.

32. Anthony B. Chan, *Li Ka-shing: Hong Kong's Elusive Billionaire* (Hong Kong: Oxford University Press, 1996); Feng, *Xianggang Yingzi caituan 1841–1996*, pp. 232–50; *Economist*, January 11, 1997, pp. 58–59.

Chinese Studies in History, vol. 31, nos. 3–4, Spring–Summer 1998, pp. 145–50.
ISSN 0009–4633/1998 $9.50 + 0.00.

PARKS M. COBLE

Comments and Reflections on Chinese Business History

In reading over the articles by Professors Hao and Chan, I would make several general observations. First, historical studies necessarily reflect the particular time and place in which they are written. In the 1950s, the nations of East Asia, China in particular, were poverty stricken, and no economic miracle was in sight. The Soviet model appeared a viable rival to capitalism as a strategy for economic development. As Yen-p'ing Hao notes in his article, dominant issues of much early scholarship dealt with explaining "China's failure to modernize," the limitations of family firms, and the weaknesses of Chinese entrepreneurship. We have, for instance, Feuerwerker's classic study that discusses the "tardy" nature of Chinese development by focusing on the limitations of the *guandu shangban* form of business organization.[1]

Today, perceptions are much different. The market appears triumphant, socialism dead and dying, and government involvement is widely seen as a certain bet to slower growth. China seems a most vibrant part of the international economy. Overseas Chinese businessmen and ethnically Chinese areas such as Singapore and Taiwan are perceived as part of "Greater China." The question is not being asked why China's growth is 'tardy' but why China's economy and business structure has become so dynamic. Is it the family firm, the Confucian heritage, or other combinations of factors? As Wellington Chan notes, we have gone from reading Max Weber on why Confucianism retarded economic development to Gordon Redding on how Confucianism promotes business culture.

From a paper presented at the workshop on Scholarly Research on Chinese Business History: Interpretive Trends and Priorities for the Future, University of Akron, October 27–29, 1995.

Parks M. Coble is on the faculty of the University of Nebraska–Lincoln, Department of History.

These reflections of the present moment dominate much of the current writing by journalists and pundits (which far outweighs in volume that of historians), as well as output by writers in business administration and management studies. A similar approach dominates much of the writing coming out of China itself, where the celebration of the economic dynamism of Chinese society permeates a great deal of what has recently been published. The difficulty of this "present-ist" euphoria is that if circumstances change, entire new sets of questions will become en vogue. One needs only to remember the sudden shift of the pundits from explaining why Japan was "number one" to explaining the collapse of the bubble economy. One day the Ministry of International Trade and Industry (MITI) and the Japanese government were working miracles in partnership with business, and the next they were accused of creating protected sectors of the economy that could not withstand international competition.

Undeniably, as both Hao and Chan indicate, academic studies of Chinese business history reflect changing circumstances. History, as I noted above, is written in a particular time and place. Yet what is striking is the enduring strength of so much of the scholarship cited in the two articles. The academic studies of Chinese business history transcend much of the "present-ism" of more popular studies. By placing the development of business in Chinese societies within the framework of a century or more of change and development, we are able to ask more enduring questions. Indeed, one can read Feuerwerker's study *China's Early Industrialization* about the *guandu shangban* style of enterprise and apply many of those insights toward understanding the hybrid businesses that have developed in China since the reforms of Deng Xiaoping. Feuerwerker's insights into the structure and problems of government-connected business offer a point of departure for examining the new forms of enterprises that have emerged in China. Indeed in his keynote address to the conference from which this volume has evolved, "Doing Business in China over Three Centuries" [see pp. 16–34], Feuerwerker reminded us of the precedence of politics over economics and the significance of particularlistic criteria over this sweep of time.

The articles by Yen-p'ing Hao [pp. 106–26] and Wellington Chan [pp. 127–44] discuss issues central to an understanding of Chinese business history: What is the nature of Chinese business organization? Is the Chinese family firm uniquely Chinese or is it similar to family firms elsewhere? Is there a lesser tendency toward the large, impersonal enterprises as described by Chandler than in other societies? What is the relationship of Chinese enterprise to government and how has that changed under different political circumstances? What is the nature of Chinese entrepreneurship? In examining these kinds of issues over historical time, much of this scholarship retains an enduring quality that is missing in so much of the contemporary writing about Chinese business.

A second observation I would make is that the academic studies cited are also very much a captive of sources. The greatest change in the study of Chinese business history in the past generation has been the opening of China for academic research. Indeed, the business records held at archival institutions in China are some of the richest in the world. Whereas many Western firms retain control and access to their archives, most economic units in China lost control of their records in 1949. When these have been made available, they have allowed work such as Sherman Cochran's examination into the Nanyang Brothers Tobacco Company.[2] Yet the process has been uneven. Far more material is held in China and listed as available in archival catalogues than has been actually accessible to outside scholars on a regular basis. Institutions in China that have been welcoming to foreign scholars have had proportionally a much greater impact on Western studies. The Shanghai Academy of Social Sciences, its scholars, its research agenda, and its publications, have had a dominant influence in our field, in large part because of the openness of the institution and its willingness to work with Western scholars.

The problems and opportunities of archival work in China contrast with those of Chinese enterprises outside of the mainland. Because much scholarly work now focuses on Chinese firms in "Greater China," we confront the reality that many business held by overseas Chinese are secretive, have often existed in environments perceived as hostile to ethnic Chinese, and have very opaque business practices and records. Indeed, the difficulties of doing extensive work on the enterprises of Dhanin Chearavanont or Li Ka-shing, to cite two businessmen mentioned by Wellington Chan, would appear daunting. Approaches used for this research are often quite different than archival work, and include extensive reliance on interviews. One thinks of Ellen Oxfeld's masterful study of Hakka leather manufacturers in India, *Blood, Sweat, and Mahjong: Family and Enterprise in an Overseas Chinese Community*, as an example of this type of study.[3]

A third observation I would make is that the two articles remind us of the dual heritage of the field of Chinese business history. Most of the scholars listed in these articles are a product of "China studies." Their academic training has been in the China field; they have demonstrated an ability to work in Chinese language sources. Because of the structure of the academic world, most teach academic courses broadly related to China or to their disciplines; few can be narrow specialists in Chinese business history. At the same time, a great part of the methodology and approach used in our studies derives from that developed in the very separate discipline of Western business/economic history. One need only look at the numerous references in the works cited to Western scholars such as Alfred Chandler, Schumpeter, Gerschenkron, and the like. These Western scholars have framed the debate to which those of us in the China field react.

Even the academic institutional affiliations reflect this dual heritage. Most of the students of Chinese business history in North America are active participants in the Association for Asian Studies. The Chinese Business History Research Group is an affiliate of this body. Yet, many have also become affiliated with business history associations primarily composed of scholars who study North America and Europe. This dual heritage gives scholars of Chinese business history an opportunity to be a bridge between these two worlds. Insights from the Chinese experience are a vital part of the global history of business enterprise; scholars of Western enterprises will benefit from reading the work of Wellington Chan and others on the Chinese family firm. At the same time, insights from the far more advanced and theoretically sophisticated field of Western business history can be applied to understanding the Chinese experience.

Finally, these articles on Chinese business history by two of its leading scholars reveal not only the richness of the field but also its infancy. Although we have many strong pioneering studies by Hao, Chan, Sherman Cochran, Robert Gardella, and Albert Feuerwerker, just to name a few, the summary of half a century of scholarship also reveals that much remains to be done. Many questions still call for answers. What are some of the questions that should be pursued?

First, both Hao and Chan make the point that we need to study individual enterprises in particular times and places. It seems quite clear that when we define Chinese business history to include virtually all forms of business operated by ethnic Chinese, we are dealing with an extraordinary range of environments. If we examine the relationship of business and government, for instance, in Shanghai, the nature of the government in question will be radically different from 1930 to 1940 to 1960 to 1990. The changes from a semicolonial international city, to a city occupied in war, to the Mao years, to today's reform era, have brought extraordinary transformations in government and the political environment. Studying the operation of enterprises in that environment is challenging and rewarding. When one moves to "Greater China," the disparity is also great. A firm operated by ethnic Chinese in Indonesia or Burma faced and faces different political issues than one operating in Singapore or colonial Hong Kong. This extraordinary range of political and social environments over time and geographical space makes the topic of government–business relations complex. Much remains to be done.

A second issue is the nature of the Chinese enterprise. Wellington Chan's article reminds us that the family firm remains a dominant form in the Chinese environment. But, Chandler notwithstanding, it is not a form that can be easily dismissed as backward and traditional. His article also reveals that evaluating the family firm is a complex and difficult task, one that would benefit enormously from studies of individual companies. In her recent study, *Native Place, City, and Nation: Regional Networks and Identities in Shanghai, 1853–1937*, Bryna Goodman examines native-place associations.[4] Usually dismissed as traditional, parochial, and particularistic, these institutions should presumably give way to the construction of modern, universalistic, and impersonal groups. Yet, Goodman argues quite successfully that the native-place groups were a very plastic form; a traditional structure that changed over time. Indeed, she makes a strong case that the modern nationalist movement was greatly strengthened by these regional associations.

In reading Wellington Chan's article on the family firm, I was struck by the parallels with Goodman's approach. The family firm would seem to be "old-fashioned," traditional, and limited. Most theorists would say that it should give way to the impersonal, corporate form of organization. However, Chan clearly demonstrates its vitality. The small family firm has served as the basis of Taiwan's miracle economy. Yet, it has also ballooned into huge enterprises such as that of Li Ka-shing. Chan even argues that some Hong Kong groups have created large, publicly held companies that still retain family control. The issues raised in Wellington Chan's article are clearly ones that require more research and should yield exciting new insights into business history, the relations between business and government, and between business and culture.

Finally, one area of research that has not been heavily discussed in either of these articles is the development of business firms in the People's Republic. Much of the work that has been done, of course, has been published in article form rather than in books. In the past ten years, hybrid structures, such as village and township enterprises and even some state enterprises, are operating in new ways. Issues of ownership are murky; connections (*guanxi*) often overrule the marketplace; and continued growth remains uncertain. Yet, in the final analysis, the economy of mainland China has been rapidly expanding in the past twenty years. The factories, businesses, and financial institutions involved in this process are changing in rapid and complex ways. The study of Chinese business history offers approaches to understanding some of these changes. The historical knowledge of the *guandu shangban* experience provides a comparative basis. Insights into the behavior of overseas Chinese firms will help understand the complex involvement of these groups as they reinvest in China. Understanding the institutions emerging in China will be a challenge for scholars of Chinese business history, but it may be the most rewarding aspect of our scholarship.

If the study of Chinese business history is in its infancy, it already shows prospects of being an important scholarly field. Potentially it should tell us a great deal about Chinese society, culture, government, and economy. In scholarly terms, it should provide a bridge from "area studies" to broadly comparative international research.

Notes

1. Albert Feuerwerker, *China's Early Industrialization: Sheng Hsuan-huai (1844–1916) and Mandarin Enterprise* (Cambridge: Harvard University Press, 1958), passim.

2. Sherman Cochran, *Big Business in China: Sino–Foreign Rivalry in the Cigarette Industry, 1890–1930* (Cambridge: Harvard University Press, 1980).

3. Ellen Oxfeld, *Blood, Sweat, and Mahjong: Family and Enterprise in an Overseas Chinese Community* (Ithaca, NY: Cornell University Press, 1993).

4. Bryna Goodman, *Native Place, City, and Nation: Regional Networks and Identities in Shanghai, 1853–1937* (Berkeley: University of California Press, 1995).

Chinese Studies in History, vol. 31, nos. 3–4, Spring–Summer 1998, pp. 151–65.
ISSN 0009–4633/1998 $9.50 + 0.00.

DANIEL NELSON

Western Business History

Experience and Comparative Perspectives

In recent decades, Western business history has grown in volume and sophistication, creating important benchmarks for students of Chinese and other non-Western business systems. At its best, it has emphasized the limitations of traditional historical scholarship, blurred customary distinctions among business history, economic history, and the history of technology, and underlined the common features of market economies characterized by diverse economic activities. Business history thus serves as a forceful reminder of the power of economics and technology over culture. It also illustrates the obstacles that lie ahead for Chinese business historians. Western business historians have emphasized change over time under conditions of relative economic freedom, where risk-taking and technical and organizational creativity are the principal routes to individual wealth and power. To study the operation of business in a context where change has been slower, economic freedom more circumscribed, and market stimuli more subdued poses challenges that the Western example cannot adequately address.

Origins

American business history dates from the early twentieth century and the particular political climate of that era. Nineteenth-century American history had been characterized by conflict between business groups, notably between farm proprietors and nonfarm entrepreneurs. The emergence of large private

From a paper presented at the workshop on Scholarly Research on Chinese Business History: Interpretative Trends and Priorities for the Future, University of Akron, October 27–29, 1995.
Daniel Nelson is on the faculty of the University of Akron, Department of History.

transportation and communications corporations during the middle third of the century had given these conflicts a new and sharper focus: The large corporation became the enemy to farm and nonfarm groups alike. The critics' intramural hostilities precluded a uniform reaction or the success of most antimonopoly and antitrust political initiatives, but they did not prevent the emergence of the trust issue as the dominant public issue of the period from the 1870s to the 1930s. The great merger movement of the turn of the century, which created large industrial (as opposed to commercial) corporations and exacerbated concerns about the future of the economy and of individual opportunity, heightened the political debate. It also provided a stimulus to business history.

By the early twentieth century, histories of large corporations and corporate executives had become powerful contributors to the assault on big business. Indeed, two historical works, Ida Tarbell's *The History of the Standard Oil Company* (1904) and Gustavus Myers's *History of the Great American Fortunes* (1909), were among the most notable muckraking exposés of their era. Designed to titillate popular audiences and mobilize support for political causes, they graphically illustrated the political character and potential of this style of historical writing.

Scholarly business history had different origins, although it, too, reflected the political environment of the early twentieth century. One stimulus was the rise of an American historical profession based on rigorous document-based German scholarship. Most professional historians devoted their attention to public policy issues and strongly identified with the critics of big business, hence the term "progressive history," which became the dominant political influence in academic history writing. Regardless of political or ideological inclinations, however, historians rejected the notion of history as propaganda. Historical scholarship was to be document-based, comprehensive, and objective insofar as possible.[1] Historian-scholars began to write histories of industries and firms that were comparable to the best studies of political institutions, and biographies that were equal to the best political biographies.

A second milestone came in 1927, when the Harvard Business School appointed N.S.B. Gras as professor of business history with a mandate to create a body of useful historical scholarship. Gras had begun his career as a student of the medieval grain trade and had no identifiable political position. Yet he was not oblivious to the School's links to the fortunes that writers like Tarbell and Myers had attacked, nor to its role in supplying apprentice managers to the corporations and banks that symbolized Wall Street to defenders and critics alike. Coupled with the obligation to be useful, that is, illustrative of how firms actually operated, this perspective dictated a cautious approach. Gras's work, and that of the scholars he gathered around him, was meticulous, detailed, nonpolitical, and descriptive.[2] It depicted, generally from the perspective of top managers, the evolution of the individual firm, often over a century or more. It examined problems associated with starting businesses, developing markets, creating new products, managing transitions between generations of owners and managers, and addressing the myriad other obstacles and challenges that executives faced in the nineteenth and early twentieth centuries.[3] The Gras studies were almost exclusively of firms that had deposited their records at the Business School. New England companies, mostly manufacturing companies, predominated. Most of them had long and successful histories. None of them was well known outside the region, none were big businesses, none was particularly controversial. Their histories were therefore success stories largely devoted to individuals and events. They are useful primarily as reference works. Finally, despite their rigorous empiricism, they probably contributed to a new, more balanced view of business that emerged in the 1920s. The executives described in the Harvard studies were conservative, hard-working, and community-spirited. They struggled to gain and retain markets, confront competitors, and survive in difficult times. There was no John D. Rockefeller or Andrew Carnegie among them. Their world, though hardly static, was vastly different from the world the muckrakers had portrayed. When Gras, in 1929, attempted to write an introduction to business history, he could do no better than a series of stages, starting in medieval Europe. He devoted less than half of the book to the nineteenth and twentieth centuries. Indeed, the twentieth-century chapters, describing what he termed "finance capitalism" and "national capitalism," are notably flaccid and unrevealing.[4] In effect, he acknowledged what any reader of the Harvard studies is likely to conclude: They did not lead to meaningful generalizations or a larger perspective.

In the meantime, the big business issue had arisen again with the onset of depression and would soon create a more enduring legacy of business history. Much of the polemical writing of the early 1930s, whether liberal, socialist, or communist, was based on the muckraking accounts of a generation before. Wall Street and big business were invariably the targets. Small business firms (including farmers) were again the victims, though not so often or so notably as in earlier accounts; the plight of individuals, especially industrial workers, was more appealing in an era of mass unemployment.[5] Nevertheless, the most celebrated work of this genre was distinctly of the old school. Matthew Josephson's *The Robber Barons* (1934) was Tarbell and Myers redux, together with a dollop of Marxian determinism. It retold the stories of Rockefeller, Carnegie, Morgan, and other nineteenth century titans who were cast as medieval outlaws. Unlike Gras and his colleagues, Josephson did no primary research and wrote nothing of value to an apprentice manager. His portrayal of the clash between good and evil was designed as a political tract, with resounding effect. Although most readers probably never got beyond the first or second chapters, Josephson's title endured. For a generation, the term "robber baron" and the implication of lawlessness, social irresponsibility, and immorality would dominate the portrayal of the origins of big business in the nineteenth century.[6]

Josephson's work might have shared the fate of most popular histories except for Allan Nevins. One of the most prolific and influential historians of the middle third of the century, Nevins wrote massive life-and-times biographies of prominent industrialists, including John D. Rockefeller and Henry Ford. His Rockefeller biography, published in 1940, was subtitled "The Heroic Age of American Enterprise."[7] Although the work is a conventional life and times, it was designed to be read as a refutation of Josephson. The effect, ironically, was to legitimize Josephson's work. Although Nevins unequivocally rejected the robber-baron label, he seemed to endorse Josephson's approach. The personal behavior and sense of social responsibility of high executives, rather than the organization or operation of the business, was the measure of business achievement. In the following years, books, articles, and especially texts with titles like *The Robber Barons: Saints or Sinners?* became popular. Explicitly or implicitly, they assumed that the task of the business historian was to render judgments on the morality of big business and the actions of big business leaders.[8]

By the late 1940s, the limitations of this perspective had stimulated a cautious revisionism. The best example was the work of the Research Center in Entrepreneurial History, which operated at the Harvard Business School in the late 1940s and 1950s. Under the inspiration of Arthur H. Cole and others identified with the Harvard school who had grown impatient with the seemingly aimless empiricism of the Gras studies and superficiality of the robber-baron debate, the Center sought to transcend the traditional bounds of business history. Cole and the scholars and graduate students he attracted derived much of their inspiration from the social sciences, notably sociology. Accordingly, they sought to make entrepreneurship, rather than the firm or a group of individuals, the intellectual foundation for business history.[9] By most measures, they failed. Although most of the Center-sponsored studies were well received and many participants became prominent scholars, "entrepreneurial history" had little enduring influence. It was too vague to have broad appeal and did not address the political issues that traditional historians associated with business history. In the following years economic history became an adjunct of theoretical economics, while business history underwent a parallel transformation that provided a new and more compelling focus.[10]

The Managerial Revolution

The modern era of Western business history dates from the late 1950s and is closely associated with two developments, one general and one specific. The general development was a derivative of the post-war economic and political environment, especially the decline of the class and interest group tensions of the late 1930s and the emergence of a new, more positive view of big business as a contributor to prosperity and social harmony. The specific development was the emergence of a dominating individual, Alfred D. Chandler, Jr. Chandler's influence, almost unimaginable in the political climate of the pre-war years, redefined the character of Western business history and provided a starting point for anyone interested in the role of big business in Western society, or in the larger context created by the emergence of big business.

Chandler's major publications include *Henry Varnum Poor: Business Editor, Analyst and Reformer* (Cambridge: Harvard University Press, 1956); *Strategy and Structure: Chapters in the History of the Industrial Enterprise* (Cambridge: MIT Press, 1962); *Pierre S. Du Pont and the Making of the Modern Corporation*, with Stephen Salsbury (New York: Harper and Row, 1971); *The Visible Hand: The Managerial Revolution in American Business* (Cambridge, MA: Belknap Press, 1977); and *Scape and Scope: The Dynamics of Industrial Capitalism* (Cambridge, MA: Belknap Press, 1990).[11]

At MIT, Johns Hopkins, and Harvard Business School (where he held Gras's old chair in the 1970s and 1980s), Chandler launched a highly successful assault on both the Gras legacy and the robber-baron tradition. More important, he argued persuasively for a new interpretation of the role of the large corporation as a reflection of economic and especially technological forces in nineteenth-century society. From his perspective, Josephson, Nevins, and their many imitators had simply asked the wrong questions. Rather than the fundamental "what happened?" they had stressed the more subjective "was it good or bad?" Chandler was no less emphatic in rejecting the idea that events spoke for themselves and that each firm was *sui generis*. Chandler's work was explicitly interpretative and revisionist. It soon became the starting point for virtually all explorations of the twentieth-century economy.[12]

Although Chandler wrote mostly about organizational innovation and the role of the manager, his starting point was the centrality of technology to economic and societal change. Small family-owned and -operated firms prevailed before the mid-nineteenth century because primitive transport and communication technologies made it uneconomical to operate on a larger scale. Steam power and telegraphy were preconditions for larger factories and more sophisticated distribution systems. Improved transportation and communications in turn encouraged technological innovation in production and the creation of a new generation of larger and more mechanized factories. Chandler also insisted that technology limited the spread of big business. Only where the firm could achieve economies of scale (reducing unit production costs) and scope (using a single production system to produce multiple products or services) did large, multifunction enterprises make sense. In other industries, small traditional firms remained viable and big businesses typically failed. Chandler thus provided a reasoned refutation to the implication common to progressive history of an ever more powerful Wall Street and an economy monopolized by a handful of plutocrats. Finally, he explained how successful large firms perpetuated themselves by investing in research and development, creating related products for their factories and distribution networks, and generating new technologies to replace declining technologies.

In the Chandlerian world, individuals counted. Corporate managers rationally evaluated operations and markets and allocated investments. Failure was common. But success depended less on individual genius or ruthlessness than on the ability to create an effective organization, one that permitted middle managers to gauge the possibilities and limitations of their environment. *Strategy and Structure* documented the process by which twentieth century big business executives adapted structure (from centralized to decentralized, divisional management) to strategy (from a single product to a diversified group of products). One of his favorite examples of the power of organization was the rivalry between Ford and General Motors (GM) in the 1910s and 1920s. Despite its initial success, Ford retained its primitive early form, misjudged its environment, thwarted the development of an able cadre of middle managers, and declined. General Motors ultimately succeeded because it created an organization that enabled its managers to realize the industry's potential.[13]

Chandler summarized his message in the title of his best-known book, *The Visible Hand* (1977). In countries where modern technologies permitted economies of scale and scope, the visible hand of the manager rather than the invisible hand of the market coordinated economic activity. The principal mechanism of coordination was the vertical integration of business functions, notably production and distribution. Thus, the rise of big business meant not only the emergence of corporations that were big in size (in assets, sales, employees, etc.) but also, and more important, in function. The classic examples were in manufacturing, where a handful of businesses took advantage of improved transportation and communications to introduce improved production methods and in-house distribution and marketing activities, making the single-function industrial firm and the independent wholesaler obsolete, and dominating industries for many years. Vertical integration was more important than horizontal combinations (mergers of like producers) because mergers did not necessarily lead to economies of scale and scope. Mergers, however, often served as a stimulus to reorganization and vertical integration.

The revisionist character of Chandler's work is apparent from a brief summary of late nineteenth-century American history. Rockefeller and Carnegie (together with Gustavus Swift, O.C. Barber, and others) were examples of entrepreneurs who recognized the possibilities of innovative technologies in transportation, communications, and manufacturing. They took advantage of those opportunities to create modern factories, efficient distribution systems, and hierarchical organizations to guide the flow of goods and services to the retailer or consumer. They were no more creative or ruthless than the many executives who misjudged their environments and failed. Nor were they pawns of Wall Street; production and distribution, not finance, were crucial to success. The losers, on the other hand, included some of the wealthiest businessmen of the time, the proprietors of the specialized single-function firms that emerged in the early nineteenth century. Most notable was the eclipse of the jobber, the wholesaler who bought from manufacturers and sold to retailers. By the early twentieth century, a pattern had appeared that would persist for most of the century. Large firms dominated transportation, communications, and high-volume manufacturing, while traditional firms dominated agriculture, most manufacturing, and most services.

In *Scale and Scope* (1990), his most recent work, Chandler showed how this pattern also characterized the business systems of Germany and, to a lesser degree, Britain. Although culture and politics modified the process at many points, technology and organization ultimately guided them as they had the evolution of the American business system. The result was a gradual convergence in economic structure and marked similarities in economic performance.[14]

Chandler in Retrospect

Chandler's message, repeated with mounting empirical support in articles and books over more than a quarter century, has left an indelible stamp on Western business history. Disciples and quasi disciples, including a growing cadre of European historians, have made complementary contributions. Critics have found Chandler equally useful. Even in Britain, where economic history writing has long emphasized industries rather than firms, Chandler's work had a catalytic effect.[15] In the 1970s and 1980s, Japanese business historians demonstrated that Chandler's paradigm was equally useful in non-Western settings.[16] Richard R. John is presently completing a detailed evaluation of post-Chandlerian writing with copious references.[17] My purpose is broader: to indicate areas where Chandler's work raises interpretive issues and to assess his intellectual (as opposed to his professional) impact.

Chandler devotes considerable attention to individuals and individual actions, as befits a historian, but virtually no attention to the human qualities that make individuals distinctive and understandable. He explicitly rejects the invisible hand of the neoclassical economist and the determinism of the Marxist, yet the people who dominate his accounts are little more than names. His two biographical studies, of Henry Varnum Poor, a nineteenth century editor who published a leading railroad trade journal, and Pierre S. Du Pont, an executive who reorganized DuPont and General Motors, are his weakest books. Poor is a remote figure who never emerges from his technical writing, and Du Pont is even more perplexing: a workaholic who retired in his fifties to devote himself to gardening and philanthropy; an ascetic who developed one of the great estates of the early twentieth century; a devotee of family life who avoided personal relationships and married his cousin at age 45, mostly, it appears, to have someone to manage his domestic affairs; a private man who was a behind-the-scenes power in the Democratic Party; Du Pont was, at minimum, an intriguing individual.[18] Yet to Chandler he was simply a representative of a new generation of well-educated, clear-thinking, rational decision makers. Studies of big business executives have documented their elite status, so it is hard to argue with this designation; Chandler is right as far as he goes. But even in this rarefied company, personality often had (and has) a decisive impact. Presumably the business historian is no less obligated than others to weigh the importance of individual characteristics and eccentricities.

If Chandler paid little attention to the human qualities of the people at center stage, he devoted no attention whatsoever to the chorus and orchestra, the employees who made up the base of the corporate hierarchy. In this respect he is not unlike Gras, Nevins, and even Josephson. Inexplicably, Western labor history has always been seen, and seen itself, as a distinctive, largely unrelated subject. There are good reasons for this de facto divorce: the practice of delegating production management and labor relations to low-level operating managers, which meant that few records reached corporate archives; the cultural divide between white and blue collar employees; and the growing geographic separation of executives from production workers. But there are even better reasons for integrating business and labor history. The large corporations of the turn-of-the-century years succeeded because they became more efficient as they became larger, contrary to the conventional assumption that impersonal relationships would lead to inefficiency. Chandler explains how this happened, but not how the people most intimately involved in the production process contributed to it.

To appreciate the workers' contribution, it is useful to consider the two fundamental choices of employees in hierarchical organizations: exit and voice. In a market economy, dissatisfied workers can quit (or be fired) or they can organize to express a collective voice.[19] The trade union is the classic expression of voice, but there are many less formal examples. Indeed, the century's most famous research on the operations of a large corporation, the "Hawthorne" studies (conducted at AT&T's Hawthorne plant, near Chicago), documented the pervasive presence of informal organizations and the techniques they used to adapt corporate policies to group goals.[20] The implication was that an authoritarian boss was a failed boss. Only by enlisting employees in the work of the organization and persuading them of the legitimacy of the organization's goals could the executive succeed over the long term.

Many of the corporate executives that Chandler features grasped these insights long before social scientists arrived on their doorsteps. Managers who sought to control markets also sought to influence the behavior of employees. The four corporations that Chandler featured in *Strategy and Structure* (DuPont, GM, Standard Oil of New Jersey, and Sears) were all pioneers in personnel management. With few exceptions, larger corporations were responsible for innovations in personnel work, industrial relations, and human resources management.[21] They sought to reduce exits by curtailing supervisors' powers and creating nonwage benefits, such as pensions and insurance plans. Some of them sought to provide acceptable outlets for the workers' voices. Though consistently anti-union, they were rarely involved in aggressive open-shop drives and other illegal or controversial activities. The most notable exceptions, the steel manufacturers, were also laggards in other areas. Most of the century's labor turmoil occurred in coal mining, clothing, and textiles, industries dominated by small, single-function firms.

In short, there is no reason apart from tradition to distinguish between the activities of executives and other employees. Although Chandler was among the most astute interpreters of production methods, he emphasized the external implications of innovations in production technology. He might just as easily have explored their impact on the shop floor. Those who have focused on workers have rarely had a comparable understanding of the larger context of business activity.

If Chandler's neglect of the workers has received little attention, his neglect of government and public policy has occasioned more notice. In the Chandlerian scenario, technology is the principal stimulus to economic change, and technological innovation is a product of individual and corporate creativity. This emphasis reflects his preoccupation with the United States and with industry in the late nineteenth and early twentieth centuries. At other times government has played a more assertive role. In agriculture, transportation, banking, communications, and energy—the regulated sectors of the U.S. economy, which embrace a variety of large and small firms—public policy has been the decisive stimulus to change, including technological change. In all industries, labor, social welfare, environmental, and civil rights laws have had a greater effect on large firms than on small firms. At the macroeconomic level, fiscal and, in particular, monetary policy have had a substantial impact on corporate policy-making. In Europe and Japan, the role of the state as planner and formal or informal allocator of investment funds, and in some cases as operator of industrial corporations, has added another layer of influence. Chandler and his followers have recognized these effects and taken them into account in their more recent studies,[22] but have resisted the temptation to accord the state a primary role in Western business systems.

In summary, Chandler has almost single-handedly changed the character of business history. The robber-baron debate is passé and no one would argue that generalizations about American or European business systems must await more company histories or business biographies. Terms like vertical integration, decentralization, throughput, economies of scale and scope, and mass production have become common. In few other areas of historical research has an individual had a comparable effect or greater influence in defining what matters and what should be studied. Still, there are limits to Chandler's influence. His neglect of labor and public policy has left significant gaps. The larger trend among historians generally toward microscopic social histories has also had an insidious effect, diverting attention from large institutions and sweeping generalizations alike. Most of all, the complexity of the Western economies has limited the utility of all generalizations, no matter how insightful.

Other Approaches

Though the Chandler school has dominated Western business history for more than twenty years, it accounts for only a small fraction of the high quality work that has appeared during that period. Ironically, as the focus of business history as a discipline has narrowed, the range of business history writing has broadened. Virtually no era or subject has been overlooked. The following comments suggest the breadth of Western business history and the range of additional examples and models available for students of Chinese business history.

While the Chandler school emphasizes patterns of activity within and between firms rather than the history of the firm per se, single company histories remain popular. A large proportion are authorized histories, commissioned to commemorate a turning point in the company's development, create an institutional memory, or communicate a corporate culture to employees or the public. Most of them focus on the actions of top executives, the development of distinctive products and services, and major external events. Most—but not all—are highly particularistic in focus and convey little sense of the evolution of an industry, a functional activity, or a national business system. This is especially true in studies of small firms. The exceptions tend to be histories of railroads, airlines, or other participants in well-defined industries that have been examined in detail.[23] Histories of industrial firms vary widely, depending on the size of the firm and its products, the availability of records, and the receptiveness of executives at the time the project was undertaken.

A notable example in which I am personally involved illustrates some of these possibilities. The history of the B.F. Goodrich Company, scheduled to appear in 1996, was commissioned to commemorate the one hundred twenty-fifth anniversary of the founding of the company.[24] The authors were given a substantial budget and access to the company's archives, including material from the 1970s, 1980s, and 1990s. The result is essentially two stories: a relatively conventional history of business growth, new product development, and responses to external challenges up to the mid-twentieth century, and a different and more intriguing history of organizational evolution and turmoil in the succeeding years as the company evolved from a classic mass producer of rubber products, mostly for the automobile industry, to a chemical manufacturer, and, more recently, a supplier to the aircraft and defense industries. Although a single company narrative, B.F. Goodrich's history includes discussions of research and development, the role of technology in corporate evolution, acquisitions and divestitures, managerial succession, and financial issues. It is unusual, perhaps distinctive, because the authors have been given unrestricted access to records and individuals and have deliberately assumed a skeptical attitude toward their patrons. Most readers, including most employees, will be drawn to the final chapters, which deal with contemporary developments, rather than to the historical material.

Although most Western business historians are preoccupied with big business, a significant minority has addressed the role of the small firm in the era of big business—recognition of the continuing vitality of small, usually family-owned enterprises, the inherent differences between big and small business, and the fact that the majority of wealthy people have always been, and continue to be, owners of small businesses, not Chandler's top or middle managers. Studies of successful small firms in industries with a significant big-business presence have demonstrated that the small producers were different. As Mansel Blackford notes, "By carving out market niches, and by developing new production methods, small businesses could remain as independent enterprises in successful coexistence with larger firms."[25] After 1900, government often helped small enterprises create and sustain a market niche. For example, government support for family farms, single-unit banks, and independent retailers was a vital influence in the evolution of those industries. In other instances, new economic relationships, such as franchising, enabled small firms to take advantage of the growth of large corporations. The underlying theme of all these studies is the adaptation of small business to the rise of big business.

Other important trends in business history writing reflect contemporary business developments. One of these, which also bears the imprint of the Chandler school, is the role of technology in business development and behavior, including the work of corporate research laboratories and of noncorporate sources of technological change. Studies of technological change as an exogenous force, similar to Chandler's treatment of the effects of railroads on manufacturing and commerce, have become more prevalent. A notable recent example is JoAnne Yates's study of the relationship between tabulating and computing technology and the life insurance industry. As users of tabulating devices, insurance companies gained or lost competitive advantage through their responses to changing technologies. As purchasers, they were also positioned to influence the product developments of the machinery makers.[26]

Another theme related to Chandler's work and contemporary interests is the growth of multinational business activity in the twentieth century. Until the 1970s, scholars focused on the flow of European capital into American transportation and mining enterprises and on U.S. investment abroad, notably in Latin America. Since the appearance of Mira Wilkins's studies of direct investment and the growth of public awareness of "global" business activity, historians' interests have broadened substantially. Particularly helpful has been a shift from investment abroad—a subject that lends itself to quantitative studies—to more expansive issues, such as the spread of ideas, values, and social institutions. Two themes on which I have worked, international differences in higher education for business, and the flow of scientific management ideas among the United States, Europe, and Japan, are illustrative of this trend.[27]

By far the most popular subject—because it involves a variety of subdisciplines besides business history—is the role of government in business decision-making. The convergence of business history and policy history, the history of the creation and implementation of public policy, is particularly promising.[28] The work of leading scholars such as Ellis Hawley and Thomas McCraw suggests that the relationship has been varied, often convoluted, and difficult to interpret. The progressive historians' portrayal of conflicts between economic interest groups and the people, with government as a surrogate for the people, is at best misleading. But is there a superior approach? Despite the ever growing volume of work, business–government relations have yet to produce a Chandler.

Finally, industrial relations and human resource policies have commanded growing attention. The decline of organized labor has emphasized the importance of labor issues that are unrelated or only indirectly related to traditional subjects like formal organization, collective bargaining, and strikes.

Other contemporary issues are likely to have substantial effects in the future. In recent years, the largest corporations have come under attack for their inability to keep pace with competition, including foreign competition. The decentralized structure that Chandler identified as a key to their success is now cited as a source of costly sloth. In many cases, middle managers have been discharged in efforts to improve short-term financial performance. Does this trend represent a short-sighted fad, like the conglomerates of the 1960s, or a reversal of the managerial revolution, as popular writers have suggested?[29] If they are right, when did the process begin and what effects is it likely to have on business and business history writing?

These speculations should not obscure the fact that big business and corporate organization, top-down histories that emphasize organization building and technological creativity, dominate Western business history and will likely dominate it for many years. Though political factors will receive more attention and transnational operations and comparisons of business activities in different countries will become more popular, the large corporation remains the overriding concern of Western business history. The process that Chandler initiated in the 1950s has transcended the milieu that originally encouraged it and has had a pervasive impact in the United States, Europe, and Japan. It should be the starting point of scholarly efforts to make sense of the role of the firm and the business community in China.

Notes

1. See Peter Novick, *That Noble Dream: The "Objectively Question" and the American Historical Profession* (New York: Cambridge University Press, 1988).
2. Gras's approach was partly utilitarian: to provide case studies used in his business history course, a practice that continues to the present.
3. Louis Galambos, *American Business History* (Washington: American Historical Association, 1967), pp. 1–4. Most of these works appeared in the Harvard Studies in Business History, which Gras edited.
4. N.S.B. Gras, *Business and Capitalism: Introduction to Business History* (New York: F.S. Crofts, 1939).
5. See, for example, Walter B. Rideout, *The Radical Novel in the United States, 1900–1954* (Cambridge: Harvard University Press, 1954).
6. See, for example, Peter D'A Jones, ed., *The Robber Barons Revisited* (Boston: Heath, 1968).

7. Allan Nevins, *John D. Rockefeller and the Heroic Acre of American Enterprise*, 2 vols. (New York: Scribner, 1940).

8. See Thomas B. Brewer, ed., *The Robber Barons; Saints or Sinners?* (New York: Holt, Rinehart, and Winston, 1970).

9. See Hugh G. J. Aitken, ed., *Explorations in Enterprise* (Cambridge: Harvard University Press, 1965).

10. See, for example, Robert William Fogel, "The New Economic History: Its Findings and Methods," in Fogel and Stanley L. Engerman, eds., *The Reinterpretation of American Economic History* (New York: Harper and Row, 1971), pp. 1–12.

11. Chandler also wrote dozens of articles and book chapters, many of which had wide influence. Indeed, his most widely read work is probably his article "The Beginnings of 'Big Business' in American Industry," *Business History Review*, no. 33 (spring 1959), pp. 1–31, and numerous reprints. For a comprehensive list of Chandler's works, see the bibliography in McCraw, *The Essential Alfred Chandler*.

12. For Chandler's career, see Thomas K. McCraw, "Introduction: The Intellectual Odyssey of Alfred D. Chandler, Jr.," in *The Essential Alfred Chandler: Essays Toward a Historical Theory of Big Business* (Boston: Harvard Business School Press, 1988), pp. 1–21.

13. See, for example, Chandler, *Giant Enterprise: Ford, General Motors, and the Automobile Industry* (New York: Harcourt, Brace and World, 1964).

14. See *Scale and Scope* and "The Competitive Performance of U.S. Industrial Enterprises Since the Second World War," *Business History Review*, no. 68 (spring 1994), pp. 1–72.

15. Though acknowledging Chandler's influence, British historians have argued that his characterization of British business in *Scale and Scope* reflects an "ethnocentric model based on the United States." Maurice W. Kirby and Mary B. Rose, eds., *Business Enterprise in Modern Britain: From the Eighteenth to the Twentieth Century* (London: Routledge, 1994), p. 13.

16. See especially W. Mark Fruin, *The Japanese Enterprise System: Competitive Strategies and Corporate Structures* (Oxford: Clarendon Press, 1992), and the International Conference on Business History Series, 1974–, published by the University of Tokyo Press. A notable example is Tsunehiko Yui and Keiichiro Nakagawa, eds., *Japanese Management in Historical Perspective* (Tokyo: University of Tokyo Press, 1989).

17. Richard R. John, "American Business History Since the Visible Hand: Elaborations, Anomalies, and Revisions," unpublished manuscript, 1995.

18. See Alfred D. Chandler, Jr., and Stephen Salsbury, *Pierre S. Du Pont and the Making of the Modern Corporation* (New York: Harper and Row, 1971). See also David E. Kyvig, *Repealing National Prohibition* (Chicago: University of Chicago Press, 1979).

19. Richard B. Freeman and James L. Medoff, *What Do Unions Do?* (New York: Basic Books, 1984), chaps. 1 and 6. See also Olivier Zunz, *Making America Corporate, 1870–1920* (Chicago: University of Chicago Press, 1990).

20. See Richard Gillespie, *Manufacturing Knowledge: A History of the Hawthorne Experiments* (New York: Cambridge University Press, 1991).

21. Sanford Jacoby, *Employing Bureaucracy; Managers, Unions, and the Transformation of Work in American Industry, 1900–1945* (New York: Columbia University Press, 1985).

22. See Richard H.K. Vietor, *Contrived Competition: Regulation and Deregulation in America* (Cambridge: Harvard University Press, 1994).

23. See, for example, Keith L. Bryant, *History of the Atchison, Topeka and Santa Fe Railway* (New York: Macmillan, 1974); H. Roger Grant, *Erie Lackawanna: Death of an*

American Railroad, 1938-1992 (Stanford: Stanford University Press, 1994); W. David Lewis and Wesley Phillips Newton, *Delta: The History of an Airline* (Athens: University of Georgia Press, 1979).

24. Austin Kerr and Mansel Blackford, *BF Goodrich* (Columbus: Ohio State University Press, 1996).

25. Mansel Blackford, *Small Business in America: A History* (Boston: Twayne, 1992), p. 38. See also Philip Scranton, "Diversity in Diversity: Flexible Production and American Industrialization, 1880-1930," *Business History Review*, no. 65 (spring 1991), pp. 27–90.

26. JoAnne Yates, "Co-evolution of Information-Processing Technology and Use: Interaction Between the Life Insurance and Tabulating Industries," *Business History Review*, no. 67 (spring 1993), pp. 1–51.

27. See the essays in Nobuo Kawabe and Eisuke Daito, eds., *Education and Training in the Development of Modern Corporations* (Tokyo: University of Tokyo Press, 1993), and the introduction to *A Mental Revolution: Scientific Management Since Taylor* (Columbus: Ohio State University Press, 1992).

28. See the new *Journal of Policy History* for a variety of articles on these issues.

29. Anthony Sampson, *Company Man: The Rise and Fall of Corporate Life* (New York: Random House, 1995).

Chinese Studies in History, vol. 31, nos. 3–4, Spring–Summer 1998, pp. 166–68.
ISSN 0009–4633/1998 $9.50 + 0.00.

KEITH L. BRYANT, JR.

Response to Daniel Nelson's "Western Business History: Experience and Comparative Perspectives"

Professor Daniel Nelson's article [see pp. 151–65] presents an overview of the evolution of business history in the United States. He notes at the outset that business historians have emphasized the limitations of traditional historical scholarship; have blurred the former boundaries between business, labor, and economic history and the history of technology; and have demonstrated the commonalities of market economies characterized by diverse economic activities. Business history, he argues, reminds us of the power of economics and technology over culture. I would not go that far, a point to which I shall return.

The early sections of the article review the evolution of business history from the emergence of the "robber baron" school and the progressive historians to the creation of the business history group at Harvard University after 1927. The scholarly output from N.S.B. Gras and his colleagues was thoroughly researched and highly descriptive. It provided no framework by which the growth of capitalism in the United States could be interpreted. By the 1930s, Allan Nevins and his army of researchers had challenged the robber-baron school and had created the "captains of industry" perspective. Ironically, both the debunkers and the defenders of the industrial giants emphasized the personalities of a few key individuals. They were not interested in the structure of enterprise or how firms actually functioned. This debate failed to advance

---

From a paper presented at the workshop on Scholarly Research on Chinese Business History: Interpretative Trends and Priorities for the Future, University of Akron, October 27–29, 1995.

Keith L. Bryant, Jr., is on the faculty of the University of Akron, Department of History.

our understanding of managerial capitalism. It would take Alfred Chandler's leadership and insights to develop a modern, broadly interpretative body of business historians.

Nelson's analysis of Chandler's contributions and influence are absolutely on target. The international impact of Chandler's theories may be seen in the constant references to him and his theories in the other articles presented in this volume. Again and again, the Chandler model has been applied to various aspects of Chinese business history. Nelson's criticisms of Chandler's analysis are also fruitful. The organizational theories of Chandler as laid out in *Strategy and Structure*, *The Visible Hand*, and *Scale and Scope* are the basis for business history in this country and in Western Europe. Technology, economies of scale, managerial leadership, and structural evolution formulated modern capitalism, Chandler contends. He emphasizes individuals within the structure, especially the professional managers, not necessarily the owners of the firm. Chandler also notes failures as well as successes. Flexibility, vision, and able subordinates were crucial to those who were successful. The "visible hand" of the manager rocked the cradle of capitalism. Entrepreneurs who grasped and seized opportunity did so through innovation, technology, and sophisticated communication. The Chandler theses dominate the field.

But, as Nelson argues, there are flaws in the Chandlerian world. Throughout his major studies there are people, but they never come alive as actors, as personalities. Chandler's innovators create giant enterprises, but where are the workers in the factories? Who are they? What do they do? And how do they respond to the changing workplace? In the Chandler analysis government's role is minimal, indeed, government is largely a passive instrument. Chandler's actors recite lines on the stage, they move vigorously, but they lack passion and fire. Managers employ millions of workers who are only numbers. The entrepreneur operates, seemingly, beyond the influence of government. As Nelson argues, these omissions are not only critical, but they also suggest the limitations in applying the Chandlerian hypotheses to Chinese business history.

While I am in basic agreement with Nelson's analysis, I believe that he stresses technology and innovation too strongly. It appears to me that cultural and societal norms are far more significant than Nelson suggests. Entrepreneurs and managerial capitalists are not always rational creatures, and their decisions are often dictated by the environment in which they operate. Corporate cultures often reflect the values of the society in which they operate to the detriment of the firm. The deterioration of IBM's position in the marketplace in the 1980s has been attributed to an ingrained corporate culture that failed to respond to a rapidly changing society. Cigarette manufacturers have largely responded with obfuscation to rising opposition to their product. Eastern Airlines and Pan American retained large first class sections in their planes, even as deeply discounted fares on competing carriers took away passengers. Such corporate behavior is not limited to capitalistic societies. The government of China continues to produce steam locomotives in large plants when it is clear that diesel electric and electric locomotives are far more efficient. A national culture, the goals of the state, and even a dominating religion can limit the choices of business managers. Firms operating in the Middle East, for example, must take into consideration the presence of Islam and the views of its adherents.

How then is the Chandlerian to use the theories of the master in Chinese business history? Obviously, with caution. There are major questions on which Chandler's concepts can inform researchers. In China, how did small firms respond to the creation of large-scale enterprises, private or state? Wellington Chan's article [see pp. 127–44] shows the importance of family relationships in the formulation of Chinese enterprises. Fathers and sons, uncles and nephews played significant roles in firms, and outsiders found little hope for advancement. Having competed with grandsons and cousins at Ford Motor Company, Lee Iaccoca could identify with this problem. Chinese family enterprises are not unlike those that resulted in the United States from the 1870s to the 1920s when family firms in the East and Middle West sent sons and nephews to the West to form banks, invest in real estate, and create mercantile firms. Some articles in this volume emphasize provincial differences in China in the formulation of enterprises and in the support, or lack of support, of the creation of business activities. Within the United States, the South has lagged behind the rest of the nation, and many Westerners see their region as a "plundered province" stripped of its natural resources. Regional differences are significant in Chandler's analysis. The rise of petroleum companies in the Southwest after 1900—Texaco, Magnolia, Humble, Sinclair, and Conoco—undermined Standard Oil Company's monopoly to a greater extent than did the use of the Sherman Antitrust Act by the federal government. Chandler's shifting focus from trade and traders, merchants and merchandising is also seen in the symposium papers. The endnotes refer to numerous studies of banks, large-scale state enterprises, the rise of manufacturing, and efforts to create heavy industry. Chandler's theories offer suggestions as to how these shifts can be interpreted.

In Alfred Chandler's work, Chinese business historians can find ways to view internal operations of firms, decision-making strategies, the employment of innovations and technology, and the evolution of business structures. But, scholars should also be aware of the need to incorporate the workers and the state into such an analysis and to turn the managers into flesh and blood with personalities. Daniel Nelson's paper provides an excellent analysis of the state of business history in the United States, and his insights should serve to enhance and enlighten the scholarship of Chinese business historians.

Chinese Studies in History, vol. 31, nos. 3–4, Spring–Summer 1998, pp. 169–88.
ISSN 0009–4633/1998 $9.50 + 0.00.

CHI-KONG LAI

Enterprise History

Studies and Archives

Recently there has been a growing interest in the study of the history of Chinese enterprises. Several conferences have been organized, and proceedings, journal articles, and books published. There are also a number of M.A. and Ph.D. theses, written either in Chinese or in English.

The history of Chinese enterprise at present is being written from a variety of historical sources such as company archives, legal records, local gazetteers, biographical materials, family instructions, novels, memoirs, personal letters, diaries, genealogies, missionary records, and foreign affairs documents. New archival sources are also being discovered all the time. The goal of this article is to review recent trends in enterprise case studies and introduce the sources and archives for the study of modern Chinese enterprise history. I will also briefly illustrate the connection between these archival sources and some possible research topics in Chinese business history.

Historiographical Review of Recent Trends in Enterprise Case Studies

There is little doubt that Chinese enterprise history (*qiye lishi*) has been receiving much attention in recent literature. Since 1956, the Shanghai Academy of Social Sciences (SASS) has collected many source materials on

From a paper presented at the workshop on Scholarly Research on Chinese Business History: Interpretative Trends and Priorities for the Future, University of Akron, October 27–29, 1995.

Chi-kong Lai is on the faculty of the University of Queensland, Brisbane, Department of History.

I thank Huang Hanmin, Andrea McElderry, Dian Murray, and especially Robert Gardella, who contributed to the revision of this article.

enterprise history in Shanghai. In the past four decades, the Economics Institute of the Shanghai Academy of Social Sciences (SASS) has compiled several source materials. The most important of these are: *Liu Hongsheng qiye shiliao* [Source Materials on Liu Hongsheng's Enterprise Group]; *Rongjia qiye shiliao* [Source Materials on the Rong Family's Enterprise Group]; *Nanyang Xiongdi Yancao Gongsi shiliao* [Source Materials on the Nanyang Brothers Tobacco Company]; *Ying–Mei Yan Gongsi zai Hua qiye ziliao huibian* [Source Materials on the British–American Tobacco Company in China]; *Shanghai minzu jiqi gongye* [Source Materials on Shanghai's Domestic Machinery Industry]; *Shanghai minzu xiangjiao gongye* [Source Materials on Shanghai's Domestic Rubber Industry]; *Shanghai shi mianbu shangye* [Source Materials on Shanghai's Domestic Cotton Cloth Industry]; and *Zhongguo baoxian shizhi* [Source Materials on Chinese Insurance].[1] Scholars of the institute have also published numerous scholarly monographs on the history of Shanghai's enterprises, most of which concern famous large-scale enterprises. These include monographs on machinery firms, textile mills, tobacco companies, drugstores, department stores, and other industrial and commercial firms.[2] The Economics Institute also publishes a journal formerly entitled *Source Materials on Modern Chinese Economic History* and recently renamed *Modern China*. This journal provides scholars with an important overview of the field of Chinese economic and business history. Currently, under the leadership of Professor Ding Richu, SASS scholars are preparing a comprehensive three-volume study entitled *Shanghai jindai jingjishi* [The Economic History of Modern Shanghai].[3]

Some of the compilations of materials in the First and Second Historical Archives, in Beijing and Nanjing, respectively, facilitate research on Chinese enterprise history, and selected materials have been published by each Archives press.[4] Some recent publications related to Chinese enterprise history concern the mining industry in the Qing dynasty; selected commercial archives from the Republican period; a three-volume collection of materials on the history of the Bank of China; and sixteen volumes of *Reports of the National Resource Commission*.[5] Compilations of materials on various modern enterprises,[6] as well as the Chamber of Commerce Archives of Tianjin and Suzhou[7] will facilitate research on the nature of modern Chinese enterprises, chambers of commerce, and the Chinese bourgeoisie.

Contemporary enterprises are showing a growing interest in having their histories written by their research teams.[8] Source materials have been published both by individuals and by local archives.[9] One of the most important publishers is the Shanghai Municipal Archives, which has published some major source materials on the stock exchange in Shanghai and the Tianyuan chemical firm.[10] Other important local presses are the Fujian People's Press and Xiamen University Press, which have published source materials on overseas Chinese investment in modern enterprises and on China's maritime customs.[11] During the past four decades, major studies on Chinese business and enterprise history in Chinese include: Liu Xiusheng's study of the commodity economy and commercial capital during the Qing dynasty; Guo Yunjing's history of commerce in Qing China; Fan Jinmin and Jin Wen's study of the silk industry in the Jiangnan area; Wang Weiguan, Wu Zhengyuan, and Zhang Yingen's history of foreign merchants; and Guo Daoyang's history of Chinese accounting.[12] Some archive-based studies provide extensive documentation on technical aspects of Chinese business enterprises.[13] Others provide an overview of the history of Chinese industry[14] or of industrial development in a particular region.[15] Still others are case studies of the Chinese bourgeoisie,[16] old firms,[17] advertising,[18] and particular industries.[19] Some enterprises have published their own histories.[20]

Compilation of the sources on Chinese maritime history will also facilitate research.[21] The most important contribution is the recent publication of Nie Baozhang's collection on the history of shipping in modern China, and a second volume, edited by Nie Baochang and Zhu Yinguei, is now underway.[22] The Nautical Association of Australia, Inc. has published a useful review of Chinese shipping companies, complete with fleet lists and illustrations.[23] In Taiwan, case studies have been done on hong merchants, the Tainan business group, an overview of the silk industry of modern China, and a study of the operational and managerial structure of the Chinese railway industry.[24] The Institute of Modern History has also published some collections of business materials and some oral histories of many business tycoons.[25] These oral histories shed light on how the participants regarded the operation of the businesses they owned or in which they worked. In Hong Kong, Professors Chuan Hansheng and David Faure supervised several M.A. and Ph.D. theses on Chinese enterprise history, some of which have been published as monographs and articles.[26]

Major Archives for the Study of Chinese Business History

The above discussion of published source materials and case studies of firms concerns pre-selected materials. Scholars obviously also need to go to archives and find new materials for their research. The following remarks offer some information about major archival holdings.

Established in December 31, 1959, the Shanghai Municipal Archives houses important materials about the records of the Wing On (Yong'an) Company, the Shanghai Chamber of Commerce, and various trading associations. During the late 1940s, although many enterprises in Shanghai were reorganized, merged, or closed, most of their archives are available in the Shanghai Municipal Archives. At present, the Archives houses 1.4 million volumes of archival sources and has materials on 400 types of enterprises, not including their subsidiaries.[27] There are materials on 300 industrial enterprises, 70 financial enterprises, and a small number of commercial enterprises as well as transport, communication, and agricultural enterprises, altogether numbering approximately 50,000 volumes.

The materials on any particular enterprise tend to be few in number, most consisting of around ten volumes. Only 10 percent of the enterprise archives comprise more than 100 volumes. For example, there are 49 volumes of materials available on the Nanyang Brothers Tobacco Company, eighty-four volumes on the Sincere Company, and 112 volumes on the Sun Sun Company. In the above archives, scholars can find a large amount of data on the native place origins of the personnel, criteria and procedures for promotion and dismissal, information about employee guarantors, and staff addresses, as well as share composition and marketing materials. Several of the personnel files should contain photographs of company staff members, but some of the photographs are missing. Very few businesses left a large quantity of records. Those businesses with a large number of volumes of archives include the Wing On Company (808 volumes), the Wing On Textile Mill (3,215 volumes), and the Agricultural Machinery Company. Most of these archives include the origin and history of the company, company regulations and organization, minutes of the Board of Directors, production and operation records, and source materials on industrial relations.

The archives also house some materials on native place associations, such as the Shanghai Textile Association Archives. There are also 330 volumes of archival materials that include documents of the anti–Japanese-goods movement and information concerning the production costs and industrial disputes. Moreover, most of these enterprises and some native place associations had their own publications. The contents of these publications are extensive and include information on production technology, management style, and company culture. Researchers have yet to utilize these rich source materials.

In addition to these company archives, the Shanghai Municipal Archives also houses the records of government organizations. These include information regarding accountants and lawyers, the registrar records of companies, their balance sheets and financial statements, information on company property, and on trademarks and legal disputes. These sources, mostly from the 1930s and 1940s, are particularly valuable for the study of Shanghai's business environment during the Sino–Japanese War period.[28]

Most of the old firms in Shanghai had offices to house their own archives and did not forward them to the Shanghai Municipal Archives. After 1949, most of the old firms as well as some foreign firms were merged into state-owned hierarchies and their records were placed under the control of the central enterprises. Thus few materials are available for enterprises that were established before 1940.

During the late 1950s, many old commercial banks were closed and most of their archival materials transferred to the research unit of the Shanghai Branch of the People's Bank of China. Archives of the native banks were likewise placed with the same unit. Although this research unit houses around 1,200 volumes of materials, these documents are still not available to the public. The same unit also houses 3,479 volumes of materials on forty-seven Chinese and four foreign insurance companies. These archives include private correspondence, operational reports, insurance contracts, regulations, minutes of the board of directors, personnel reports, and introductions to the insurance business. They contain a large quantity of the private correspondence of the Bao Hua Insurance Company, including books, auditing reports, and maps of Shanghai and other port cities. The pawnshop archives contain the debit and credit accounting books of dividends, cash diaries, and contracts. The Trust Company's Archives contain several minutes of the board of directors, lists of shareholders, operational regulations, telephone books, personnel records, and salary records.

In August 1994 the research unit of the Shanghai Financial Archives of the People's Bank of China began to transfer its materials to Shanghai Municipal Archives. However, because of the process of cataloguing, the materials are still not open to the public. The materials include the records of some trust companies, insurance companies, native banks, foreign banks, and government-owned banks.

The Industrial and Commercial Administrative Bureau of the Shanghai city government (Shanghai shi gongshang xingzheng guanliju) has a research branch that has collected source materials on industrial and commercial enterprise history and banking history. The Industrial and Commercial Enterprise Alliance of Shanghai (Shanghai shi gongshangye lianhehui) has sponsored oral history projects on former Shanghai entrepreneurs who commissioned them to write their autobiographies, and these materials, which can be found at the agencies' offices and at the Shanghai Municipal Archives, are important for the study of enterprise history.[29]

The Center for the History of Chinese Enterprises Studies (Zhongguo qiye lishi yanjiu zhongxin) is part of the Economics Institute of the Shanghai Academy of Social Sciences.[30] Its director is Shen Zuwei and its deputy director, Huang Hanmin. The center houses both photocopies and original copies of some major archives of Chinese and Western firms. Materials from the Nanyang Brothers Tobacco Company, the British–American Tobacco Company, the Swire Group, Liu Hongsheng's enterprise group, the Rong family's enterprise groups, and other enterprises are available for researchers. In addition, the center houses surveys of Shanghai factories done in the 1930s and 1940s as well as industry-wide surveys. The surveys, such as the Shanghai Industrial Report and the Silk Factories of Shanghai, are in both Chinese and English and are useful sources for information on workers' wages, working conditions in the factories, and local economic conditions. Other materials include the correspondence of managers and some background materials on firms and on management styles.

Papers from Liu Hongsheng's match enterprises contain some interviews (totaling around 600,000 words) with the enterprises' former managerial staff, the result of a large-scale interviewing project carried out between 1961 and 1964. The personal business account books of Liu Hongsheng are also accessible.

The four volumes of material on the British–American Tobacco (B.A.T) Company published in 1983 represent only a fraction of the 1.2 million words of BAT materials in the Center's holdings. These volumes contain materials on the firm's organization and its subsidiaries, including financial statements, information on shareholders and dividends, the firm's operations, distribution networks, and workers' conditions. The Swire Group holdings have materials on its comprador system, its activity in China, and its competition with the China Merchants' Steamship Navigation Company, as well as information on its piers and warehouses in Shanghai and elsewhere.

At the Center, there are also files of clippings from the Shanghai Commercial and Savings Bank and selected economic materials from forty Chinese, English, and Japanese newspapers, such as *Shenbao*, the *Commercial Press* and the *Central Press*. These materials include economic editorials, financial and economic news, and various forms of Republican era economic data. Finally, the Center houses a particular law firm's archives that contain materials on accounting as well as legal and enterprise correspondence. These materials enable scholars to have access to the accounting records of 900 native and foreign enterprises, including pawnshops, factories, banks, schools, and public institutions.

Many owners of firms and their forebears have collected materials about their enterprises. Some, such as Liu Hongsheng, have also left memoirs that preserve some records from their own firms and information about investments in other enterprises. One of the most valuable private sources is family correspondence, which provides personal information on entrepreneurs. The Center for the History of Chinese Enterprise Studies has some such materials. Most private correspondence and diaries, however, are still controlled by private individuals. This would be most important data if it were readily accessible to scholars, but not many are able to do surveys on this kind of data.

The library collection in the Economics Institute of the Chinese Academy of Social Sciences in Beijing is very rich and contains some source materials on Chinese business history, notably the enterprise reports in manuscript form by the team of Wu Chengming. The Institute also houses photocopied materials from some major firms.

For studies of enterprise history, the People's Republic of China's (PRC) national archives—the First and Second Historical Archives—are extremely important resources. The First Historical Archives in Beijing houses Qing materials with information on traditional industries, such as copper mining. Much information on the operation of the Imperial Household Department can be found in the Imperial Household Archives at First Archives. Many have been microfilmed and are for sale. (More recently, archives in China are putting materials on CD-ROM.) Some of these records are also available in libraries, including the libraries at the Institute of Modern History in Taipei and at the Genealogical Association in Salt Lake City, Utah.

The Second Historical Archives in Nanjing houses one of the largest collections on Republican business history and also publishes many archival sources on the subject.[31] A huge collection of archival sources from Republican China's four largest national banks: the Central Bank, the Bank of China, the Bank of Communications, and the Chinese Farmers' Bank are available. Other business records available are from the Chinese Tea Company (1937–1945), the Chinese Oil Company, Ltd., the Central Shipbuilding Company, Ltd., and the Yangtze Electricity Joint-Stock Company, Ltd. There are also large holdings of materials related to the business affairs of government agencies, such as the Finance Ministry, the Department of Industry, and Commerce, the Department of Enterprises, the Department of Economics, the Bureau of Trademarks, the National Resources Council, the Central Credit Bureau, the Department of Communications, the Department of Railways, and regional railway bureaus. The archives also contain personal records and papers of individuals such as H.H. K'ung (Kong Xiangxi), whose activities were related to business affairs in the Republican period. Drawing on these personal papers of major figures, researchers can better understand their personal networks and their roles in Chinese business development.

The Second Historical Archives also preserves some materials on late Qing enterprises and institutions, such as the China Merchants' Steam Navigation Company and the Imperial Chinese Maritime Customs Administration. The China Merchants' Company collection is one of the largest on this company. It contains 7,117 volumes of enterprise records, including account books, financial statements on private and government loans and assets, minutes of the Board of Directors meetings, private correspondence, lists of shareholders, ledgers, reports on special projects, management plans, personnel records, official memorials, magazines, annual reports, warehouse management reports, maps, photographs, legal documents, documents of other enterprises, and so on. These materials enable scholars to examine the managerial side of a Chinese business operation.

The Shanghai Municipal Library houses the Sheng Xuanhuai archives, which contain private correspondence between Sheng and his associates, as well as account books, enterprise regulations, and confidential documents on real estate speculation.[32] These materials provide a complete picture of the operation of some of Sheng's self-strengthening enterprises. Some of these materials have been published by the Shanghai People's Press and some are awaiting publication. This archive is in the process of being catalogued and the projection is that it will be open to the public in three or four years. (There are also plans to put some of the materials on CD-ROM.) The Sheng Xuanhuai Archives at the Chinese University of Hong Kong Library include a wealth of materials for understanding business activities in the late Qing period. They include Sheng's letters and papers as director of several of China's first business corporations. Some of these have been published by the Chinese University of Hong Kong Press and the Institute of Modern History of the Academia Sinica in Taipei.[33] There are still some unpublished materials on merchants' participation in charity work, and Sheng's own family genealogies.

The Hong Kong Public Record office houses the records of the former colony's registered companies. According to Stephanie Po-yin Chung, it has a large quantity of materials on insurance companies, shipping companies, department stores, and banks, including the records of the Sincere Life Insurance Company and Wing On Maritime Insurance Company.[34] According to Wai-Keung Chung, these archives are records of the reregistration of about 200 Hong Kong businesses during the Japanese occupation, mostly from 1943. Each company file includes the original business registration documents, such as memoranda and articles of association, in English. The reregistration documents include a list of the board of directors, a list of shareholders, assets, balance sheets, and so on. These reregistration documents are in Chinese, but some companies have included a Japanese translation.[35]

The South China Research Centre of the Hong Kong University of Science and Technology houses some of the source materials collected by

James Hayes (as does the Hoover Institute at Stanford University). These include business records from a Hong Kong trading firm and commercial contracts of lineage groups in nearby Nanhai and Dongguan counties. The Centre also has some commercial contracts of firms and business organizations in South China. The University of Tokyo has been publishing these business materials (there will be six volumes of materials published).[36] This will enable scholars to have a deeper understanding of Guangdong's lineage structures and business operations at the village level, including examples of account books and business contracts.[37]

In the Taipei area, the Institute of Modern Chinese History at Academia Sinica, Nankang, holds a large amount of material on registered companies, both public and private, from 1926 to 1948. These records fall largely into the categories of banking, pawnshops, insurance companies, trusts, stock markets, cotton textiles and cloth, silk, steel, chemical, rubber, electricity, paper, commerce, trade, medical supplies, restaurants, the food industry, tobacco companies, department stores, salt, transport, agriculture, the building industry, and printing. Most of the records have lists of shareholders, regulations, a description of the company, and records of changes in capitalization. These are the best records for the studies of Republican enterprise history. For example, the records of the Sun Sun Company detail the minutes of shareholders meetings and the records of disputes among shareholders. We also have a list of the firms' accountants, with basic data on who these accountants were—their names, ages, addresses, qualifications, and appointment dates. This is valuable data as we seek to understand the technical staff of businesses in the Republican period. For an overview of other source materials in the Taipei area, see the spring/fall 1995 issue of *Chinese Business History*.[38]

The National Archives of Taiwan holds archives from various Republican era government agencies, including the Ministry of Finance, the Ministry of Communications, the National Resources Council, and the Economic Reconstruction Council, as well as some materials on public and private firms. Archives from the Ministry of Finance contain materials on different types of taxation, financial organizations, salt management, local finance as well as personnel records. The Ministry of Communications' archives have materials on railways, water transport, telecommunications, maps of roads, and customs department records. The National Resources Commission archives have materials on their personnel, operations, maps, and accounting records, and include some English materials. The private correspondence of major managers of the National Resources Commission is also available. The Joint Commission on Rural Reconstruction (JCRR) archives house important materials on agricultural planning and operations in Taiwan from

1948 to 1979. The Economic Planning Council Archives hold materials on American foreign aid to Taiwan.

The Chinese have had a strong presence in Australia since their first migration to the continent in the 1840s. In the past decade there has been a growing literature on Australian Chinese businesses in the late nineteenth and early twenty centuries. Conferences, such as the one on Australian Chinese held in Melbourne in 1993, have focused attention on this topic, and some books and articles have been published on the subject. In two separate case studies, Wellington Chan and Yen Ching-hwang have used the Wing On Company to illustrate the successful development of Australian Chinese department stores in Hong Kong and Shanghai.[39] They contend that the success of this Australian Chinese company depended on the entrepreneurship of its founders—the Kwok brothers. Janis Wilton's case study of a Chinese department store in northern New South Wales also provides us with examples of Australian Chinese entrepreneurs and their marriage networks.[40] However, there are no comprehensive case studies of other Australian Chinese department stores, such as the Ta-Hsu Company and the Sun Sun Company. All of these major Chinese department stores were established by Chinese immigrants from Xiangshan (now Zhongshan) County in Guangdong Province, who constituted 80 percent of the Chinese population in Sydney in the early twentieth century. Their successful enterprises deserve further study.

A few archives are available to study Australian Chinese businesses and businessmen, notably those of the tea merchant Mei Quong Tart, whose papers are held in the Mitchell Library's Genealogical Society Records in Sydney. The Mitchell Library also has some nineteenth-century Australian newspapers in both Chinese and English, and some archives of individual merchants.[41] In Melbourne, the Chinese Museum has some Australian Chinese business papers.[42] According to one source, the "most significant items in the Chinese Museum's collection are the extensive set of receipts and other documents in Chinese and English that relate to the conduct of the Foon Kee Chinese grocery business in Chinatown in the first half of this century."[43] Other sources at the same institution include a business language text for Guangchao merchants and account books of some Chinese firms and stores in Australia. The archives of the Chinese Chamber of Commerce of New South Wales (and its predecessors), 1890–1950, are available in Canberra at the Noel Butlin Archives of Business and Labour, Australian National University. This archive includes minutes of meetings, correspondence, and lists of officers, as well as some Wing On Company records.[44] The Butlin Archives also have materials on the Australia–China trade and on sugar-company compradors in various Chinese ports, as well as a very small portion of the Jardine Matheson Papers. The

Australian National University Library holds a set of Wing On Company publications. Customs records for the port of Melbourne are available at the Victoria State Archives.

For the study of Australian Chinese business networks, scholars can draw on documentary sources, such as Xiangshan County gazetteers, source materials on Macau,[45] the newspaper *Shenbao*, the Guangchao Gongsuo Archives, and the Chinese Chamber of Commerce of New South Wales Archives in the Butlin Archives Centre of Business and Labour at the Australian National University.

Very valuable as well are archival holdings in England and the United States, such as the Chinese Maritime Customs and John Swire and Sons, Ltd. Archives at the School of Oriental and African Studies Library (SOAS), the Jardine, Matheson and Co. Archives at the Cambridge University Library, the H.B. Morse Archives at Harvard University, and the British–American Tobacco Company papers at Duke University.[46] The Baker Library's Manuscript Division at Harvard University houses materials from various American firms, such as the Perkins Company. These materials provide us with data on the inside operations of foreign firms in China. In the past, business historians drew on these materials to write monographs on B.A.T and other foreign firms in China. Scholars can also draw on oral history materials in the Singapore National Archives. The oral history office has interviewed many successful entrepreneurs, and the transcripts and tapes are available to researchers.[47]

A new generation of scholars can combine these materials with newly available materials in the PRC to examine topics related to Chinese business development. Nonetheless, a number of obstacles continue to inhibit archival research in the PRC. For example, in the course of the recent economic reforms, publishers are not able to publish source materials because of funding problems. Some of the source materials themselves are endangered because of damage done by insects that are eating the paper; thus, some of the archives will not allow researchers to photocopy documents.

Finding Sources: Research Guides on Chinese
Business History

Most students of Chinese business history are not familiar with the various primary source materials that are essential for research in the field. Recently, libraries, archives, research institutes, government agencies, and individual researchers have published increasing numbers of source books aimed at educating researchers and graduate students about various types of source materials on modern Chinese history. Guidebooks identify records held in each collection in archives and some are particularly helpful in providing to scholars some hints on what is available in each archive. *A Brief Guide to the Second Historical Archives of China*, was published in 1987.[48] The Archives has also published a detailed guidebook on some of its collections. Some general guidebooks can help researchers to identify available archival records held in each record group before going to China and Taiwan.[49] Information on each record group can also be located through catalogues available in an archive. *The Universal Dictionary of Foreign Business in China* is a useful briefing on the history of foreign enterprises.[50] Chinese local archives also often publish guidebooks.[51] Major source books on archives are:

1. Alan Birch, J.C. Jao, and Elizabeth Sinn, eds. *Research Materials for Hong Kong Studies*. Hong Kong: Centre for Asian Studies, University of Hong Kong, 1990.

2. Man-houng Lin, comp. and ed. *Taiwan suocang Zhonghua Minguo jingji dang'an* [Taiwan's Holdings of the Republic of China's Economic Historical Archives]. Taipei: Institute of Modern History, Academia Sinica, 1995.

3. William Kirby and Man-houng Lin, eds. *Business Archives in the Republican Period*. Cambridge: Fairbank Center, Harvard University, forthcoming.

4. Ye Wa and Joseph W. Esherick, eds. *Chinese Archives: An Introductory Guide*. Berkeley: Institute of East Asian Studies, University of California, China Research Monograph 45, 1996.

Since many successful businessmen who formerly operated businesses in China are still active, future research methodology may combine both archival and library research with interviews of Chinese businessmen in Taiwan, China, Hong Kong, the United States, or Australia. For example, Wellington K.K. Chan and I have been interviewing a former managing director of the Sun Sun Company, Mr. C.C. Lee.[52] Interviewing former businessmen can provide us with more personal forms of information for reconstructing the lives of Chinese entrepreneurs and managers. Janis Wilton's *Hong Yuen: A Country Store and Its People* is a case in point.[53]

The resources discussed here, and particularly the newly available sources in the PRC, offer the opportunity to address existing issues and frame more in-depth questions about Chinese business history. Sherman Cochran has provided some valuable suggestions on the direction of the field.[54] The following are some of my own suggestions for future research:

1. The relationship between the central office of an enterprise and its branches: In the past historians have had to look at the operation of a business as a whole unit. Newly available sources will enable scholars to look at how branches dealt with the central office or how the central office monitored and controlled the branches.

2. The emergence of corporate structures: Recent studies on stock markets and other newly available materials will enable scholars to look at company law and corporate structures. These kinds of studies depend on company archives.

3. Marketing strategies and management styles: The company records include their own magazines, catalogues, and posters. These kinds of materials help researchers better understand marketing strategies. Some newspapers, such as *Shenbao* and the *North China Herald*, also have marketing intelligence sections.

4. Consumer styles: Business historians could draw on autobiographies, company promotion materials, pamphlets, calendar posters, and paintings to reconstruct changing consumer preferences in modern China.

5. Legal disputes: Available in company archives are many contracts and documentation of legal disputes, which could support solid research on the legal aspects of Chinese business. For example, did law or custom weigh heavier in resolving business disputes?

6. Chinese business networks: We have a number of studies of Chinese business networks, but there is still no clear consensus on what a Chinese business network is, or what is particularly "Chinese" about such business networks. The new material can help us to better understand topics such as how patterns of emigration and different forms of trading affected the network structure. In the past, scholars have focused primarily on the positive sides of networks, but interviews could provide insight on the negative/dysfunctional aspects of networks.

7. Industrial technology: Some company archives contain information on industrial designs and engineering and industrial technology. The University of California at Berkeley Library houses materials on some translations of Western science texts into Chinese. These kinds of materials could help us to understand one of the more neglected topics in this field.

In sum, we need to have more case studies of individual enterprises in order to analyze these and other issues; thus, access to archives and new materials matters. After we have a sufficient number of cases, we can piece them together into more conclusive images of how Chinese business has functioned in the distant and more immediate past, a past that will continue to shape a rapidly evolving present.

Notes

1. *Liu Hongsheng qiye shiliao* [Source Materials on Liu Hongsheng's Enterprise Group], 3 vols. (Shanghai: Shanghai renmin chubanshe, 1981); *Rongjia qiye shiliao* [Source Materials on the Rong Family's Enterprise Group], 2 vols. (Shanghai: Shanghai

renmin chubanshe, 1980); *Nanyang xiongdi yancao gongsi shiliao* [Source Materials on the Nanyang Brothers Tobacco Company] (Shanghai: Shanghai renmin chubanshe, 1958); *Ying–Mei yan gongsi zai Hua qiye ziliao huibian* [Source Materials on the British–American Tobacco Company], 4 vols. (Beijing: Zhonghua, 1983); *Shanghai minzu jiqi gongye* (Source Materials on the Shanghai Domestic Machinery Industry), 2 vols. (Beijing: Zhonghua, 1966); *Shanghai minzu xiangjiao gongye* [Source Materials on the Shanghai Domestic Rubber Industry] (Beijing: Zhonghua, 1979); *Shanghai shi mianbu shangye* [Source Materials on the Shanghai Domestic Cotton Cloth Industry] (Beijing: Zhonghua, 1979); Yan Pengfei, Li Mingyang, and Cao Bu, eds., *Zhongguo baoxian shizhi* [Source Materials on the Chinese Insurance Industry] (Shanghai: Shanghai shehui kexue yuan chubanshe, 1989).

2. Zhang Zhongli, Chen Zengnian, and Yao Xinrong, *The Swire Group in Old China* (Shanghai: Shanghai renmin chubanshe, 1991); Zhang Zhongli and Chen Zengnian, *Shasun jituan zai jiu Zhongguo* [The Sassoon Enterprise Group in Old China] (Beijing: Renmin chubanshe, 1985); Xu Weiyong and Huang Hanmin, *Rongjia qiye fazhan shi* [The Development of the Rong Family Enterprises] (Beijing: Renmin chubanshe, 1985); Fang Xiantang, *Shanghai jindai minzu juanyan kongye* [History of the Cigarette Industry in Modern Shanghai] (Shanghai: Shanghai shehui kexue yuan chubanshe, 1989); Zheng Yukui, Cheng Linsun, and Zhang Chuanhong, *Jiu Zhongguo di ziyuan weiyuanhui: shishi yu pingjia* [The National Resource Council in Old China: Historical Fact and Evaluation] (Shanghai: Shanghai shehui kexue yuan chubanshe, 1991); Xu Xinwu, *Jiangnan tubu shi* [The History of Domestic Cloth in the Jiangnan Area] (Shanghai: Shanghai Academy of Social Sciences Press, 1992); Xu Dingxin, *Zhongguo jindai qiye di keji liliang yu keji xiaoying* [Chinese Modern Enterprise and Its Technological Power and Efficiency] (Shanghai: Shanghai shehui kexue yuan chubanshe, 1995); Pan Junxiang, *Zhongguo jindai guohuo yundong* [The National Goods Movement in Modern China] (Beijing: Zhongguo wenshi, 1996); Jingji suo, Shanghai shehui kexue yuan [Economics Institute, Shanghai Academy of Social Sciences], ed., *Jiangnan zaochuanchang changshi, 1865–1949* [The History of Jiangnan Arsenal] (Nanjing: Jiangsu renmin chubanshe, 1983); *Shanghai jindai wujin shangye shi* [The Metal Industry of Modern Shanghai] (Shanghai: Shanghai shehui kexue yuan chubanshe, 1990); *Zhongguo jindai zaozhi kongye shi* [The Paper Industry of Modern China] (Shanghai: Shanghai shehui kexue yuan chubanshe, 1989); *Shanghai Yong'an gongsi di chansheng fazhan he gaizao* [The History of the Origins, Development, and Reconstruction of the Wing On Company] (Shanghai: Shanghai renmin chubanshe, 1981); *Shanghai jindai baihuo shangye shi* [The History of Modern Department Stores in Shanghai] (Shanghai: Shanghai shehui kexue yuan chubanshe, 1988); *Longteng huyue bashinian Shanghai Zhonghua zhiyue chang chang shi* [The History of the Zhonghua Drugstore in Shanghai] (Shanghai: Shanghai shehui kexue yuan chubanshe, 1991); Jingji suo, Shanghai shehui kexue yuan, and Shanghai shi liangshiju [Bureau of Food Supply of Shanghai], eds., *Zhongguo jindai mianfen gongye shi* [The History of China's Modern Flour Industry] (Beijing: Zhonghua, 1987); Jingji suo, Shanghai shehui kexue yuan, and Zhongxi yaochang (Zhongxi Store), eds., *Zhongxi yaochang bainian shi* (The Hundred-Year History of the Zhongxi Drugstore) (Shanghai: Shanghai shehui kexue yuan chubanshe, 1990).

3. Ding Richu, ed., *Shanghai jindai jingjishi* (The Economic History of Modern Shanghai) vols. 1 and 2 (Shanghai: Shanghai renmin chubanshe, 1994, 1997). Professors Huang Hanmin and Sheng Zuwei are responsible for editing vol. 3 in the set.

4. A leading journal on archives, *Republican Archives*, is published by the Second Historical Archives, Nanjing. Another major journal, *Archives and History*, is published

by the Shanghai Municipal Archives. These journals have published a variety of archival materials from the Republican period.

5. Zhongguo renmin daxue qingshi yanjiusuo and Dang'anxi [Department of Archives, People's University, and Research Institute of Qing History, People's University], eds., *Qingdai di kuangye* [The Mining Industry of the Qing Dynasty] (Beijing: Zhonghua, 1983); Jiangsusheng shangyeting and Zhongguo di er lishi dang'anguan [Commercial Bureau of Jiangsu Province and the Second Historical Archives], eds., *Zhonghua minguo shangye dang'an ziliao huipian* [A Collection of Commercial Archives from the Republic of China] (N.p.: Zhongguo shangye chubanshe, 1991); Zhongguo yinhang and Zhongguo di er lishi dang'anguan [Bank of China and the Second Historical Archives], eds., *Zhongguo yinhang hangshi ziliao huipian* [A Collection of Materials on the History of Bank of China] (Nanjing: Dang'an chubanshe, 1991); Zhongguo di er lishi dang'anguan [Second Historical Archives], ed., *Guomin zhengfu ziyuan weiyuanhui gongbao* [The Bulletins of the National Resource Commission During the Republican Period], 16 vols. (Nanjing: Dang'an chubanshe, 1990).

6. Chen Xulu, Gu Tinglong, and Wang Xi, eds., *Sheng Xuanhuai dang'an ziliao xuanji: Hanyeping gongsi* [Source Materials on Sheng Xuanhuai: The Hanyeping Company], vols. 1 and 2, (Shanghai: Renmin chubanshe, 1984, 1986); *Sheng Xuanhuai dang'an ziliao xuanji: Xinhai geming qianhou* [Source Materials on Sheng Xuanhuai: Before and After the Revolution of 1911] (Shanghai: Shanghai renmin chubanshe, 1979); *Sheng Xuanhuai dang'an ziliao xuanji: Jiawu Zhong–Ri zhanzheng* [Source Materials on Sheng Xuanhuai: The First Sino–Japanese War] (Shanghai: Shanghai renmin chubanshe, 1980); Department of Economics, Wuhan University, ed., *Jiu Zhongguo Hanyeping gongsi yu Riben guanxi shiliao xuanji* [Source Materials on the Relationship Between the Hanyeping Company and Japan in Old China] (Shanghai: Shanghai renmin chubanshe, 1985); Archives of Hubei Province, comp., *Hanyeping dang'an guanbian* [Selected Archives on the Hanyeping Company] (Beijing: Zhongguo shehui kexue yuan chubanshe, 1992, 1994).

7. Tianjin shi dang'anguan [Tianjin Municipal Archives], eds., *Tianjin shanghui dang'an huibian, 1903–1911* [Collected Archives on the Tianjin Chamber of Commerce, 1903–1911], 2 vols. (Tianjin: Tianjin renmin chubanshe, 1989); *Tianjin shanghui dang'an huibian, 1912–1928* [Collected Archives on the Tianjin Chamber of Commerce, 1912–1928], 4 vols. (Tianjin: Tianjin renmin chubanshe, 1992); *Tianjin shanghui dang'an huibian, 1928–1937* [Collected Archival on the Tianjin Chamber of Commerce, 1928–1937], 2 vols. (Tianjin: Tianjin renmin chubanshe, 1996); Suzhou Municipal Archives, ed., *Suzhou shanghui dang'an congbian, 1905–1911* [Collected Archives on the Chamber of Commerce of Suzhou, 1905–1911] (Wuchang: Huazhong shifan daxue chubanshe [Huazhong Normal University Press], 1991). For an overview of Tianjin archives, see Xiaobo Zhang, "A Treasury for Chinese Business Historians: The Tianjin Chamber of Commerce Archives," *Chinese Business History* 4, no. 2 (spring 1994), pp. 1–3.

8. For example, see Jia Xueshi and Zhang Keliang, *Angang shi* [The History of the Angang Steel Mill] (Beijing: Yejin gongye chubanshe, 1984); Zhongguo Beijing Tongrentang gongsi and Beijing Tongrentang bianwei hui, eds., *Tongrentang shi* [History of the Tongrentang Corporate Group] (Beijing: Renmin ribao, 1993).

9. For example, see Mu Xuan and Yan Xuexi, *Dasheng shachang gongren shenghuo di diaocha, 1899–1949* [A Survey of Working Conditions in the Dasheng Textile Mill, 1899–1949] (Nanjing: Jiangsu renmin chubanshe, 1994); Chen Jiawu, ed., *Zhang Jian nongshang zongzhang renqi jingji ziliao xuanbian* [Selected Economic Sources on Zhang Jian's Tenure as the Minister of the Department of Agriculture and Commerce] (Nanjing: Nanjing daxue chubanshe, 1987); Nantong dang'an guan and Nanjing daxue, lishi suo, comp., *Dasheng qiye xitong dang'an xuanbian* [Selected Archives on the

Dasheng Enterprise Group] (Nanjing: Nanjing daxue chubanshe, 1987); Zigong dang'an guan, Beijing jingji xueyuan, and Sichuan daxue, eds., *Zigong yanye qiyue dang'an xuanji* [Selected Archives on Salt Contracts in Zigong] (Beijing: Zhongguo shehui kexue yuan chubanshe, 1985); Zhongguo yinhang, Shanxi fenhang, and Shanxi caijing xueyuan [Financial Institute of Shanxi], comps., *Shanxi piaohao shiliao* [Source Materials on Shanxi Native Banks] (Taiyuan: Shanxi jingji chubanshe, 1990); Editorial Board of Yudahua fangzhi ziben jituan shiliao bianjizu, ed., *Yudahua fangzhi ziben jituan shiliao* [Source Materials on the Yudahua Textile and Financial Group] (Wuhan: Hubei renmin chubanshe, 1984).

10. Shanghai shi dang'an guan, ed., *Jiu Shanghai di zhengjuan jiaoyi suo* [The Stock Exchange in Old Shanghai] (Shanghai: Guji chubanshe, 1992); *Wu Yunzhu qiye shiliao: Tianyuan huagong changjuan* [Source Materials on Wu Yunzhu's Enterprises: The Tianyuan Chemical Firm] (Beijing: Dang'an chubanshe, 1989).

11. Lin Jinzhi and Zhuang Weiji, eds., *Jindai huaqiao touzi guonei qiye shi ziliao xuanji, Fujian juan* [Selected Materials on Overseas Chinese Investment in China's Modern Enterprises, Fujian] (Fuzhou: Fujian renmin chubanshe, 1985); Lin Jinzhi and Zhuang Weiji, eds., *Jindai huaqiao touzi guonei qiye shi ziliao xuanji: Guangdong juan* [Selected Materials on Overseas Chinese Investment in China's Modern Enterpriese, Guangdong] (Fuzhou: Fujian renmin chubanshe, 1989); Lin Jinzhi, ed., *Jindai huaqiao touzi guonei qiye shi ziliao xuanji, Shanghai juan* [Selected Materials on Overseas Chinese Investment in China's Modern Enterprises, Shanghai] (Xiamen: Xiamen daxue chubanshe, 1994); Dai Yifeng, ed., *Xiamen haiguan lishi dang'an xuanbian* [Selected Historical Archives on the Maritime Customs of Xiamen], vol. 1 (Xiamen: Xiamen daxue chubanshe, 1997).

12. Liu Xiusheng, *Qingdai shangpin jingji yu shangye ziben* [The Commodity Economy and Commercial Capital in Qing China] (Beijing: Zhongguo shangye chubanshe, 1993); Guo Yunjing, *Qingdai shangye shi* [A History of Commerce in Qing China] (Liaoning: Renmin chubanshe, 1991); Fan Jinmin and Jin Wen, *Jiangnan Suzhou shi yanjiu* [A Study of the Silk Industry in the Jiangnan Area] (Beijing: Nongye chubanshe, 1993); Wang Weiguan, Wu Zhengyuan, and Zhang Yingen, *Waishanghi* [A History of Foreign Merchants] (Beijing: Zhongguo caizheng jingji chubanshe, 1996); Gao Daoyang, *Zhongguo kuaiji shigao* [A History of Chinese Accounting], 2 vols. (Beijing: Zhongguo caizheng jingji chubanshe, 1982, 1988).

13. Zhang Baichun, *Zhongguo jindai jiqi jianshi* [A General History of Modern Chinese Machinery] (Beijing: Beijing ligong daxue chubanshe, 1992).

14. For example, see Gong Jun, *Zhongguo xin gongye fazhanshi dagang* [A Brief History of Industrial Development in New China], reprint of 1933 original (Taipei: Huashi chubanshe, 1978); Liu Guoliang, *Zhongguo gongye shi* [A History of Chinese Industry], 2 vols. (Nanjing: Jiangsu kexue jishu chubanshe, 1990, 1992); Zhu Zishou, *Zhongguo gudai gongye shi* [A History of Chinese Ancient Industry] (Shanghai: Xuelin chubanshe, 1988); Zhu Zishou, *Zhongguo gongye jishushi* [A History of Chinese Industrial Technology] (Chongqing: Chongqing chubanshe, 1995); Zhu Zishou, *Zhongguo jindai gongye shi* [A History of Modern Chinese Industry] (Chongqing: Chongqing chubanshe, 1989); Zhu Zishou, *Zhongguo xiandai gongye shi* [A History of Chinese Industry since 1949] (Chongqing: Chongqing chubanshe, 1990); Fan Xicheng and Lu Baozhen, *Zhongguo jindai gongye fazhan shi* [A History of Industrial Development in Modern China] (Xi'an: Shanxi renmin chubanshe, 1991); Gao Jiren, *Zhongguo gongye jingji shi* [A History of Modern Chinese Industrial Economy] (Kaifeng: Henan daxue chubanshe, 1992).

15. Duan Benluo and Zhang Qifu, *Suzhou shougongye shi* [A History of the Suzhou Handicraft Industry] (Nanjing: Jiangsu guji chubanshe, 1986).

16. Kong Lingren, *Zhongguo jindai qiye di kaituozhe* [Pioneers of Modern Chinese Enterprises], 2 vols. (Jinan: Shandong renmin chubanshe, 1991); Zhongguo renmin zhengzhi xieshang huiyi Shanghai shi weiyuanhui wenshi ziliao gongzuo weiyuanhui, comp., *Jiu Shanghai di waishang yu maiban* [Foreign Merchants and Compradors in Old Shanghai] (Shanghai: Shanghai renmin chubanshe, 1987).

17. Xie Mu and Wu Yongliang, *Zhongguo di laozihao* [Old Firms in China] (Beijing: Jingji ribao chubanshe, 1988); An Guanying and Han Sunfang, *Zhonghua bainian laoyaopu* [A Century of Old Drugstores in China] (Beijing: Zhongguo wenshi chubanshe, 1993); Hou Shiheng, *Beijing laozihao* [Old Firms in Beijing] (Beijing: Zhongguo huanjing kexue chubanshe, 1991); Gan Ku, *Shanghai bainian mingchang laodian* [A Century of Old Firms in Shanghai] (Shanghai: Wenhua, 1987); Zhongguo renmin zhengchi xieshang huiyi, Beijing shi weiyuanhui wenshi ziliao yanjiu wei yuanhui, eds., *Zhuming jinghua di laozihao* [Famous Old Firms in Beijing] (Beijing: Wenshi ziliao chubanshe, 1986).

18. Yi Bin, *Lao Shanghai guanggao* [Old Shanghai Advertisements] (Shanghai: Shanghai huabao chubanshe, 1995); Feng Yiyou, *Lao xiangyan paizi* [Old Trademarks of Cigarettes] (Shanghai: Shanghai huabao chubanshe, 1996); Lu Shaohui and Song Zilong, eds., *Zhongwai xiangyan guanggao jicui* [A Collection of Chinese and Western Cigarette Advertisements] (N.p.: Anhui meishu chubanshe, 1997); Ng Chunbong, Cheuk Paktong, Wong Ying, and Yvonne Lo, comps., *Chinese Women and Modernity: Calendar Posters of the 1910s–1930s* (Hong Kong: Joint Publishing, 1996).

19. Li Kuo-ch'i (Li Guoqi), *Zhongguo zaoqi de tielu jingying* [The Management of China's Early Railroads] (Taipei: Institute of Modern History, Academia Sinica, 1976); Huang Qianhui, *Zhongguo yinhangye shi* [A History of Chinese Banking] (Taiyuan: Shaanxi jingji chubanshe, 1994); Feng Bangyan, *Xianggang Yingzi caituan* (British Financial Groups in Hong Kong) (Hong Kong: Joint Publishing, 1996); Peng Jiusong, *Zhongguo qiyue gufenzhi* [The System of the Chinese Contractual Stock] (Chengdu: Chengdu keji daxue chubanshe, 1994).

20. Baogangzhi bianzuan weiyuanhui, comp., *Baogangzhi* [A History of Baogang] (Shanghai: Shanghai shehui kexue yuan chubanshe, 1995).

21. See Chi-Kong Lai, "The Historiography of Maritime China since c. 1975," *Research in Maritime History*, no. 9 (December 1995), pp. 53–79.

22. Nie Baozhang, *Zhongguo jindai hangyunshi ziliao* [Source Materials on the History of Shipping in Modern China] (Shanghai: Renmin chubanshe, 1983), vol. 1.

23. H.W. Dick and S.A. Kentwell, *Beancake to Boxboat: Steamship Companies in Chinese Waters* (Canberra: Nautical Association of Australia, Inc., 1988).

24. Kuo-tung Ch'en, *The Insolvency of the Chinese Hong Merchants, 1760–1843* (Taipei: Institute of Economics, Academia Sinica, Monograph Series No. 45, 1990); Hsieh Kuo-hsing (Xie Guoxing), *Tainanbang de ge'an yanjiu: Qiye fazhan yu Taiwan jingyan* [Corporation Development and the Taiwan Experience] (Taipei: Institute of Modern History, Academia Sinica, 1994); Ch'en Tsu-yu (Chen Ciyu), *Jindai Zhongguo di jixie saosi gongye 1860–1945* [The Silk Industry of Modern China] (Taipei: Institute of Modern History, Academia Sinica, 1989); Chang Jui-te (Zhang Ruide), *Pinghan tielu yu Huabei di jingji fazhan, 1905–1937* [The Peking–Hankou Railroad and Economic Development in North China] (Taipei: Institute of Modern History, Academia Sinica, 1987); *Zhongguo jindai tielu shiye guanli de yanjiu: Zhengzhi cengmian di fenxi, 1876–1937* [The Railroad in Modern China: Political Aspects of Railroad Administration] (Taipei: Institute of Modern History, Academia Sinica, 1991).

25. Materials published by the Institute of Modern History of the Academia Sinica in Taipei include *Haifangdang* [Archives on Maritime Defense], a photo-offset reproduction of Zongli yamen papers, 1957; *Kuangwudang* [Archives on Mining], 1960; Tai

186 CHINESE STUDIES IN HISTORY

Chih-li (Dai Zhili), comp., *Sichuan baolu yundong ziliao huizuan* [A Collection of Historical Materials on the Sichuan Railway Protection Movement], 1994; *Qingji Huagong chuguo shiliao* [Source Materials on the Emigration of Chinese Coolies in the Qing Period], 1995. Oral histories published by the Institute of History include Ch'en Tsun-kung (Chen Cungong), interviewer, "Zhao Zhengkai xiansheng fangwen jilu" [The Reminiscences of Mr. Chao Chen-kai], 1993; Hsieh Kuo-hsing (Xie Guoxing), interviewer, "Wu Xiuqi xiansheng fangwen jilu" [The Reminiscences of Mr. Wu Hsiu-chi], 1992; Hsu Hsueh-chi, interviewer, "Minying Tang Rong gongsi xiangguan renmu fangwen, 1940–1962" [Forging the Future: An Oral History of the Teng-Eng Iron Co., 1940–1962], 1993.

26. For example, see Ho Hon-wei (He Hanwei), *The Early History of the Beijing Hankou Railroad* (Hong Kong: Chinese University Press, 1979); Lee Muk-miu (Li Mumiao), *The Development of Yungs' Enterprises, 1912–1921* (Hong Kong: Modern Chinese History Society of Hong Kong, 1989).

27. Shanghaishi dang'an guan, ed., *Shanghaishi dang'an guan jianming zhinan* [Concise Introduction to the Shanghai Municipal Archives] (Beijing: Dang'an chuban-she, 1991). In the following discussion, I also draw on a guide to the Chinese Business History Research Center published by the Economics Institute, Shanghai Academy of Social Sciences: *Zhongguo qiyeshi ziliao yanjiu zhongxin jianjie* [A Brief Guide to the Center for the Study of Chinese Enterprise History] (Shanghai, 1994), and on Huang Hanmin, "Business Archives," unpublished paper presented at the conference "Business in Shanghai: Past and Present," University of Queensland, Brisbane, March 28–30, 1997. See also Andrea McElderry, "Shanghai Municipal Archives" and "Shanghai Academy of Social Sciences Libraries," *Chinese Business History* 5, no. 2 (spring/fall 1995), pp. 8–9.

28. The Shanghai Historical Museum has a few contract materials on a drug firm. A huge collection of material on Zhang Jian is available in the Nantong Museum, some of which has been published, most recently Zhang Jian yanjiu zhongxin, Nantong shi tushuguan, and Jiangsu guji chubanshe, comp., *Zhang Jian quanji* [Complete Works of Zhang Jian], 7 vols. (Nanjing: Jiangsu guji chubanshe, 1994). On the the materials in Nantong, see Elisabeth Köll, "Nantong: Archives, Libraries, Museums," *Chinese Business History* 5, no. 2 (spring/fall 1995), pp. 3–5.

29. Some local archives, such as those in Chongqing, Sichuan, house source materials related to wartime enterprise relocation from Shanghai to Chongqing during World War II.

30. See also Kai-yiu Chan, "Chinese Business History Research Center," *Chinese Business History* 5, no. 2 (spring/fall 1995), pp. 6–8.

31. See Chi-Kong Lai, "The Second Historical Archives," *Chinese Business History* 5, no. 2 (spring/fall 1995), pp. 2–3.

32. For information on the collection, see Feng Jinniu, "Sheng Xuanhuai dang'an de zhengli yu liyong" [The Compilation and Use of the Sheng Xuanhuai Archives], unpublished paper, 1997.

33. Three titles compiled by Wang Erh-min (Wang Ermin) and Alice Lun Ng (Wu Lun Nixia) have been published in Taipei by the Institute of Modern History, Academia Sinica: *Sheng Xuanhuai shiye pengliao hangao* [Letters from Business Associates and Acquaintances to Sheng Hsuan Huai, 1874–1914], 3 vols. 1997; *Sheng Xuanhuai shiye handiangao* [Sheng Hsuan Huai's Letters and Telegraphs on Modern Industry in the Late Ch'ing Period], 2 vols. 1993; *Qingji waijiao yiuying handian ziliao* (Sheng Hsuan Huai's Letters and Telegraphs on Foreign Affairs in Late Ch'ing China), 1993; another title is Wang Erh-min and Chan Sin-wai (Chen Shanwei), *Qingmo yiding Zhongwai shangyue jiaoshe: Sheng Xuanhuai wanglai handiangao* [Docu-

ments on Commercial Treaty Negotiation Between China and the West in Late Qing], 2 vols. (Hong Kong: Chinese University Press, 1993).

34. See *South China Research Resource Station Newsletter* 2 (January 1996), pp. 1–2.

35. Wai-keung Chung to C.K. Lai, e-mail, June 19, 1997.

36. See *South China Research Resource Station Newsletter* 1 (October 1995), p. 1.

37. Tokyo University has also published six volumes of materials on the trade guilds in Beijing, and source materials on the correspondence of Shanxi native banks. The Institute of Oriental Culture at Tokyo University houses materials on Shansi banks and will continue to publish these in the future.

38. Andrea McElderry, "Taipei: Resources," *Chinese Business History* 5, no. 2 (spring/fall 1995), pp. 12–13.

39. Wellington K.K. Chan, "The Origins and Early Years of the Wing On Company Group in Australia, Fuji, Hong Kong, and Shanghai: Organization and Strategy of a New Enterprise," in Rajeswary A. Brown, ed., *Chinese Business Enterprises in Asia* (London: Routledge, 1995), pp. 80–95; "Personal Styles, Cultural Values and Management: The Sincere and Wing On Companies in Shanghai and Hong Kong," *Business History Review* 70 (summer 1996), pp. 141–66; "Chinese Business Networking and the Pacific Rim: The Family Firm's Roles Past and Present," *Journal of American–East Asian Relations* 1 (summer 1992), pp. 171–90; Ching-Hwang Yen, "The Wing On Company in Hong Kong and Shanghai: A Case Study of Modern Overseas Chinese Enterprises, 1907–1949," *Proceedings of the Conference on Eight Years of History of the Republic of China*, vol. 4 (Taipei, 1991), pp. 77–117.

40. Janis Wilton, *Hong Yuen: A Country Store and Its People* (Armidale, New South Wales: University of New England Printery, 1988).

41. I thank Dr. M. Diamond, who drew my attention to some of the Australian archives.

42. See Paul MacGregor, "The Material Heritage of Chinese Australians: A Survey and Evaluation of the Collection of the Museum of Chinese Australian History," in Paul MacGregor, ed., *Histories of the Chinese in Australasia and the South Pacific* (Melbourne: Museum of Chinese Australian History, 1995), pp. 409–18.

43. *China Talk,* (April 1991), p. 15.

44. Noel Butlin Archives Center, *List of Holdings as of December 1993* (Canberra: Noel Butlin Archives Center, Australian National University), p. 10.

45. See, for example, *Ao'men zhuandang* [Special Collection on Macau] (Taipei: Institute of Modern History, Academia Sinica, 1992, 1993, 1995, 1996).

46. The microfilm collection of the British–American Tobacco papers from the William R. Perkins Library at Duke University has recently been published by Adam Matthew Publications in its *China Through Western Eyes Series*, vol. 3, 1997.

47. Singapore Archives and Oral History Interviews Department, ed., *Pioneers of Singapore: A Catalogue of Oral History Interviews* (Singapore: Archives and Oral History Department, 1984); Chan Kwok Bun and Claire Chiang, *Stepping Out: The Making of Chinese Entrepreneurs* (Singapore: Prentice-Hall, 1994).

48. *Zhongguo di'er lishi dang'an guan* [A Brief Guide to the Second Historical Archives of China] (Beijing: Dang'an chubanshe, 1987).

49. See Qin Guoqing, *Zhonghua Ming–Qing zhendang zhinan* [Guidebook to Valuable Archives from the Ming and Qing Dynasties] (Beijing: Renmin chubanshe, 1994); Institute of Modern History, Academia Sinica, *Collection of Catalogues for Documents on Modern China's Economic Affairs*, vols. 1–3 (Institute of Modern History, Academia Sinica, 1987, 1993, 1994); Guo Shiguan, *Guoshiguan xiancang guojia dang'an gaizhu* [A Brief Description of the Recently Opened Archives in the National Archives] (Taipei: Guo shiguan, 1996).

50. Huang Guangcheng, comp., *Weiguo zaihua gongsheng qiye cidian* [The Universal Dictionary of Foreign Business in Modern China] (Chengdu: Sichuan renmin chubanshe, 1995).

51. The Dang'an chubanshe [Archives Press] in Beijing has published the following local guidebooks: *Heilongjiang sheng dang'an guan zhinan* [Guide to the Heilongjiang Provincial Archives], 1994; *Yuyangshi dang'an guan zhinan* [Guide to the Yuyang City Archives], 1994; *Hubei sheng dang'an guan zhinan* [Guide to the Hubei Provincial Archives], 1994; *Wuhan shi dang'an guan zhinan* [Guide to the Wuhan City Archives], 1994; and *Liaoning sheng dang'an guan zhinan* [Guide to the Liaoning Provincial Archives], 1994.

52. See Lee Ch'eng-chi (Li Chengji), *Di'er guxiang* [My Second Home] (Hong Kong: N.p., 1997).

53. Wilton, *Hong Yuen: A Country Store and Its People*.

54. Sherman Cochran, "An Assessment of Chinese Business History Five Years After Our Inaugural Issue," *Chinese Business History* 6, no. 1 (spring 1996), pp. 1–2.

Chinese Studies in History, vol. 31, nos. 3–4, Spring–Summer 1998, pp. 189–90.
ISSN 0009–4633/1998 $9.50 + 0.00.

Author Index to Volume 31
(Fall 1997–Summer 1998)

————. "The Modern Women's Rights Movement (January 18, 1922)," in *Chinese Studies in History*, vol. 31, no. 2 (Winter 1997–98): 24–28.

————. "Transforming the Family," in *Chinese Studies in History*, vol. 31, no. 2 (Winter 1997–98): 61–62.

————. "Women's Education," in *Chinese Studies in History*, vol. 31, no. 2 (Winter 1997–98): 34–35.

————. "Women's Movements," in *Chinese Studies in History*, vol. 31, no. 2 (Winter 1997–98): 15–16.

Li Dazhao. "The Postwar Woman Question (February 15, 1919)," in *Chinese Studies in History*, vol. 31, no. 2 (Winter 1997–98): 17–23.

————. "The Modern Women's Rights Movements (January 18, 1922)" in *Chinese Studies in History*, vol. 31, no. 2 (Winter 1997–98): 24–28.

Lin, Man-houng. "Interpretative Trends in Taiwan's Scholarship on Chinese Business History: 1600 to the Present," in *Chinese Studies in History*, vol. 31, nos. 3–4 (Spring–Summer 1998): 65–94.

McElderry, Andrea. *See* Gardella, Robert.

Nelson, Daniel. "Western Business History: Experience and Comparative Perspectives," in *Chinese Studies in History*, vol. 31, nos. 3–4 (Spring–Summer 1998): 151–65.

Qi Wenxin. "The Case for Yi Yin and Huang Yin Being Two Persons," in *Chinese Studies in History*, vol. 31, no. 1 (Fall 1997): 3–22.

Samarani, Guido. "Italian Studies of the Guomindang and Its Historical Origins," in *Chinese Studies in History*, vol. 31, no. 1 (Fall 1997): 86–96.

Shen Yanbing. "How Do We Make the Women's Movement Truly Powerful? (June 5, 1920)," in *Chinese Studies in History*, vol. 31, no. 2 (Winter 1997–98): 84–87.

Tang Jicang. "Public Child Care and Public Dining Halls (August 10, 1920)," in *Chinese Studies in History*, vol. 31, no. 2 (Winter 1997–98): 78–81.

Wang Jianhong. "The Center of the Women's Rights Movement Should Move to the Fourth Class (December 10, 1921)," in *Chinese Studies in History*, vol. 31, no. 2 (Winter 1997–98): 95–97.

Xiang Jingyu. "A Plan for Women's Development: A Letter from Xiang Jingyu to Tao Yi (December 20, 1919)," in *Chinese Studies in History*, vol. 31, no. 2 (Winter 1997–98): 50–54.

Yun Daiying. "A Refutation of Yang Xiaochun's 'Against Public Child Care' (April 8, 1920)," in *Chinese Studies in History*, vol. 31, no. 2 (Winter 1997–98): 69–77.

Zelin, Madeleine. "Critique of Scholarship on Chinese Business History in the People's Republic of China and Taiwan," in *Chinese Studies in History*, vol. 31, nos. 3–4 (Spring–Summer 1998): 95–105.

Zhang Weici. "Emancipating Women by Reorganizing the Family (August 10, 1919)," in *Chinese Studies in History*, vol. 31, no. 2 (Winter 1997–98): 63–68.

For Product Safety Concerns and Information please contact our EU
representative GPSR@taylorandfrancis.com
Taylor & Francis Verlag GmbH, Kaufingerstraße 24, 80331 München, Germany